# TENNYSON

SIR HAROLD NICOLSON, born in 1886 in Teheran, where his father, Sir Arthur Nicolson, was British chargé d'affaires, spent his youth in Persia, Hungary, Bulgaria and Morocco. After his graduation from Oxford in 1909, he entered the Diplomatic Service, joining the Foreign Office, and has served as a delegate to the Versailles Peace Conference, the First Secretary of the Diplomatic Service and Foreign Office counsellor. In 1929 he resigned from the Diplomatic Service to work on the London *Evening Standard,* later becoming literary editor of the *Daily Express,* and in 1935 a Member of Parliament. Sir Harold's first book was published in 1921. Most widely acclaimed for his critical biographies and political studies, he has also written two novels. His works include *Swinburne, The Development of English Biography, Byron: The Last Journey, Some People, Peacemaking, 1919, People and Things,* and *Age of Reason,* published by Doubleday in 1961. He was knighted in 1953 by Queen Elizabeth. He and his wife, novelist V. Sackville-West, live with their two sons in London and in Sir Harold's ancestral home, Sissinghurst Castle, Kent.

# TENNYSON

*Aspects of his Life,*
*Character & Poetry*

*1809-*

HAROLD NICOLSON

Anchor Books
Doubleday & Company, Inc.
Garden City, New York
1962

*This book is dedicated*
*to*
*Dorothy Wellesley*

ἔγνων οὖν καὶ περὶ τῶν ποιητῶν
τοῦτο, ὅτι οὐ σοφίᾳ ποιοῖεν
ἃ ποιοῖεν, ἀλλὰ φύσει τινὶ καὶ
ἐνθουσιάζοντες·
        ΑΠΟΛΟΓΙΑ ΣΩΚΡΑΤΟΥΣ

# INTRODUCTORY NOTE

I find some difficulty in acknowledging the many sources on which I have drawn in the preparation of this volume. The British Museum catalogue records some two hundred and fifty books bearing directly upon Tennyson himself or upon his writings, and there is scarcely a work on the literature or life of the Victorian age in which he is not mentioned. To acknowledge all such sources would be to overload the text with notes or unduly to encumber the preface. It is only fitting, however, that I should specifically record my indebtedness to those works which I have found of greatest value. First among these must always come the present Lord Tennyson's *Memoir* on his father, and the companion volume, *Tennyson and his Friends*, which we also owe to his industry and filial devotion. The *Memoir* is not only the standard work upon the poet, but is itself, in its clear construction and outright simplicity, a remarkable literary achievement. I would next mention the brilliant, but unfortunately posthumous and incomplete, work of Professor Lounsbury, published by the Yale University Press, under the title of *Life and Times of Tennyson, 1809–1850.* From this delightful book I have drawn largely but I hope not unscrupulously. Among the shorter biographies of the poet the best is perhaps that by Mr. Arthur Waugh; the studies by Andrew Lang, S. Gwynn, A. C. Benson and Sir A. Lyall have also been invaluable. I have found some useful material in Canon Rawnsley's *Memories of The Tennysons*, in Mr. Masterman's *Tennyson as a Religious Teacher*, and in Sir N. Lockyer's *Tennyson as a Student and Poet of Nature.* For the bibliographical side Mr. Churton Collins' *Early Poems of Tennyson* has proved an essential book of reference, while Mr. Wise's two volumes of Bibliography, which were published for private circulation, contain in a scholarly form all the information which may be desired. As regards criticism, the monograph by Mr. Stopford Brooke, and the two commentaries on *In Memoriam* by Bradley and Genung, cannot be ignored, while the *Cambridge History of English Literature*, the works of Professor Saintsbury and Mr. Gosse, and the *Survey of English Literature, 1830–1880*, by Professor Elton, have been used as text-books for the literary history of the period.

Finally I am much indebted to my friend, Mr. Edward Marsh, for his kindness in reading the proofs and for the many valuable and scholarly suggestions which he has made.

H. N.

*October 1, 1922.*

# CONTENTS

# TENNYSON

CHAPTER ONE

# THE TENNYSON LEGEND

## I

We smile to-day at our Victorians, not confidently, as of old, but with a shade of hesitation: a note of perplexity, a note of anger sometimes, a note often of wistfulness has come to mingle with our laughter. For the tide is turning and the reaction is drawing to its close.

It is a matter, in the first place, of historical perspective. As the Victorian age recedes from our vision, the lesser accidents and accessories, which had seemed to us, but a decade ago, to be so characteristic and so humorous, sink down together in the haze of distance, and from behind them emerges slowly the long line of mountain landmarks, bleak and dominant, and our merriment is for the moment stilled.

The individual emotions aroused by this change of aspect will vary according to temperament. For some the immensities of the Victorian background will but emphasise what they regard as the complacent futilities of the foreground; others, again, will feel a stirring of indignation at the thought of so vast an opportunity having fallen to a generation seemingly so ignorant, so optimistic and so insincere. And there will be some who, from the troubled waters of our insecure age, will look back wistfully at what may

appear to them as the simple serenities, the sun-lit confidence, the firm dry land which formed the heritage of that
abundant epoch.

I am not concerned with such opinions, whether they be
accurate or the reverse; still less is it my intention to furnish
any history of the political, economic or imperial development of nineteenth-century England. From the material
point of view, the actual statistics, the stupendous upward
curves of quantitative progress, are familiar or at least available: they need to be borne in mind as ultimate facts, ac-
counting, in their incontrovertible way, for much of the self-
satisfaction with which that uneasy age would seek to cover
its perplexity; and, as such, they are illuminating enough.
For the nineteenth century was not, as the unwary may
sometimes suppose, a sedate and static period; it was anything but that: it was furiously dynamic; it moved, as Dr.
Inge has told us, with the large excitement of "a religious
revival," and in the rush and thunder of it all our ancestors
became a little bewildered. We can well believe it. They
saw their daily lives—their meals, the very hours of their
meals, the way the post came, the daily paper, the games
one played after supper, those things one's wife and daughter embroidered round the fire—changing before their eyes
with a startling and jerky rapidity; they saw political power
wrested from the hands of the territorial aristocracy by the
industrial middle classes only to fall finally to the masses;
they saw local authority passing gradually from the squire
and the rector to end in an autonomous parish council;
they saw the idea of Empire emerging from the old planta-
tion conception, through the purely geographical phase,
through a wholly emotional transition, towards the broader
aim of Commonwealth; they saw science and invention
opening illimitable and fantastic vistas into the unknown;
they saw the very foundations of their faith and conscience
cracking before the advancing billows of criticism and
analysis; they felt obscurely that unaccountable forces had
been released, that vast and hidden tides were sucking them

out from the old familiar roadsteads to some unknown and restless ocean. They were afraid. They yearned for control and for direction. It was all very magnificent; but they yearned to be reassured.

We can thus trace in the full-flowing, muddied stream of the nineteenth century two psychological currents, mingling sometimes the one with the other, blurred at moments by other swirls and eddies, but in the main distinct and clearly recognisable. The first of these is the conception of progress—in its worst form a mere complacent materialism, but in its clearer essence an earnest if puzzle-headed desire for betterment, a realisation of the responsibility of each individual to contribute something to the common improvement. The second current appears as a peculiar form of individualism, a specialisation of type—a conception so general and so persistent that it dotted every phase of contemporary life with the personification of its appropriate quality, with a series of appropriate heroes. And it is with this second element in the psychology of the nineteenth century that I am primarily concerned.

The hero-worship of the Victorian age, that predominant and imposing factor, was in its essence a reaction against the spirit of the time. The generation which flourished from 1780 to 1850 had passed from a period of great national danger to one of great personal perplexity. The French Revolution and the Napoleonic Wars had instilled into the average mind of that generation an abiding horror of excess, and abiding distaste for adventure. They were tired of romance, they were disillusioned of idealism: they wanted only to settle down in their homes, in homes finally secure; to lead a domestic, enlightened and above all a sane existence. Peace and prosperity became their gods, and Jeremy Bentham was there conveniently to serve as prophet. But gradually as the century progressed a great many unpleasant developments came to disturb this placid illusion: there was the Reform Bill, and the Corn Law agitation, and Niebuhr, and the Railways and the co-operative movement, and geology and astronomy, and the industrial population and the first uneasy hints of evolution; and with these disappeared all hope of peace and sanity, or of the new, easy, selfish England which, while in their strenuous Napoleonic days, they had forecasted so confidently. By the middle of the century such unpleasant problems had increased. Even as Copernicus had displaced the earth from its central position in space, so did the first half of the nineteenth century displace man from his predominate position in the scheme of animal creation. Instead of the old simple authoritative conceptions, it was now suggested that man was but a recent, but an unimportant, sport of nature; that, far from being God's deliberate and crowning achievement, it was at least questionable whether man had been meant to exist at all. The implications of it all were terrible: the Victorians, the great mass of the Victorians, refused to listen to them. Troubled and unhappy, they turned their backs upon these sardonic suggestions; defiantly they insisted upon the pre-eminence of human personality. The more the scientists succeeded in shaking their belief in God, the more did they invest their own leading contemporaries with divine attributes. The scientists could explain away many things, but they could not explain away the *soul;* they could not explain why, in every man and woman, in every Victorian man and woman, was implanted an instinctive, ultimate desire to be good. The scientists might say that the genus man was but an accidental sport of nature, that man was different in degree only from the other animalculæ; the radicals might urge that all men were equal, that the attributes of virtue, culture and intelligence were but the accidental trappings which diversified an essential uniformity—the Victorians refused to be convinced: such cynicism could apply only to the dull and unenlightened mass, it could not apply to the higher, nobler characters which, nay *who,* towered as landmarks above their kind; it might be true of men, it could not by any possibility be true of super-men.

And in this way the qualities of truth and courage, wisdom and duty, the characters of soldier, statesman, patriot and priest, were reduced to their simplest and most convincing expression, and were attached, thus simplified and enhanced, to the more eminent among their contemporaries. As the century proceeded, the whitewashed effigies of these heroes glimmered through the uncertain tempest to guide and hearten the uneasy and the perplexed. And finally, if they survived it, these divinities began themselves to take quite kindly to their own apotheoses, and the postures which were expected of them became the very attitudes which they happened, quite naturally and quite sincerely, to adopt.

And in our irreverent age the Victorian idols have suffered accordingly.

## II

Of these many mythologies it was perhaps the Tennyson legend which attained the most exaggerated proportions. For over fifty years his votaries prostrated themselves before the shrine which they had built for him, and he, moving a little clumsily at times within his sacerdotal vestments, became inevitably less and less the lyric poet, and more and more the civic prophet—the communal bard. There were grave disadvantages in this process. In the first place, it has rendered him, for some at least of the successors of his own generation, an object of derision and even of dislike. And, in the second place, what is more important, it hampered seriously the expression of his own essential genius. For whereas Tennyson was an extremely good emotional poet, he was, unfortunately, but a very second-rate instructional bard. His gift of emotion, had he indulged it less reservedly, was powerful and immense; his capacity for thought, which he indulged effusively, was of a quite different quality. Thus if Tennyson the poet is to mean anything to the present generation, he must from the outset be differentiated, and somewhat ruthlessly, from Tennyson the bard. The Tennyson laurels have grown by now into vast thickets, dusty, cumbersome and unvisited. It is necessary to let in the sun, and in the process much dead wood will have to be rejected and much destroyed. The task of destruction will, I fear, be wearisome: there will be moments when it will seem not only ruthless, but impertinent. But in the end, I think, a clearing will have been made such as will justify a labour seemingly so negative, and will give to the completed task the excuse of having disengaged the essential Tennyson from some, at least, of the undergrowth which now obstructs our vision. For the purpose of this book, if not the method, is very far from being destructive, and if, at the end, its constructive intention is not apprehended, I shall most signally have failed.

There are several alternative devices by which Tennyson might be rendered almost palatable to modern readers: I have worked out the several theses which could potentially be adopted. One might embark, for instance, on the theory that the real Tennyson, the poet Tennyson, was not a Victorian at all but a later Georgian. This contention could be elaborated and maintained with more detail and conviction than might be supposed: one can see the general outlines and the few high lights on which such a composition would be based. As frontispiece, of course, there would be the fierce and adventurous Tennyson of the Sam Lawrence portrait—the fine brown forehead, the brown, defiant eyelids, the ugly, ill-tempered mouth, the huge stock and collar. Much would be made of his youth and boyhood: of George III, of the Regency, of George IV, of press-gangs and crimping, of cock-fights and professional boxers, of Hessian boots and the smugglers' stories at Mablethorpe. Circumstantial detail would be provided by the drinking parsons who would ride across Lincolnshire to dine at 5 p.m. with his father in the Rectory hall, by the Bishop of Lincoln in his wig, by his father's knee-breeches and silver buckles, by the cake and negus in the parlour, by his sisters playing

bilbo or embroidering fire-screens in Berlin wool, by the
tinder-box and tallow dip at his bedside, by the thieves
swinging in chains against the sunset on Gibbet Hill. The
Cambridge period would be dated (perhaps ante-dated)
by similar touches: there would be a picture of the fireworks
at the accession of William IV, of the mulled claret, the
rat hunts and the churchwarden pipes, of the port-besotted
dons in Trinity Common room, of Sunderland's kerseymere
breeches and of the Byronic manner in which Arthur
Hallam discarded his stock. London would come with a reference to the haymakers in Bayswater, the stile into the
fields at the end of Portland Place, and the snipe-shooting
in Kensington; Tom Moore and Rogers would figure
prominently, and Leigh Hunt would flit contemporaneously
through the picture; there would be much about curiously
shaped bottles of heavy port at the Cock Tavern, and Government lottery tickets, and M. Dubourg's cork models of
Roman antiquities at his exposition in Bond Street. One
would thus arrive in a rich Hanoverian atmosphere at the
volumes of 1830 and 1832, at the composition of all that is
most valuable in the 1842 volume, at the earlier versions of
*In Memoriam,* and one could emerge triumphantly in 1837
having proved that all the most durable of Tennyson's work
was either published or composed before the accession of
Queen Victoria. If determined still further to prove such a
contention, one might extend the time limit a few years by
maintaining that the first decade of the young Queen's
reign had still a dash about it of the old Brunswick hilarity,
and that the real Victorian fog did not settle upon England
till close on 1850. One would, by such a paradox, gain *The
Princess* for the theory, and even the final version of *In
Memoriam,* and could kill Tennyson off fairly securely by
the date of the first Exhibition.

A great many people would doubtless be angered and
stimulated by such a thesis: I doubt whether very many
would be convinced.

Another and even more alluring performance would be

to work backwards. To start from Mr. Gosse and Swinburne and struggle back to the Pre-Raphaelites, and thus to the 1842 volume. In other words, to drape Tennyson in the fabric of the middle 'eighties, and to ignore the less effervescent period from 1842 to 1866. But such a contention would, after all, get seriously out of hand.

One can but mention such possible theses: their elaboration might be entertaining, and would serve at least to remove many current misconceptions and prejudices, would serve to startle the average reader out of his accepted assumptions of Tennyson, and to correct what is obviously a false perspective; as a negative business, the process might be valuable enough.

If, however, any practical zest for Tennyson is to revive in this generation, some more positive theory will be required; some formula such as will enable the modern reader, while accepting with kindly resignation Tennyson's undoubted deficiencies, to come upon his virtues with a shock of sudden and delighted surprise. Such a formula will not be attained by the negative processes which I have adumbrated; still less will it be attained by the comparative method, always dangerous, but in the case of Tennyson actually deceptive. I have carefully eschewed the temptation of emphasising obvious differences or of drawing farfetched resemblances between Tennyson and his contemporaries; and indeed to seek, as some have sought, analogies between Tennyson and Browning, or Tennyson and Clough, or Tennyson and Patmore, or Tennyson and Swinburne, or Tennyson and the now popular Morris appears of all tasks the most mistaken and unremunerative.

The formula, moreover, will not be attained by suppressing or ignoring the Victorian element in Tennyson's poetry: it will be attained only by analysing and defining that element with a view to isolate it from the central lyrical throb which pulsates through his work. It can only be discovered and conveyed by following the thread of Tennyson's life and work from his unhappy and puzzled boyhood to his puzzled and prosperous old age, and by examining, and endeavouring at times to disentangle, the diverse strands which are interwoven so curiously as to give to the superficial observer a mistaken impression of uniformity. For the secret of Tennyson is to be sought not in the apparent harmony between his work and character, but in the essential conflict between the two: in the conflict, that is, between the remarkable depth and originality of his poetic temperament and the shallowness and timidity of his practical intelligence.

Temperamentally Tennyson possessed all the qualities which should have rendered him one of the greatest and most original of our lyric poets. With the strong, full blood of his yeoman forebears mingled the black and bitter strain of some obscurer ancestry; through the arteries of an athlete fluttered the frightened, sensitive pulses of a mystic; and under the scent and music of delicate and tender things pierced the coarse salt savour of the wold and marsh.

That Tennyson's genius was essentially of a subjective, and not of an objective, quality will, I suppose, be now generally admitted; it is tempting even to consider how his genius would have developed had not the force and passion of his poetic temperament been hushed by quite ephemeral considerations. For had his lot fallen among other circumstances, or in a less cloying age; had that unfortunate element of caution been absent from his character; had some whim of fate let loose the vast reserves of emotion which were in him, and had he realised that what he *felt* was infinitely more important than what he *thought,* we might well have had a greater Francis Thompson, or maybe—for who can tell?—an earlier Swinburne. I am not so illiterate as to suggest that Tennyson would have been a better poet had he been a less reputable man and citizen. Yet even if he had retained his austerity, even if he had lost nothing of the sombre stateliness of his manner, a little more emotion, a little less accuracy, might well have rendered him our supreme poet of despair—a broader and

more human Alfred de Vigny. He was intended to be a subjective poet, and was forced by circumstances into fifty
years of unnatural objectivity. He chose the easier and more
prosperous course: he became the Laureate of his age; he
subordinated the lyric to the instructional. And his poetry
thereby has lost one half of its potential value.

### III

I have said that the reaction of the twentieth century
against Tennyson is very largely due to the exaggerated
worship with which he was regarded by our grandfathers,
and that this adulation is, in its turn, to be explained by the
general tendency of the Victorians to magnify their more
eminent contemporaries. I have implied also that a deeper
and more permanent explanation of the very secondary
place which he is now allotted, is to be found in the fact
that he allowed a very unconvincing intelligence to hamper
and restrict a very full and forceful temperament. Both
these contentions require to be qualified. In the first place,
Tennyson's success and popularity were by no means of
rapid growth, and throughout his lifetime there were many
of the more enlightened who said about him very much
what we are saying to-day. In the second place, although
his "message" now appears to have been a very inconclusive
business, although he seems to us to provide no effective
formula for any essential problem, yet it must be remembered that upon the majority of his contemporaries it acted
as a very potent sedative, and that to hundreds of thousands
of perplexed and anxious minds he brought complete intellectual and moral relief. It cannot be expected that this
narcotic influence of Tennyson will by the present generation be regarded as very admirable: we are not to-day to
a similar extent tortured by spiritual anxieties; our attention
is diverted into more material channels such as social and
sexual problems. But it is essential for any historical criticism (which is, after all, the only generous and intelligent

form of criticism) to bear in mind that the age of Tennyson
was an age of real spiritual agony, and that a poet would
have indeed been limited and selfish if he had failed to the
extent of his capacity to respond to the crying spiritual
needs of his contemporaries. We may regret that Tennyson
clung so timidly to the sedate and middle course, we may
feel angered at his material prosperity being built up on
foundations which appear to us unsound and insincere, but
we must remember that the poetry of Tennyson, even those
many pieces which we now deride, brought great solace to
many unhappy people, and we must admit that even if, to
us, his thought seems shallow and insincere, it was hailed
by millions of his countrymen as penetrating, audacious and
profound. The fact that many of Tennyson's contemporaries
imagined Bailey's "Festus" or Tupper's "Proverbial Philosophy" to be works of even greater comfort and acumen,
shows how general was the demand for ethical poetry, and
explains perhaps the easy superiority which Tennyson attained in this style of composition. Nor should we forget
that it was Huxley himself who called Tennyson "the modern Lucretius"—an epithet which, to-day, leaves us agape.
It is this, I think—this conviction that, although perhaps not
very deeply rooted in eternity, Tennyson was very deeply
rooted in his age—which in the end throws a real dignity, a
feeling of something so inevitable as to be immune to
transitory expressions of taste and bias, on the totality of
his work and character. We speak glibly of the "optimism"
of the Victorians, but the word is misleading: at best it was
a courageous confrontation of the ruins of an easier, happier world; at its worst it was a real inability—an inability
based on sheer terror of the consequences—to face the facts.
And now that we no longer care so much for the things
that they were terrified of losing, we are mildly entertained
by their psychological heroics; confident as we are in our
own preference for realities, their idealism strikes us as
pathetic and rather engaging. But the point, I fear, is not
whether we are justified in our amusement: it is whether

we are justified in having ceased to care. And if humanity means anything, the answer can only be that we, not they, are wrong.

I will not recur to this aspect of the question: my endeavour is, frankly, to induce some people to approach Tennyson with an unbiased mind—to read him, for their pleasure, profit and even their amusement, as a poet who flourished prodigiously between the years 1832 and 1892. I shall not attain this object by propounding ethical considerations; my only hope is to approach his writings from the purely literary standpoint, and his life from our usual scavenger point of view. But I admit my sense of irreverence in doing so; I admit that by Tennyson the man, especially by Tennyson the old man, I am very considerably overawed. And if this feeling of awe will not (as I trust) be very apparent in the pages which follow, I should wish it, for several reasons, to be presupposed.

It is legitimate, perhaps, or at least desirable, in discussing a poet whose work is before us as a completed whole, to ignore what is bad in his poetry and to concentrate upon the task of illuminating what is good. It is unnecessary to imagine that because a great poet may have published certain verses which are silly or insincere, we are thereby obliged to qualify our admiration of what he had produced of excellence. There is no poet who would not be marred by so vain and unprofitable a process of criticism. A mood of zest and appreciation is essential to any useful discussion of poetry; a mood of reverence is perhaps helpful to any examination of a poet's life and character. One admits this theory as a platitude, and one proceeds to recognise that to the life and work of Tennyson it cannot, at this date, usefully apply. For Tennyson has already suffered more than enough from the admiration of his critics and the reverence of his biographers. That he should have inspired these sentiments is inevitable; that he should have ceased to inspire them may be regretted; but, for the purpose of explaining Tennyson to the modern generation, the one impression which it is essential to convey is the impression of *reality*, and to this object the elements of reverence and admiration can contribute only indirectly: they must be kept in the background.

## IV

I have of late been importuning my friends and acquaintances with the question: what, after all, they thought of Tennyson? The answers were varied. The majority replied that they did not think of Tennyson at all. A few said that they liked the Catullus and Virgil odes but didn't like the other things. Those who were in the movement assured me that Tennyson was "coming back." A few, more intelligent spirits, expressed the view that the man could write well enough but couldn't think, and that the whole thing reminded them too vividly of their schoolroom days to constitute a pleasant reminiscence. One of them quoted an illuminating passage from Samuel Butler: "Talking it over," he said, "we agreed that Blake was no good because he learnt Italian at sixty in order to study Dante, and we know Dante was no good because he was so fond of Virgil, and Virgil was no good because Tennyson ran him, and as for Tennyson—well, Tennyson goes without saying." And there was one, an undergraduate, who said that he liked the classical poems but couldn't stand the romantic. The latter opinion interested me greatly. For although I am second to none in my admiration of *Demeter and Persephone, Ulysses, Tithonus* and the first *Oenone,* I do not feel that *Tiresias* is as good a poem as *Maud,* and I am personally, and combatively, convinced that *Lucretius* is a very bad poem indeed. I did not understand why that undergraduate should have been so assured about it all; at the time I endeavoured to point out to him that the classical poems were not classical in the least, that the romantic poems were very spuriously romantic, and that the one category was, after all, just as Victorian as the other. He said that he knew all about that, but that the classical poems were none the less better than the romantic. And when I thought about it afterwards, I realised that what he had really meant to say was that Tennyson was better in form than in inspiration. And this discovery made me very angry.

For such a type of criticism is so nearly true, so easily substantiated, that it appears an almost hopeless task to controvert it. And, on considering the matter carefully, I realised that it would take me at least eighty thousand words to repudiate what people still imagined to be the Tennyson legend, and that this would leave me with but little space in which to indicate the possible lines of ultimate rehabilitation. So that the book has become but a tentative, sketchy sort of thing; an attempt, merely, to clean the paper for some other more appropriate hand to fill in the picture. But even with this restricted programme, it may prove of some utility.

My own views on Tennyson—the views I held as a child, the views I held at school and at the University, or in the period when I also did not think of Tennyson at all, or in the recent period when I have read and re-read him carefully—have undergone the most conflicting developments. It was the *Idylls* at first, and *Lady Godiva,* and *Lady Clare,* I fear, and a vague and plangent memory of my nurse intoning *Crossing the Bar.* And then came *Oenone* and *The Lotos-Eaters* and *Ulysses* and the period when I liked *Lucretius.* By the time I was sixteen, *In Memoriam* meant, as it still means to me, something very important; and then came Oxford, and Swinburne, and a wave of shame at having ever admired anything so smug and insincere as the Laureate of the Victorians. And gradually I was brought back to him by things like the Catullus ode, and the bit about Virgil, and *The Daisy,* and the lines to Lord Dufferin, and the dedication to FitzGerald, and I read *Maud* and *The Two Voices;* and then I read *Crossing the Bar* again, and after that I had no doubt at all that Tennyson was a very great poet. Of late I have read and re-read the poems as a whole, and have experienced curious fluctuations of opinion. I also have been through the phase of thinking him perfect in form and deficient in emotion; I have passed from that to feeling that his form was a mere mannerism, a trick of alliteration, onomatopœia and the like, and that it was his thought and purpose which, however much we might disagree with them, were the essential Tennyson; I have traversed a stage of thinking that the early poems were excellent and the later poems very bad indeed—there were moments when I felt that a few cantos in *In Memoriam* and the songs in *The Princess* were his only claims to immortality—and I have emerged with a very deep admiration for the great muscular mass of it all, for the sheer efficiency of style; and with a conviction that if one could separate the two Tennysons—the prosperous Isle-of-Wight Victorian from the black, unhappy mystic of the Lincolnshire wolds —one would find in the former the secret of his weakness, and in the latter the secret of his preponderating and triumphant strength.

And, as I read of his life and his friends, and as I visited the place where he was born, the places where he lived, this duality of purpose and inspiration became even more apparent, and I thought that, after all, it might be possible to represent Tennyson as something quite real and human, and to place his work, his life and character in a perspective which would be a little less legendary, a little less untrue, and which might offer some possibility of his being apprehended, if not admired, by an age which does not appreciate illusions, however soothing and successful they may be.

For Tennyson, if he survives at all, will survive in spite of, and not because of, the Tennyson legend, even as his poetry will survive in spite of the instructional and objective tenour which was forced upon it by the Victorians. Throughout his life and writings we can trace his sensitive poetic temperament struggling against the "mission" and "message" imposed upon it by the circumstances of his age. From early days the gloom and mystery of the wold and marsh were softened for him by the tender domestic atmosphere of his mother's parlour; the large excitement of Cambridge, the passionate inspiration of Hallam, were directed into objective channels by the moral earnestness of his particular set at Trinity, by the conceptions they instilled into him of an ethical purpose, of the importance to the poet of "a conscience and an aim." The death of Hallam, the ten years of sorrow and loneliness which followed, constituted the great opportunity, and he produced *The Two Voices* and *In Memoriam;* and in the end the "mission" conquered, and after the last defiant flash of *Maud* he settled down to the routine of marriage and Farringford, and the soft sweet smell of the laburnum, and success.

And it is thus that, in reviewing Hallam Tennyson's biography of his father, a former intimate could write, quite seriously, as follows:—

"No poet, perhaps, has ever come so close to the type of the Seer-prophet of the Old Testament as Tennyson, for I think none was ever so penetrated through and through as he was with the sense of the divine source of the gift of poetry imparted to him. He told me that this sense was *almost awful* to him in its intensity, because it made him feel as a priest who can never leave the sanctuary, and whose every word must be consecrated to the service of Him who had touched his lips with the fire of heaven which was to enable him to speak in God's name to his age. And so, he went on to say, nothing he had ever written seemed to him to have reached the standard of perfection short of which he must never rest; all he could hope was that he had brought men a little nearer to God. And it is just because, all through his life as a poet, Tennyson felt that he had a divine purpose to further, that the inner springs of that life, now revealed more fully than ever before in his son's biography of him, are of such surpassing interest."

The reasons which induced two whole generations to go so wrong—so irritatingly wrong—about a great poet; the causes which led that great poet to go so wrong—so tragically wrong—about himself, will require further elucidation. The explanation resides very largely in the state of English literature, in the state of English literary taste, between the years 1825 and 1840.

## V

In the concluding chapter of that remarkable work of art, the "Histoire de la Littérature Anglaise," Taine has amused himself by painting in delicate colours the soft and prosperous background of Tennyson's life, and by depicting the complacent propriety of the bourgeois public to which the Laureate appealed. From the artistic point of view—for the purpose, that is, of enhancing his own strident, gas-lit *finale* on Alfred de Musset—Taine may well have been justified in thus setting Tennyson among the roses and the honeysuckle; but when he proceeds, in perfect seriousness, to represent the Laureate as the cheerful dilettante of our later literature, one is forced to wonder whether he can have done more than turn the pages of the 1830 volume. There is one aspect, however, of Tennyson's literary development which Taine has brought out very admirably—the connection, that is, which exists between the more obvious inspirations of Tennyson's poetry and the average literary taste of his age. It was not a high average; it was not calculated to inspire any very adventurous flights of genius; and it created a circumambient atmosphere—a soft, clinging, relaxing atmosphere, which must be examined, and if possible discounted, before we can hope to reach any sensible appreciation of Tennyson's poetry.

"When," says Taine, "Tennyson published his first poems, the critics gave them a bad reception. He relapsed into silence: for ten years his name disappeared from the reviews, even from the booksellers' catalogues. By the time he again came forward his poetry had won its way subterraneously and by itself: he was at once hailed as the greatest poet of his country and his age. The public were surprised by Tennyson, surprised and delighted. The mighty generation of poets which had just disappeared had passed over the face of England like a thunderstorm. Even as their predecessors of the sixteenth century, they had flung themselves into extremes. They had seized on gigantic and forgotten legends, they had piled vision upon vision, they had ransacked Greece and Arabia, the East and the Middle Ages, and had surfeited the imagination of their contemporaries with the colours and fantasies of every clime. Some, rising to the heights of ethics and metaphysics, had pondered indefatigably upon the conditions of humanity, and had passed their lives in the monotony of the sublime. Others had exhibited, against a background of clouds and lightning, a procession of fantastic and fearsome personages writhing in remorse or aureoled by their essential magnificence. The English public, after all these energies and excesses, desired a rest. As a relief from all this satanic, sentimental, imaginative business, Tennyson struck them all as perfectly delicious. All the formulæ, all the ideas which had recently been so popular, were reproduced by Tennyson in a sweeter, simpler form, framed for the ear in a style of gold. In Tennyson we find the close of an epoch; it was given to him to enjoy what had disturbed his predecessors: his poetry can be likened to a soft summer evening—the lines of the landscape are the same as in the day, but the glitter of the cupola is veiled, the flowers lift their heads refreshed, and the sun sinks calmly in the west, blending in its purple haze the woods and meadows which had glared so fiercely in the noonday heat."

There is much bias, of course, and some wilful misconception, in this dramatic passage; but it embodies, vividly enough, a truth, the realisation of which is an essential preliminary to any study of Tennyson—it implies, I mean, that Tennyson was terribly unfortunate in the literary taste of his age. A supremely great man would doubtless have triumphed over the taste of his contemporaries and directed it into better channels; but Tennyson, though great, was not supremely great. And the atmosphere of his age affected him most perniciously.

It is customary to define the years between 1825 and 1842—the years, that is, in which Tennyson's literary manner was formed—as a period of transition; but it was less than that—it was a period of mental lethargy. For the interregnum between the gospel of Rousseau and the gospel of Carlyle was but a shilly-shally period, in which no one knew exactly what was wanted in literature and very few felt that they wanted anything at all. There existed during those seventeen years no general literary excitement, no general effervescence even: the period is but an interval of nervous prostration between the glories and excitements of the preceding decades and the spiritual perturbations that were to come. An age, in fact, "incapable of being sung to in any but a trivial manner"; an age which, as Carlyle himself recognised, required "intelligible word of command, not musical psalmody and fiddling."

Keats, Shelley and Byron had all died between 1821 and 1824. Their predecessors, although they outlived them, had ceased to produce work of poetical value. Wordsworth was, it is true, to publish *Yarrow Revisited* in 1837, but his later compositions are no more than the magnificent sunset flickers of a waning genius. Coleridge was up at Highgate mumbling metaphysics, and had, when he died in 1834, been silent for nine years. Southey, Campbell, and, with a few exceptions, Landor, had all ceased to write poetry; Crabbe and Scott both died in 1832. Tom Moore, who survived them by twenty years, had written little of value since the publication of *Lalla Rookh* in 1817; and Samuel Rogers, preferring St. James' Place to the "cot beside the hill," decided after 1828 that his immortality was secure, and refrained for the twenty-seven years which still remained to him from competing with the rising literary generation. In a word, "The marvellous bloom was over and the petals were scattered on the grass."

The field was clear. The critics were searching for a new poet. Christopher North, writing in February 1832, remarks that "all the great schools seem effete. I know not from what fresh fountains the waters may now flow. The future is all darkness." And in 1834 we find *Fraser's Magazine* bewailing that there are "no sun, no moon, no stars in the poetical heavens—nothing but a miserable sprinkling of wretched glow-worms." The unfortunate thing, however, was that the public, as distinct from the critics, did not want a new poet at all. "Many a well-educated man," we read in *Fraser's Magazine* in 1834, "can no more read poetry than he can Chinese." And as late as 1839 we find the *Edinburgh Review* maintaining that "even while many of our best poets are yet alive, poetry herself is dead or entranced." The critics were puzzled by this indifference, and they contradict themselves in endeavouring to find a remedy. Thus we find the *Edinburgh Review* explaining in March 1831 that "what we desire . . . is that poetry nowadays should not so much instruct as that it shall interest and delight. . . . We require that it shall appeal to the imagination and our feelings rather than to our judgment." And in the same authority, in the same year, we find the following: "The public taste has been cloyed with dainties: what they now want is information." And again, in the same Review for 1831: "Non satis est pulchra esse poemata: dulcia sunto."

In all this contradiction and bewilderment of the critics,

in all this indifference and satiety of the public, in all the vagueness and triviality which we find in the literary production of the period, there is one dominant *motif* which is essential to the understanding of what followed. There is the reaction against Byron.

We are apt, I think, to underestimate the position occupied by Byron throughout the earlier decades of the nineteenth century. Up till 1830, Shelley, it must be remembered, was known, if known at all, for his religious and political views rather than for his poetry. The first complete authorised edition of his works did not appear till 1839, and even then *Queen Mab* was omitted from the collection. The recognition of Keats was even more curiously retarded, and as late as 1842 we find that a man like Bulwer could still write of him as "Keates." The point is important and interesting: it meant that the intellectuals between 1825 and 1840 were occupied with Wordsworth, Coleridge, Southey, but still more with the exciting but tardy discovery of Keats and Shelley; it meant that when the great mass of the public, to whom poetry meant Byron and predominantly Byron, began to react against their idol, they reacted into the soft but inevitable arms of Felicia Hemans or Laetitia Landon; it meant that when the old reviews boomed and thundered, the great public were impressed, of course (for had not an article in the *Quarterly* in 1829 caused a drop of 2 per cent in the stocks?), but were not quite clear what it was all about. It meant, not that there were no poets existing, but that the general atmosphere was curiously unfavourable to the birth of any but the most trivial verse. It meant, finally, that the reaction against the magnificent muscular poetry of the Byronic period was complete.

I do not think that the extent and depth of this reaction are sufficiently realised. It explains a great many things: it explains the Annuals, and much of Tennyson's early poetry, and the popularity of the Keepsake style, and the fact that Darley and Beddoes were dismissed as odd and excessive (as indeed they were), and that Robert Pollok sold eighty thousand copies of his *Course of Time,* and that within a year Montgomery's *Omnipresence of the Deity* had run into eight editions. It explains how by 1838 the public, both of England and America, had achieved a condition of taste in which Tupper's *Proverbial Philosophy* sold well over one hundred thousand copies and brought him twenty thousand pounds. It furnishes us with a reason why the English-speaking public desired, above all things, not to be stimulated or surprised; why the commonplace, and particularly the moral commonplace, was accepted as being "true" or "tender"; why every poet, if he wished to be appreciated, felt obliged to appeal to the sane and gentle emotions, and to avoid all impulses of passion; and why that arid civil servant, Sir Henry Taylor, became, and to some extent remained, the literary idol of the age.

We have the whole theory adumbrated in the preface to Taylor's *Philip van Artevelde,* which appeared in 1834, and the influence of which upon the early Victorians in general, and upon Tennyson in particular, was profound. For Henry Taylor, sitting in his room there at the Colonial Office, had been deeply distressed by the lack of purpose in the poetry of his immediate predecessors, a style of poetry which, he admits, "will always produce a powerful impression upon very young readers. But," he continues, "from this unbounded indulgence in the mere luxuries of poetry, has there not ensued a want of adequate appreciation for its intellectual and immortal part? . . . A feeling came more easily to them than a reflection, and an image was always at hand when a thought was not forthcoming. . . . It did not belong to poetry in their apprehension to thread the mazes of life in all its classes and under all its circumstances, common as well as romantic, and, seeing all things, to infer and to instruct." From this general attack upon writers whose "appeal is made so exclusively to the excitabilities of mankind," Taylor launches out on a particular diatribe against Lord Byron. "The decline," he explains, "in popular estimation which he has suffered for the last few years, may be rather attributed to a satiated appetite on the part of the public than to rectified taste. What I would be understood to oppugn is the strange opinion which seems to prevail amongst certain of our writers and readers of poetry that *good sense* stands in a species of antagonism to poetical genius, instead of being one of its most essential constituents."

And having enunciated his theory, Sir Henry Taylor embarks upon the tedious but quite sensible heroics of his famous drama.

Not only, however, was it the duty of the poet to elevate and to instruct: it was his function also to interest and to please. I quote the following from the *Edinburgh Review* of October 1837:—

"It is gratifying," says the reviewer in discussing a contemporary Annual, "to find that a more agreeable and settled state of things is indicated by the poetical meteorology of 1837. The Germans, not long before us, had had their *Sturm und Drang periode* in literature: . . . Our 'storm and stress' period, we rejoice to think, is now also over; for if we take up any collection of poems, such as this, a more rational, healthy and natural tone of feeling on the part of our writers, indicating a corresponding state of the public mind, is obvious. The melodramatic tricks, both of conception and execution, which debarred and alloyed the real force and power of our poetical literature . . . seem nearly exploded: in all poetry which becomes in any degree popular, contemplation is visibly assuming the ascendancy over wild and irregular action; and the sources of emotion are sought less in the low, the startling and the transitory, than in the elevated, the calm and the enduring. This at least is the case with the volume before us: it indicates plainly enough a decided decline in the taste for the poetry of *excite-*

*ment,* and a return to what we must always consider as the highest and truest vocation of the Muse—the poetry of intellect, humanised and brought home to the heart by *sentiment* at once elevated and familiar, at once of individual and universal application."

## VI

It was inevitable that Tennyson should have been profoundly influenced by this almost universal reaction against all that Byronism was supposed to entail. In the "Poems by Two Brothers," published three years after Byron's death, he had worked off, in a series of vapid imitations, the literary influence which his great and virile predecessor had exercised upon his boyhood. In the *Timbuctoo* of 1829 it is already apparent that Keats had supplanted Byron in his admiration, and by the 1830 volume all traces of Byronism have completely disappeared in the pervading Shelleyan atmosphere of Cambridge. But the effect of the reaction went deeper than any merely literary renunciation; from his very early days Tennyson was influenced by the contemporary demand for calm elevation and for human sentiment. His mother's fondness for Felicia Hemans could not fail to leave a tremulous impression; the society of the young ladies at Horncastle, the types of verses which these young ladies expected and received, increased, and for the moment justified, what was, we must admit, an inherent predilection for the dainty and the elegant. On leaving the intensive domestic atmosphere of Somersby for a Cambridge in which the new generation, under the fomenting influence of men like Hare and Connop Thirlwall, were convinced that to them alone had been entrusted the enlightenment of a dull lethargic age, Tennyson fell, inevitably also, under the influence of the Trinity "Apostles," and the strength that was in him was diverted into ethical, and not, as one might have wished, into emotional channels. By the time he left Cambridge the harm had been done. The great lyric poet who had been born up there among the Lincolnshire wolds had been already tamed, controlled, labelled, and given a function unnatural to his genius; the wild, unhappy animal that lurked within him had been caged and shackled, and the real intention and meaning of the man had been for ever veiled—even from himself.

We must realise that against the insidious influence of his age, against the sheer misfortune of having been born at exactly the wrong moment, Tennyson had, in fact, but little chance. He was by no means the only writer of that time who so succumbed. Had he arrived a generation earlier, he would have been a great Romantic; had he delayed a generation later, he would have been greater than any of the Pre-Raphaelites; even as it was, he might well have emerged an immortal had his intelligence been equal to his poetic temperament. But it was not equal. And there is a great deal, therefore, which needs to be explained away.

It avails, I recognise, but little to contend that it was the fault of the age, and not of the poet, that Tennyson was thus or thus. It would be easy, indeed, to show that those characteristics of Tennyson which estrange him the most from modern readers are but the passing reflection of the thoughts and manners of his time—that his sentimentality, his commonplace morals, his caution, his shallow thought, his maddening accuracy, are merely incidentals which should not affect our estimate of his poetry. It avails still less to indicate what a very remarkable poet Tennyson would have become had he been different in himself or had he fallen upon other circumstances. If an impression is to be made by any advocacy of Tennyson, it is necessary at the outset to diagnose the real nature of the aversion with which he is now regarded, and, having done so, to examine whether this aversion is superficial only or profound.

It may be assumed that every generation, and indeed every individual, will evolve their own particular definition of what constitutes the highest poetry. Such definitions are entertaining, and may even be useful so long as they are advanced as relative only, and not as absolute. The most that one may hazard is that the scattered individual definitions of any given generation, if fused together into a composite formula, do actually constitute an indication of the particular aspect upon poetry which is prevalent in, or natural to, that generation. And I think it may be said without fear of contradiction that what the early twentieth century primarily demands from poetry is a reality of emotional impulse. One can amplify this formula if desired: one may exact, with Mr. Drinkwater, that poetry should be the "announcement of spiritual discovery"; one may demand "a coincidence of unfettered imaginative ecstasy with superb mental poise"; one may apply to it the definition which Mr. Middleton Murry applies to style—"a combination of the maximum of personality with the maximum of impersonality; . . . a concentration of peculiar and personal emotion . . . a complete projection of this personal emotion into the created thing." We may do all this, and more; but we shall come back, I think, to the simple conclusion that what people look for to-day is this reality of emotional impulse. They look for it in Tennyson, and they find, or think they find, little reality, less emotion and scarcely any impulse at all. They accuse him, therefore, of being no true poet; and this accusation, I contend, rests on a complete misconception of his peculiar genius.

For although the great mass of Tennyson's poetry, however skilful it may be in form, appears in substance to be lacking in these important qualities of impulse, reality and emotion; although one must admit that his prosperous assurance, his laborious and careful revisions, his accuracy and caution, lead one at times to doubt the compelling force of his inspiration, and even, perhaps, to question his sincerity; although he was apt on all occasions to exploit sentiments and situations which were certainly superficial and perhaps unreal; although he flinched alike before the flame of passion and the cold nakedness of truth, yet there

are sudden panting moments when the frightened soul of
the man cries out to one like some wild animal caught in
the fens at night-time—moments when he lies moaning
in the half-light in an agony of fear. And at such moments
the mystical genius of Tennyson comes upon one in a flash,
and there can be no question of the reality of his emotion
and his impulse.

I advance this theory not as a paradox but, for what it
is worth, as an absolute personal conviction. For me, the
essential Tennyson is a morbid and unhappy mystic. He
is the hero of *The Sensitive Mind*, of *The Two Voices* and
above all of *Maud*. He is a spirit for whom there was an
"ever-moaning battle in the mist"—a soul whose fancies
mingled

> "With the sallow-rifted glooms
>   Of evening, and the moanings of the wind";

and thus at times there comes

> "A cry that shiver'd to the tingling stars,
>   And, as it were one voice, an agony
>   Of lamentation, like a wind, that shrills
>   All night in a waste land, where no one comes
>   Or hath come, since the making of the world."

For those who accept this theory no great difficulty will
arise in reconciling the essential Tennyson with the Tennyson of the legend. One would prefer not to fall back upon
the jargon of the psycho-analysts, but the application of the
Freudian system to the case of Tennyson is quite illuminating. For Tennyson was afraid of a great many things: predominantly he was afraid of death, and sex, and God. And
in all these matters he endeavoured instinctively to subli-
mate his terrors by enunciating the beliefs which he desired to feel, by dwelling upon the solutions by which he
would like to be convinced. The point does not require further elaboration: my contention is merely that once one
accepts the realisation of Tennyson, and particularly the

younger Tennyson, as a man who was morbidly afraid, one must admit that the processes by which he conquered his afflictions cannot by any possibility be described as consciously insincere. And once one is able to dispose of this fatal suspicion of insincerity, the real beauty of Tennyson's poetry will triumph of itself.

## VII

I have endeavoured in this introductory chapter to indicate some of the reasons for which Tennyson is so little esteemed by the present generation, and to suggest the processes by which an interest in his poetry might be encouraged to revive. I have explained that to some extent the reaction against him is to be attributed to the exaggerated adulation accorded to him by the Victorian age; and I have admitted that a contributory cause of this reaction is the fact that so subjective a poet should have been forced, however justifiably, into a perpetual straining after objective expression. I have urged, as an excuse for this, the peculiar circumstances of the period when Tennyson first appeared as a poet and the unfortunate condition of contemporary literary taste. I have contended that, if we still desire to be fair to Tennyson, it is necessary to realise the duality which exists between his temperament and his intelligence, between his lyrical genius and the peculiar qualities which were imposed upon him by his age; and I have concluded with the theory that the essential inspiration of Tennyson was the inspiration of fear, and that, if once this view is accepted and realised, the most damaging criticism against him—the criticism that he was both morally and intellectually insincere—will cease to trouble or to disconcert.

I do not imagine that I have at this stage convinced anyone by this thesis: it is a theory at which I have arrived myself only after much doubt and hesitation. I ask only that it may be accepted as a working basis for what follows, and that it will be allowed to give a certain thread of consistency to the chapters, otherwise inchoate, in which the development of the poet is traced from his childhood days at Somersby to the final dignity of his old age.

And in the end, as always with any poet of value, it matters little what theories are propounded or what discoveries are made. In the end Tennyson will be appreciated, not in the least because the ingenious critic has toyed for an hour or two with some fresh or forgotten aspect of his genius. He will be appreciated because he wrote *Ulysses* and *The Lotos-Eaters;* because he wrote *Tithonus;* because he wrote *The Two Voices;* because he wrote *Maud;* because he wrote:—

"Now lies the Earth all Danäe to the stars,"

and *Crossing the Bar*.

And, after all, *In Memoriam*.

# CHAPTER TWO

# SOMERSBY

## *1809–1828*

## I

It is preferable, I think, to approach Somersby from Mable-thorpe, and (if your zest is sufficient) on foot; for if you drive from Lincoln, from Horncastle, or even from Alford, you will miss the full contrast between wold and marsh, between the curve and the straight, between "the garden and the wild."

It is otherwise with the road from Mablethorpe. One turns away from the dunes and the long line of yellow, white-fringed sea. The road for some eight miles runs straight across the marsh—the "glooming flats," the "level waste and rounding gray" which one had come to find. Behind is the thud of the sea and the long bulwark of the dune, dotted with sallow-thorn and sword-grass; in front, the faintly pencilled outline of the Lincolnshire wolds: not hills exactly—not high enough, not sufficiently indented, to reckon as hills—merely a sudden upward curve of plough-land beyond the wide slabs of pasture, a smooth grey curve upon the sky, the tilth showing hoary as it dries in the wind from the North Sea. And here and there rises a clump of elms under the immense soft circle of the clouds. One crosses the bleak uplands of Harrington hill and drops down again among the lesser swellings and undulations which encircle

Somersby. The lane which had cut sheer and stark across the higher wold begins to swerve among the hedgerows; the earth assumes a more delicate covering, and there are violets and cuckoo-flowers among the ash roots, and the sound of birds and water.

And so, almost unexpectedly, one comes on Somersby.

A cluster of elms, as first impression; a dip merely in the hills where the lanes deepen in their banks and converge together round a larger tree tottering upon its triangle of roadside grass. Then, above the lane, is the churchyard, and, to the right, a farm; and beyond them the squat little church, with a white gate in the hedge. Directly opposite the church is reared a red building, castellated and incongruous, with its rows of white-sashed Italian windows. Baumber's farm, it is called, and Baumber was identified, much to Tennyson's fury, as the original of the Northern Farmer. The design has been attributed to Vanbrugh; the house has been described, and wrongly, as the Moated Grange of Mariana. But it is a curious building, and it looks down rather grimly upon its neighbour—the low white Rectory of Somersby, and upon the Rectory lawn of poignant association.

The Rectory stands a few yards back from the lane, from which it is separated by a short curve of gravel and a hedge pierced by two gates and enlivened on the house side with daffodils. There are no poplars at the door to-day, but the elm-trees remain, and there is a notice to say that visitors are admitted to the garden on Wednesdays and on Fridays. Across the road, and upon a slight mound, is the churchyard, where old Doctor Tennyson lies buried under a flat, moss-greened slab. And the church itself, tiled now in place of the original thatch, sleeps small and unpretentious among its little yews, the slim Gothic cross which rises from the grave-stones forming its one claim to architectural interest. A tiny tabernacle it appears within; only the old font where Alfred was christened and behind it the bronze Woolner bust erected by the Lincolnshire gentry in 1911. A little strip of pathway edged with primulas cuts down from the churchyard, and one crosses the lane diagonally to the Rectory gate.

The southern, or garden, aspect of the house remains unaltered, familiar from the endless engravings which are to be seen in the illustrated periodicals of the later nineteenth century. There is the bay window on the left, the window of the room where Tennyson was born, the attic window of the "darling room" where he wrote his juvenilia, and on the right the two Gothic windows of the dining-room. There are the creepers, woodbine and passionflower, against the whitewashed brick, and on each side the flanking mass of elms and larches dappling the lawn with sun and shade. Only the large conifer in front of the bay window has now disappeared.

In all this exactitude of expected recognition there is, however, for the student of Tennyson, a definite element of surprise at his first sight of Somersby. It is a shock occasioned by the unforeseen modesty of its proportions; by the way it cowers rather than nestles among its trees. It is not a high house—two stories only, with a dormer here and there—and yet it seems short and truncated in comparison to its stature. The Gothic hall, baronial in Dr. Tennyson's intention, has a curtailed, almost a telescoped appearance. The lawn, which played so enduring a part in Tennyson's emotional experience, is but a trim and tidy affair, a few square yards only in measurement. The herbaceous garden, the garden

> ". . . bower'd close
> With plaited alleys of the trailing rose,
> Long alleys falling down to twilight grots,
> Or opening upon level plots
> Of crowned lilies, standing near
> Purple-spiked lavender——"

consists of two beds on either hand with a narrow grass walk ending in a rustic bench against the hedge; and finally

a short meadow falling down to the willows of the famous
brook.

There is nothing, indeed, in any of Tennyson's own and
endless references to Somersby which could justify so instinctive a misapprehension of its size. The "long alleys" and
the "twilight grots" above quoted are, after all, purely relative expressions: there is nothing in the 94th section of *In
Memoriam* which implies a more extensive Somersby. Nor
is it wholly that the park-like effect of that familiar and
magnificent passage—the glimmering of the white cows in
the distance, the long arms of the trees, the full foliage of
the elms and sycamores—had deluded one into a false sense
of spaciousness. The surprise proceeds, I think, quite pro-
saically, from the actual numbers of the original inmates.
Nor is it only this sheer weight of numbers (two parents,
eleven surviving children, an occasional aunt, indefinite
servants, intermittent guests, an eventual governess) which
perplexes one, but the actual physical bulk, taken individ-
ually, of the occupants. And indeed, the seven lanky, six-
foot sons, the four slender daughters, the stark old Rector
and gentle mother, must, even out in the garden, have got
very considerably in each other's way. One's surprise is thus
legitimate; I do not know that it is very important. It en-
tails, of course, some readjustment of the particular imaginative setting in which one had placed the family, or
visualised the Somersby episodes of *In Memoriam*—the
harp, the Tuscan poets, and the urn. It involves a realisation of a more concentric, more overcrowded, huddled and
even insanitary existence than had previously been conceived. It may even indicate, or substantiate, certain incidental theories of Tennyson's character—his almost morbid
domesticity, his effeminacy, his sociability coupled with his
aloofness and other traits. But apart from this it is interesting merely: one cannot contend that it is material.

Far more important is the general feeling of Somersby,
its peculiar atmosphere. The geography of it, in the first
place. The sense of distance and of isolation; the sense of

seclusion. The sense that to the north the wolds stretch wind-swept to the Humber, that to the south they dip again into the wide sadness of the fens. The sense, to the east there over the hill, of marshes moaning in the gale from the North Sea; the sense, to the west there over the hill, of the fog loitering from dyke to dyke. The sense of protection. The sense of Somersby, one's own Somersby, an island of green-sand in a waste of chalk, coddling down among its elms and hedgerows with the grey curve of the wold above it and the darkening flats beyond; the sense that here the gentler beauties of Nature come as some rarer and more exclusive privilege; that the gifts of warmth and scent and colour, the song of birds and the sound of running water have a more detailed, more concentrated, significance, are infused with the delicate intimacy of personal and domestic things.

And, in contrast to this, the sense of the stark plough-land on the hill; the twisted thorn; the sunbeam flying across the flattened counties; the view out to the eastern sand-dunes; the straight glimmer of the trenches among the reeds; the ragged trail of storm upon Warder Hill; the wide sweep of luminous sky; the low moon over the flats at harvest-time; the distant thunder of the sea.

## II

One would wish to know something more about the origin of the Tennysons. The accounts which have come down to us are either too vague to be useful or too romanesque to be convincing. We are told, on the one hand, that the family were of Danish origin and came from north of the Humber. This may well be true. But it does not account for one dominant and curious characteristic in the Tennyson family which is still unexplained—namely, the Tennyson type. "Foreign" they called them in Lincolnshire; even in those early days Alfred was stared at in the lanes. Swarthy, at all events, and with a perplexing swarthiness;

not English, anyhow; not Celtic even. For there is little similarity between the six-foot slouch of the Tennyson brothers and the small-boned, beady-eyed Celticism of the ordinary type. And dark they were, not only in appearance, but in temperament. "We Tennysons," the Laureate growled out later, "are a black-blooded race." Frederick alone, the eldest surviving brother, was pink and fair like his Lincolnshire contemporaries; but in other respects Frederick, for his part also, was very odd indeed. Again and again one finds in references to first meetings with Tennyson evidence of the surprise occasioned by his dark and lowering complexion. We have no clue to the reason: the explanation furnished in the memoir by Hallam Tennyson is not intended, perhaps, to be taken very seriously. "This foreign colouring," he says, "may possibly have been derived from a Huguenot ancestor, a relation of Madame de Maintenon." We pass over this hypothesis, but the problem remains. Not Plantagenet, certainly; not, as possibly with Browning, mulatto; presumably not Spanish or Italian: there was no heritage of the south in Alfred's veins. Semitic, possibly: Charles Tennyson, in his old age, became decidedly rabbinical. And gipsy possibly: even then not Triana gipsy, not Andalusian; but derived preferably from some nomadic denizen of the central European wastes: Hungarian, Czech or Polish. One is tempted by the fantasy of such an idea: one would like to connect it with some substantial evidence. It would explain many things. It would explain not only the Tennyson physique, but also the rancour and the self-pity; the lonely walks at night-time; the wistfulness and the gloom; the obsession of wide, wet, twilight spaces; the indifference to cold. It would explain much of what is best and most permanent in Tennyson's lyrical genius.

But the problem, with such material as is before us, can only be stated and emphasised as a problem. And there is a second, equally curious but less absolutely hypothetical theory which decorates Tennyson's heredity. We are told that the poet was descended through his great-grand-mother, Elizabeth Clayton, from the d'Eyncourts and the Plantagenets. It was his grandfather, George Tennyson, of Bayon's Manor, who, with the assistance of the College of Heralds, elaborated and, to his own satisfaction, established this romantic ancestry. The elder George Tennyson, the poet's grandfather, appears, in other respects, to have been a shrewd and capable man of business. He studied at first as a solicitor, promoted the construction of the docks at Grimsby, and thus trebled the value of the Clayton property around that town. His marriage with Miss Turner of Caistor brought him further wealth; he became a Member of Parliament; he bought the estates of Bayon's Manor and Usselby, near Tealby, on the north-western ridge of the wolds, and lived there to a healthy old age, diversified by his "zeal for pedigree" already noted. He had two sons, George and Charles, and two daughters, and he subjected them to a curiously individual treatment which, although the underlying causes are obscure, is important as influenc-ing the circumstances of Tennyson's own childhood. The elder of the two sons, George, the poet's father, was, for some hidden reason, disinherited in favour of his younger brother Charles. It was Charles who succeeded to the estate of Bayon's Manor; who in due time became the Member of Parliament and, indeed, a Privy Councillor; who was obliged, under the old man's will, to assume the surname of d'Eyncourt, and who constructed around the old house at Bayons the vast baronial edifice which exists to-day. George, in compensation for all this, was sent into the Church, for which, admittedly, he had neither liking nor vocation. For his maintenance were provided the livings of Somersby, of Bag Enderby and Great Grimsby, and the incumbency of Benniworth. In this manner, in those days of pluralities, did the old Squire of Bayon's Manor salve his conscience towards his elder son. He went further, and as, year by year, the household at Somersby increased to such alarming proportions, he insisted that the sons, the whole

eight of them, should also, when the moment came, enter
the Church, and be sprinkled over the livings which his
county influence could secure for them. The grandsons, for
their part, were not very amenable to this suggestion.
George, the eldest, died in infancy; Frederick, the second,
after studying for holy orders, refused at the last moment,
and went off to the Ionian Islands as secretary to the High
Commissioner; Charles, the third son, did actually live and
die as Vicar of Grasby; but Alfred refused consistently to
do anything at all—not that much pressure appears to have
been put upon him so long as his father lived, but in March
1831 the Rector died, and the family were left entirely at
the mercy of the old man at Bayon's Manor. We find a letter from Arthur Hallam to Merivale dated in August of
that year. "What I have to say," he wrote, "is this. Alfred,
not intending to go into the Church, as the grandfather who
has *patria potestas* over him wishes . . . is desirous of put-
ting his wits to profit, and begins to think himself a fool for
kindly complying with the daily requests of Annuals without getting anything in return." I have anticipated in this
way, in order to dispose of George Tennyson of Bayon's
Manor, the fine-featured old gentleman of the Lawrence
portrait, who in his turn was to disappear in 1836 and to
have no further influence upon his grandson's future. The
fact, however, that Alfred Tennyson so narrowly escaped
the Church has a speculative interest: his career there, we
can have little doubt, would have been much on the lines
of those of F. D. Maurice and Kingsley; the theology of
his poems would have more meaning; he would have been
a formidable "révolté," and, as such, his reputation to-day
would perhaps have gained that element of spice which
for the present generation is so regrettably lacking. But, as
I have said, the grandfather died, and by the time the other
four sons came of age the pressure was relaxed.

The influence of all these theories and circumstances
upon Tennyson himself was perhaps more permanent than
appears from the Memoir. Even the Plantagenet legend,

which, when questioned about it later, he would repudiate
as trivial, was not without a superficial effect. It would lead
him in his middle years to Westminster Abbey, where he
would stand in front of the tomb of Edward III, ruminating
on a family resemblance, which, with the fine nose and the
marked furrow from lip to nostril, was, and especially after
1857, when the Laureate began to grow a beard, indeed
remarkable. And then, later still, when it came to building
Aldworth, the arms and emblems of the d'Eyncourts offered
a useful and decorative variation for the Tudor fireplaces.

But more serious, and far deeper, was the effect upon
his father, and through his father upon Tennyson himself,
of the perplexing and bitter story of the disinheritance. The
congenital bile of the Tennysons was further envenomed for
the Rev. George Tennyson by this wanton freak of fortune,
which had bound him to an uncongenial and unprofitable
calling. Tall, swarthy and despondent, the Rector would
moon about the lanes, or loom in the low passages of his
home; stern always, stingy generally, "amazing sharp" to
his children, and with outbursts of black irritation succeeded by long spells of even blacker gloom. "A thousand
admirable qualities," wrote the Rt. Hon. Charles d'Eyncourt, his younger brother, rather jauntily perhaps, after
his death, "a thousand admirable qualities of heart which
would have contributed to his own happiness and that of
those around him if he had not given way to failings arising
out of a nervous temperament."

And yet not wholly a sinister figure. A scholar, in the first
place, and a lover of books. And then a man who was interested, it appears, in the plastic arts and in the work of
his own hands. For it is he who, with the help of the old
servant Horlins, built the refectory (the "hall" which figures
so domestically in *In Memoriam*) in which to feed, to edu-
cate, and possibly to isolate, his amazing family. It is not
perhaps a very great architectural success, this Somersby
dining-room; the roof-beams had been cut from the neighbouring woods and erected while still in the green. The
room is too high for its length and has a somewhat wobbly

appearance; but it still subsists, with its groined ceiling and its wooden oriels, with the scratchy sandstone corbel-heads and reliefs, in the manner of Lincoln cathedral, and the moulded architrave within. And then there is the fireplace, which at Christmas time the eleven surviving children of the house would twine with holly—a dumpy, plaster, Gothic fretted erection painted chocolate to resemble oak.

Nor are there absent some slight indications of a more human side to Tennyson's father before the cloud of his responsibilities settled upon him. The reference in *In Memoriam* applies probably to old Mr. Lushington at Maidstone:—

> "How many a father have I seen,
>     A sober man among his boys,
>     Whose youth was full of foolish noise,
> Who wears his manhood hale and green;
>
> And dare we to this fancy give,
>     That had the wild oat not been sown,
>     The soil, left barren, scarce had grown
> The grain by which a man may live?"

One may doubt the wild oat in Dr. Tennyson's past; but there exists a detached and curious story of an adventure in Russia, and how at a dinner-party at the Embassy he blurted out the name of one of the Emperor Paul's murderers in the presence of that then important individual, and how forthwith he had to fly the country in disguise.

Be this as it may, it was undoubtedly his father's scholarship, his father's library, which gave to Alfred that wide general culture, classical and romantic, which would not have come to him with the same breadth through the more precise curriculum of a private or public school. And yet one is tempted to feel that the more permanent effect of the Rector's temperament upon his son was the impression of his moods and outbursts, of the sense of wrong and injustice which brooded over the little home and increased the morbid despondencies of his own nature. There is evi-

dence enough of this in the "Poems by Two Brothers." And
there is a story, somewhere, of Alfred sobbing after one of
his father's spells of solemn gloom, sobbing by himself at
night in Holywell Glen, sobbing with a sense of intolerable
guilt and oppression.

### III

The Rev. George Tennyson did not settle at Somersby till
1808. In August 1805 he had married Elizabeth Fytche,
daughter of the Vicar of Louth. A son George was born
at Tealby in 1806, and died the same year; in June 1807
Frederick appeared, and by July of the following year,
when Charles followed, the Tennysons were already established at Somersby. It was there, in the little upstairs room
with the iron balcony, that Alfred was born at midnight
on August 6th, 1809.

Elizabeth Tennyson, the poet's mother, has been portrayed in several of the poems, and notably in that entitled
*Isabel*, which appeared in the 1830 volume. We read
there of:—

> "Eyes not down-dropt nor over-bright, but fed
>     With the clear-pointed flame of chastity,
>     Clear, without heat, undying, tended by
>         Pure vestal thoughts in the translucent fane
> Of her still spirit; locks not wide-dispread,
>         Madonna-wise on either side her head;
>         Sweet lips whereon perpetually did reign
>     The summer calm of golden charity."

We read of:—

> "The intuitive decision of a bright
>     And thorough-edged intellect to part
>         Error from crime; a prudence to withhold;
>         The laws of marriage character'd in gold
>     Upon the blanched tablets of her heart."

We read of "an accent very low in blandishment"; of "a hate of gossip parlance"; of "a courage to endure and to obey."

We read, also, and with some surprise, of:—

"The mellow'd reflex of a winter moon;
A clear stream flowing with a muddy one,
        Till in its onward current it absorbs
            With swifter movement and in purer light
                The vexed eddies of its wayward brother:
            A leaning and upbearing parasite,
            Clothing the stem," etc.

We read, finally, of:—

"The stately flower of female fortitude,
        Of perfect wifehood and pure lowlihead."

More convincingly, perhaps, we can turn to the passage in *The Princess*:—

"Not learned, save in gracious household ways,
Not perfect, nay, but full of tender wants,
No Angel, but a dearer being, all dipt
In Angel instincts, breathing Paradise. . . .
                                Happy he
With such a mother! faith in womankind
Beats with his blood, and tho' he trip and fall
He shall not blind his soul with clay."

A gentle, timid, delicate woman, it appears. Rather frightened of her sombre husband during his lifetime; rather frightened of her big, sombre sons after his death. For the first ten years of Alfred's life she must of necessity have led an immobile existence, and have had little time to give to the elder children. But there remain a few slight pictures of her: a story of her protecting some animal against the brutalities of the village children; a picture of her in a wheeled chair drawn by a Newfoundland dog reading to her sons from the works of Mrs. Hemans and Beattie's Calendar. And in after life, when she was settled at Cheltenham, and later in Hampstead, for she lived till 1865, there are some further reminiscences: a record of her facility for tears, and of Alfred stalking about the room exclaiming, "Oh, damn your eyes, Mother! damn your eyes!"; a mention of her tame monkey; a picture of her, after 1850, sitting in the omnibus at Cheltenham and informing her fellow-passengers of her identity: "It may interest you to know that I am the Mother of the Laureate." And finally there is one illuminating and suggestive letter which is produced by Mr. Horton,[1] and which was written to the poet by his mother from Hampstead at a moment when the bitter taste of *Maud* had been sweetened by the appearance of the *Idylls*. "It does," she wrote, "indeed give me the purest satisfaction to notice that a spirit of Christianity is perceptible through the whole volume. . . . O dearest Ally, how fervently have I prayed for years that our Merciful Redeemer would intercede with our Heavenly Father to grant thee His Holy Spirit, to urge thee to employ the talents He has given thee, by taking every opportunity to impress the precepts of His Holy Word on the minds of others. My beloved son, words are too feeble to express the joy of my heart in perceiving that thou art earnestly endeavouring to do so. Dearest Ally, there is nothing for a moment to be compared to the favour of God: I need not ask thee if thou art of the same opinion. Thy writings are a convincing proof that thou art."

There are, of course, other influences which reacted upon Tennyson during the Somersby period. There were the local farmers and cottagers, with whom he consorted freely, and from whom he imbibed much that remained with him in after life. Their dialect, in the first place, reflected not only in the deliberately dialect poems, but in a certain Doric quality, a certain noticeable breadth and drawl, in his own subsequent pronunciation, in the "hollow o's and a's" which

[1] Robert F. Horton, "Alfred Tennyson." Saintly Lives Series. London, J. M. Dent. 1900.

so impressed the later visitors to Farringford. And, in the second place, their broad rustic humour—a little coarse in quality, with a salt, earthy flavour, and with the necessary attendant of guffaw. It was, fundamentally at least, the only kind of humour which Tennyson evolved: in its ultimate development we may call it Johnsonian; but, in spite of Mr. Desmond MacCarthy, I cannot really contend that Tennyson's humour ever ascended much above the agrarian. That it was earthy enough cannot be contested. It disconcerted some people—it disconcerted Jowett, who only liked little silver-toned sallies about the Holy Trinity, quite considerably—and unfortunately it is not communicable or producible; its effect depended upon the breadth and manner of its production, often upon the actual dramatic mimicry for which Tennyson had so pronounced a gift—even in his Cambridge days he had evoked shrieks of laughter by his well-known imitations of George IV and the sun coming up from behind a cloud—and thus it is lost to us, and, in our ignorance, we are apt to imagine Tennyson as a wholly unhumorous person. Which is perhaps inexact.

Then there were the county neighbours—the Barings, the Edens, and the Rawnsleys. And the dances and quadrilles on occasion at Horncastle Assembly Rooms, when Alfred, who was a fervent and awe-inspiring dancer, would make friends with Rosa Baring or Sophy Rawnsley and would send them next day those album verses some of which were reproduced, regrettably perhaps, in the 1830 volume. And, indeed, we are assured by Canon Rawnsley that "Thy rosy lips are soft and sweet" was addressed to Rosa Baring. And that "Airy fairy Lilian" is to be identified as Sophy Rawnsley. All of which was, and is, of no importance either to Tennyson or to ourselves.

Other influences there were also, and particularly in the home circle: the four younger brothers; the two elder sisters, Mary and Emilia or Emily; the two younger sisters, Matilda and Cecilia; the sisters' governess, to whom, during his very short absence at school, he would write letters in a facetious vein addressed "Dulcinea"; and finally there were aunts, and particularly a Calvinist aunt, Mrs. Mary Bourne, of Dalby, who was strong on the subject of original sin: "Alfred," she said to him one day, "Alfred, when I look on you I think of the words of Holy Scripture: 'Depart from me, ye cursed, into everlasting fire.'"

## IV

At the age of eight Alfred was sent to the grammar school at Louth, some ten miles north of Somersby across the wold. He was intensely miserable. He hated the noise and the loneliness; he missed the soft presence of his mother and sisters. He was bullied by the Master, the Rev. T. Waite, who used to slam and bang one over the head with a book; he was bullied also, we may suspect, by his schoolfellows. He took no part in their games; the description of a cricket match in *The Princess* is, I am assured, one of the very rare instances of his indulgence in the inaccurate; he was not, except in physique, a very manly boy. He would mope in odd uncomfortable corners with a book, and on Sunday there were his mother's relations to visit and on Mondays it all began over again. He was there for more than three years. He hated it so much that long afterwards, when visiting Louth, he had not the physical courage to go down the lane where the school was situated. And when he was twelve he was taken away, and came home to the Rectory, to the hollyhocks and the lilies, and the little white attic upstairs, with the dimity curtains, the smell of honeysuckle and the hooting of the owls at nighttime:—

> "O darling room, my heart's delight,
>   Dear room, the apple of my sight,
>   With thy two couches soft and white,
>   There is no room so exquisite,
>   No little room so warm and bright
>   Wherein to read, wherein to write."

He would say in later years that Louth had done nothing for him beyond a single tag of Latin lingering in his memory —"sonus desilientis aquæ." This may be so; the particular quality of his erudition is certainly of the Rectory study rather than the grammar-school type. But they had left their sting right enough, those three unhappy years at Louth: an almost morbid horror of the hostility of his fellow-creatures, and, as a reaction against this, a no less morbid love of the admiration of the chosen few. And into this warm circle of admiring relations he relapsed, for eight further years, with a soft sigh of contentment.

Not that they were idle years. For a short period he attended a village school in Holywell Glen which went by the local name of Gadneys. But after a while the Rector, for some reason, quarrelled with Mr. Gadney, and Alfred was withdrawn from his tuition. There ensued a long period of private instruction from his father, diversified by lessons in elementary mathematics, and incidentally in the Lincolnshire dialect, from a certain William Clerk of Bag Enderby.

That he took these studies, and himself, very seriously, is not to be doubted. There is a letter quoted in the Memoir written at the age of twelve to his Aunt Marianne Fytche of Louth. It is a terrible letter for a child to have composed. "Going," it reads, "into the library this morning, I picked up 'Sampson (*sic*) Agonistes' . . . on which I shall send you my remarks." These remarks fill several pages: there are quotations and analogies from Dante and Horace; there is a considerable borrowing from Bishop Newton's notes; there is a comment upon Milton's avoidance—unfortunate avoidance in Alfred's opinion—of the artifice of alliteration; and the letter concludes:—

"I have not, at present, time to write any more: perhaps I may continue my remarks in another letter to you; but (as I am very volatile and fickle) you must

not depend upon me, for I think you do not know any
one who is so fickle as

> "Your affectionate nephew,
> "A. TENNYSON."

It is evident certainly that in all these years at Somersby
the boy became proficient enough in classical literature;
that his education in such subjects was wide rather than
scholastic, imaginative rather than precise. And for this his
father deserves great credit. One hears early of original
compositions. Apart from the pieces included later in
"Poems by Two Brothers," there are some even earlier
verses, written between the ages of fourteen and fifteen,
which are reproduced in the Memoir—extracts from unfinished plays; ballads in the manner of Sir Walter Scott;
echoes of Byron.

We learn also of still earlier compositions. As a small
child he would rush about shouting Tennysonian formulæ
such as "far, far away," and "I hear a whisper in the wind."
At eight he covered two sides of a slate with blank verse
in the manner of Thomson's Seasons; by ten he had written
endless verses in the rhymed couplets of Pope; and at
twelve he had composed an epic in twelve books which
he would "go shouting about the fields in the dark." From
very early years he was puzzled by the problem of personality, and would sit upon the damp moss of Holywell
Glen saying, "Alfred, Alfred," to himself, and again "Alfred," until every thing became very poignant, mystical and
hazy. And before he left for Cambridge he had written
in Greek hexameters an Homeric composition on the "Seven
against Thebes," and an Ovidian poem on the death of a
young lady who had died for love of the Apollo Belvedere.
This latter poem, unfortunately, was subsequently suppressed.

And of public events, through all this, only the faintest
ripple can have reached Somersby: the Battle of Waterloo
came to them as a belated rumour, only very belatedly con-

firmed; the accession of George the Fourth passed in a still vaguer impression of rosettes and ribbons one morning at Louth. Byron died, and when he heard of it Alfred climbed up to the quarry and scratched the words "Byron is dead" upon the sandstone. From time to time a neighbouring Vicar would ride over to Somersby and there would doubtless be some talk of the Unitarians, and Queen Caroline, and, as Cambridge became nearer, some mutterings about Catholic emancipation. But the period from 1820 to 1828 stretches a sudden lull between the Napoleonic tempest and the political and theological agonies which began in the 'thirties. A quiescent period, during which Alfred, by now a long-limbed, swarthy creature, would tramp moodily over the wolds in the dark, or curl up in the attic room reading the works of his poetic predecessors, reading his own juvenilia to his two brothers, or listening to his brothers reading their own compositions to each other. And there was a great deal of mutual approval and encouragement.

## V

It was perhaps inevitable that so intensive a system of culture, so confined an atmosphere of domestic admiration, the sheer vacuity of their rather sedentary, slouching lives, should have tempted the three elder boys into joint and premature publication. It is true that the Rector himself scoffed at such diversions; it is true that the old grandfather, up there at Tealby, if he knew about them, approved only in a broad, incidental, eighteenth-century fashion, as of a pastime gentleman-like by tradition and of late rendered actually baronial. For him, it may have seemed fitting enough that the Somersby brood should spend their spare moments in writing poems. He even encouraged Alfred, the third son, to compose some memorial verses to his grandmother. They were pretty enough, these verses, when they were shown to him, and he gave the boy half a guinea for his pains. "That is all," he chuckled, "that you will ever make from poetry." And in this, as in other things perhaps, the elder George Tennyson was singularly mistaken.

With their father it was different: the whole business for him must have been uncomfortable and distressing. We can well sympathise with his anxiety, with his perplexed petulance, with his puzzle-headed gloom at the growing problem of what to do with his children. Frederick was all right: he would inherit the Grimsby property and was going into the Church. Charles was all right: he would get Aunt Turner's money and was also going into the Church. But Alfred, Mary, Emily, Edward, Arthur, Septimus, Matilda, Cecilia and Horatio? The perspective of his children, the merely physical perspective, was enough to appal any man. Can we wonder that his mind turned constantly to the thought of fellowships and curacies as possible avenues of hope and irresponsibility, or that he would be "amazing sharp" on overhearing Alfred declaim in his adolescent Lincolnshire voice Byronic stanzas on the subject of "Mithridates presenting Berenice with the cup of poison"?

Not that the Rector was, in his inner soul, averse from poetry: he rather liked it on the whole, and on rare occasions he would actually read and comment on his children's productions. There is a story also to the effect that he exclaimed once that if Alfred died the world would have lost one of her greatest poets. I fear that I do not wholly believe this story: I am more inclined to credit the other stories—the stories which present him as going about "keeping them to their sums." Nor does he seem to have done even this very effectually: he did not enable Alfred to get his degree at Cambridge; he did not prevent him writing poetry; he did not prevent him scribbling astronomical diagrams on the fly-leaves of his lesson-books; nor, indeed, and more specifically, did he prevent "Poems by Two Brothers," published in December 1826 (typographically 1827) by Mr. Jackson of Louth at the price of seven shillings and sixpence.

It may seem curious, to-day, that a provincial bookseller

should have accepted so unpropitious a volume. It is still more astonishing that he should have paid the authors so large a sum as twenty pounds. It is true that half of this was furnished in kind in the shape of books; it is true that Mr. Jackson's heirs, had they realised it, would since then have reaped a bumper harvest from the bibliophils; it is true that the manuscript was sold to America in 1892 for four hundred and twenty pounds and has now only reached the Library of Trinity through the narrow gate of munificence; but all this *paullo post futurum* does not explain Mr. Jackson's generosity, and we must look, I conceive, to the personal interest which Mrs. Tennyson's family, the Fytches, were able to arouse in the breast of the local bookseller. For Mrs. Tennyson, unlike her husband, was positively thrilled by the poetic aptitudes of the elder children. During those long stretches of time, those so recurrent and protracted interludes, when she would be upon the sofa or be dragged up the hills in her basket chair, the boys would recite to her their latest compositions, and she, as we have said, would read to them in her gentle exhausted voice her favourite extracts from Felicia Hemans or from Beattie's Calendar. There was a pleasant element of confederacy in all this—of conspiracy, almost, against the Rector; and for all of them remained the memory of one wonderful afternoon when their mother had stood at the cross-roads waiting for the Louth carrier and his parcel of Mr. Jackson's proofs.

"Poems by Two Brothers" were, as I have said, issued by Mr. Jackson of Louth in December 1826. There were three brothers, really, and not two, since Frederick also contributed to the volume. As I have also said, the publication brought them in ten pounds on credit and ten pounds in cash—the latter being expended in a jaunt to Mablethorpe and much shouting and recitation by the side of the North Sea. It cannot be said that the volume secured much appreciation at the moment. And yet it did not pass unremarked: there was a notice in the *Sunday Mercury;* there

was another notice in the *Literary Chronicle and Weekly
Review*. In the *Gentleman's Magazine* there was an actual
review. "These poems," it said, "are full of amiable feelings,
expressed, for the most part, with elegance and correctness.
Are we to complain that they want the deep feeling of
Byron, the polished grace of Moore, or the perfect mastery
of human passions which distinguishes Crabbe? . . . The
volume is a graceful addition to our domestic poetry, and
does credit to the juvenile adelphi."

One is bored, in general, by juvenilia, and I do not contend that the "Poems by Two Brothers" are, in themselves,
very remarkable. But they indubitably reflect the Somersby
atmosphere as it inspired Tennyson before the Hallam period, and they illustrate in a surprising way how deep and
how early were the influences which throughout his sixty-
five years of literary production hampered his peculiar lyric
temperament. The allocation of the individual poems is,
however, uncertain. The handwritings in the manuscript
discovered in 1892 are different, it is true, but not conclusive. The manuscript as it can be seen to-day next to *In
Memoriam* in Trinity library shows no very definite hand-
writing. It is possible that Mrs. Tennyson sometimes, and
one of the sisters now and then, copied out the poems before they were sent to Mr. Jackson. In any case the at-
tribution of the poems as given in the reprint of 1893 is
admittedly arbitrary. Tennyson himself, when shown the
manuscript poems in his old age, merely grunted out an
expression of surprise at their high general standard, and
of uncertainty as to who of the three had written which.
There was one point, however, which he was constrained
to make clear for ever. The original preface had stated that
the poems were written between the ages of fifteen and
eighteen. "I," wrote the Laureate, "was between fifteen and
seventeen, Charles between fifteen and eighteen."

Be this as it may, the poems are obviously immature.
They are concurrently diffident and ostentatious. The endless notes, while supporting some possibly hazardous references in the text, are designed to give an indication of a

very wide and discriminating culture. The epigraph from Martial—which, incidentally, is misquoted—purports to forestall the possible critic, whereas the preface itself is a very timid little piece of writing. "To light," explain the juvenile adelphi, "to light upon any novel combination of images, or to open any vein of sparkling thought untouched before, were no easy task: indeed the remark itself is as old as the truth is clear; and, no doubt, if submitted to the microscopic eye of periodical Criticism, a long list of inaccuracies and imitations would result from the investigation. But so it is! We have passed the Rubicon, etc. . . ."

We are not, ourselves, concerned with the "inaccuracies and imitations." If it comes to that, the preface itself is a crib on Byron's to *Hours of Idleness*. Nor are we concerned, except in so far as they show the literary influences of the time, with the obvious echoes of Byron, Ossian, Mrs. Hemans, Moore, Scott, Gray and Campbell. Nor is it particularly interesting to realise that at the age of sixteen Tennyson had read, if not studied, Apollonius Rhodius and Aelius Lampridius. We are, however, concerned with the poems themselves, and with their considerable psychological if not literary interest.

Of the three contributors it is Frederick who figures the least. The scanty pieces attributed to him are interesting only as showing that the Tennysonian morbidity was most strongly developed in the eldest of the three brothers. The verses signed with Charles' initials are more valuable, in that they manifest certain unmistakable Somersby characteristics. There is domestic contentment: "Oh! never," he exclaims:—

"Oh! never may frowns and discussion molest
    The pleasure I find at the social hearth,
A pleasure the dearest—the purest—the best
    Of all that are found or enjoyed on the earth."

There is the caution and accuracy of the Rectory study, as in the ode to Lord Byron, with its absurdly Tennysonian footnote, and there are other curious and arresting elements.

There is, for instance, the complete failure of his two jocose poems, *Anacreontics* and *Phrenology,* the latter of which is almost as mawkish as Tennyson's own eventual *Amphion.* There is the interest in modern inventions and the determination to explain and illustrate them in the forms of verse; and there are the more general themes, such as flower-gardens, death, family relationships and the Deity, which haunt so many of Alfred's own earlier and indeed later verses.

But I am not concerned with Charles or Frederick. The verses initialled A. T. in the 1893 edition are more copious, and require more detailed treatment.

## VI

It should be observed that none of Tennyson's contributions to "Poems by Two Brothers" was republished in volume form during his own lifetime. The book had been forgotten—had, indeed, disappeared—and it was only republished in 1893. The title "Juvenilia" given by the Laureate to the opening poems of the collected edition applies not to these schoolroom compositions, but to some of the verses which he had in 1842 discarded from the previous volumes of 1832 and 1830. There is no evidence, of course, as to the exact date when most of these posthumous juvenilia had been composed, but they were certainly published, and some must even have been written, when the poet was between the ages of twenty-one and twenty-five. The title of "Juvenilia" is thus a little misleading, and would have applied more convincingly to the verses initialled A. T. in the Two Brothers volume, which were, as we know, written before the age of seventeen.

And, as such, they are remarkable enough.

There is in them, of course, a large element of imitation; a large element of pseudo-romanticism; and the copious footnotes irritate and interrupt. But there are many passages which reach a precociously high level, and the whole collection, illustrating as it does Tennyson's pre-Cambridge temperament, has been too little regarded.

If one excludes the occasional clumsiness of expression and metre, which is due to lack of technical proficiency, if one excludes those passages which are obvious imitations of Byron (whom he was afterwards to tire of) or mere echoes of other occasional reading, one is left with a residue of definitely personal poetry, and one can readily divide and analyse this residue into what is characteristic of the later poetry and what is not. Nor is such a differentiation without value. For much that is most permanent in Tennyson can be traced back to those early years at Somersby among the wolds, and much that is most temporal and transitory can be attributed to subsequent influences. And in the "Poems by Two Brothers" one is able, at the cost of but little investigation, to discover the seeds of many later inspirations, to observe the tender roots of various familiar growths which were later to become so well established. And, what is more interesting, one finds evidences of other growths which failed to achieve fruition, and one notes the absence, even in seed or germ, of those particular preoccupations, theological and other, which were to sprout at Cambridge and to choke and overshadow the whole.

In the first place, to take the un-Tennysonian elements in this first volume, there is a curious reflection of the Calvinism of his aunt, Mrs. Bourne. The doctrine of original sin appears to have troubled the young Tennyson almost as deeply as the later Tennyson was disturbed by the immortality of the soul. "Oh! 'tis," he exclaims at the age of sixteen:—

"Oh! 'tis a fearful thing to glance
　　Back on the gloom of mis-spent years,
What shadowy forms of guilt advance
　　And fill me with a thousand fears!

The vices of my life arise,
    Pourtray'd in shapes, alas! too true,
    And not one beam of hope breaks through. . . ."

Nor is this all: in another passage the effect of Mrs.
Bourne is even more apparent:—

"And I was cursèd from my birth,
 A reptile made to creep on earth,
 An (sic) hopeless outcast, born to die
 A living death eternally!
With too much conscience to have rest,
Too little to be ever blest,
To yon vast world of endless woe,
    Unlighted by the cheerful day,
    My soul shall wing her weary way;
    To those dread depths where aye the same
Throughout the waste of darkness glow
        The glimmerings of the boundless flame."

A curious passage this, both Tennysonian and un-Tennysonian, characteristic only in the "too much conscience"
and in the lingering sound of the last line; but uncharacteristic utterly in its sense of an original sin leading to an eventual hell, a doctrine which became increasingly so obnox-
ious to the poet that fifty years later, in his poem *Despair*,
he revenged himself on Calvinism, and on Mrs. Bourne, by
a cautionary tale of peculiar violence. "I know you,"
boomed the Laureate in a volume of 1885:—

               "I know you of old—
Small pity for those who have ranged from the narrow
    warmth of your fold,
Where you bawl'd the dark side of your faith and a
    God of eternal rage."

But there is a further and lighter element in this early
volume—an element of considerable potentiality had it been
exploited. I mean the inspiration of the exotic. In the course

of a later chapter I shall refer to the purely imaginative
side of Tennyson's poetic temperament, and shall indicate
that he was constitutionally incapable of visualising anything that he had not actually seen, heard, smelt or handled. This deficiency leads to many weak passages throughout the poems, but it leads also to a deliberate avoidance,
whenever possible, of all unfamiliar landscapes. The distant,
the different, the adventurous had little claim on the Laureate's attention or interest. But in these earliest of his poems
we find a real note of excitement about foreign countries,
a note, almost, of *Wanderlust*. There are poems entitled
*Persia, Egypt,* and *Lines written by an Exile of Bassorah.*
The ode to Sublimity is a cataract of tropical and hyperborean evocation. An echo of this stimulus appears indeed
in *Recollections of the Arabian Nights,* published in the
1830 volume, but after that single splendid experiment the
glamour of travel and horizon failed to awaken in him any
deep or even sincere response.

So much for the unexpected elements in this first volume; the expected, or characteristic, elements are perhaps
equally interesting. There is the note of caution and diffidence, the abiding fear of excess or exaggeration; there is
his sensitiveness to "the hot shafts of baleful calumny," his
hostility to "the tinsel works of art," his robust if irritable
insularity, his suspicion of the French. Nor indeed did his
matured views on foreign policy ever advance much beyond this early schoolroom jingle on the subject of Switzerland:—

> "O! when shall Time
>   Avenge the crime
>     And to our rights restore us?
>   And bid the Seine
>   Be chok'd with slain
>     And Paris quake before us?"

There is again that curious feminine or parlour note
which ran through so much of his early and middle work,

and brought upon him the fury of Christopher North, and Bulwer's gibe of "School-miss Alfred." "Where's now," he lisps in the poem on Memory:—

> "Where's now that peace of mind
>     O'er youth's pure bosom stealing,
> So sweet and so refin'd,
>     So exquisite a feeling?"

And in conjunction with this one finds a very Tennysonian treatment of the subject of love. The unquestionable inadequacy of the following line on Antony and Cleopatra may be due merely to immaturity:—

> "O Cleopatra! fare thee well,
>     We two can meet no more,
> This breaking heart alone can tell
>     The love to thee I bore";

but the longer poem entitled *Love* is obviously of a later date, and has a definitely characteristic touch. "Almighty Love!" he begins:—

>        "whose nameless power
> This glowing heart defines too well."

and then he proceeds:—

> "The glittering fly, the wondrous things
>     That microscopic art descries;
> The lion of the waste which springs
>     Bounding upon his enemies;
> The mighty sea-snake of the storm,
> The vorticella's viewless form,"—

and to the last line there is asterisk and footnote to explain the vorticella. "See," he said, "Baker on Animalculæ."

We smile at these things, doubtless seeing in them not merely the naïveté of the schoolboy, but the promise of that wider naïveté which could lead the later Laureate into such strange quirks of accuracy, such sudden vacuous drops in the continuous level of his flight. But there are more permanent things to be found in this first volume. And indeed in these immature verses one catches now and then the diapason of the assured Tennyson manner: in the metre, here and there; in the movement; in the epanaphora, for instance, of the following:—

> "Why should we sorrow for the dead?
>     Our life on earth is but a span;
> They tread the path that all must tread,
>     They die the common death of man.
>
> The noblest songster of the gale
>     Must cease when winter's frowns appear;
> The reddest rose is wan and pale
>     When autumn tints the changing year."

And in the longer poem *Remorse* are combinations which forecast even more definitely the *In Memoriam* stanza.

In some of the Nature verses, again, and notably in that entitled *Midnight,* one finds side by side the two contrasting currents of Tennyson's Nature poetry—the love of the garden and the love of the wild—and, dominating this contrast, the sense of night-time, the dark trees and the "uncertain moon."

And, with it all, the strong black undercurrent of melancholy, the gipsy wistfulness, which here, as in all his work, suddenly wrings from him that poignant note of loneliness, and which abides with us always as the most sincere and permanent element in Tennyson's lyrical inspiration:—

> "I wander in darkness and sorrow,
>     Unfriended and cold and alone,
> As dismally gurgles beside me
>     The bleak river's desolate moan,
> The rise of the volleying thunder
>     The mountain's low echoes repeat:
> The roar of the wind is around me,
>     The leaves of the year at my feet."

And finally, a curiously prophetic cry arises from the very heart of all this melancholy to some imagined friend idealised already in the imagination, who will be able to understand, to help and to inspire.

"But where art thou, thou comet of an age,
    Thou phoenix of a century? Perchance
Thou art but of those fables which engage
    And hold the minds of men in giddy trance?
Yet, be it so, and be it all romance,
    The thought of thine existence is so bright
With beautiful imaginings and the glance
    Upon thy fancied being such delight,
That I will deem thee Truth, so lovely is thy might!"

And by then, of course, he was wholly prepared for Cambridge.

## CHAPTER THREE

# CAMBRIDGE

## *1828–1831*

### I

It was in the first week of February 1828 that Charles and Alfred left Somersby for Cambridge. An exciting journey in those days: the carrier's cart bumping in the dawn along the familiar road to Spilsby, the last look back from Gibbet Hill, and then on to Lincoln and the dash and jingle of the Tally-ho coach at the "Spread Eagle" Inn. That first night with Charles in the "Clinton Arms" at Newark, and then next morning the excitement of the Royal Mail, the cold midday stretch to Stamford, with the glimpse of Burleigh House among the trees, and in the evening the halt at Caxton and the group of undergraduates waiting for gig and curricle to take them the last ten miles; and finally, dusk and darkness and the lights of Cambridge flickering across the fens.

A little stiff, a little cold doubtless on arrival; a bad start, in the first few minutes, owing to an encounter with the proctor in Trumpington Street; but not so bewildered, not so utterly lonely as might have been supposed. For, after all, Charles was with him, sharing the same tremulous confusion; and then Frederick was at hand to help and to advise. For Frederick had already been a year at Trinity, and had won a medal for a Greek ode on the Pyramids, and before that had been quite a personage at Eton, the Captain of the school. And Frederick, with all his eccentricity, could tell one the way to Hall, and not to talk so loud, and where to put one's cap. And so one could go to bed there that first evening at 12 Rose Crescent, with the sense of Charles and Frederick, and the tea-things and the firelight, and the Somersby books to be unpacked, and Somersby up there in the half-light, remote and rather childish, and the swaying of the coach, and the voices of men, young fellow-undergraduates, rising up from the narrow pavement, and the large excitement of to-morrow.

But the next morning, the succession of following mornings, brought with them a reaction: a sense of some disturbing contrast, doubtless, between himself and all those confident, well-dressed young men who would call so intimately to each other across the courts, or stroll arm in arm along the Backs; the meetings, the gay recognitions, at street corners or in the narrow passage-way of Rose Crescent, of men who had been at school together, at public schools, where each had learnt to be so amicably like everyone else; a certain lack of enthusiasm in his tutors, an absence of that deep if stern personal interest which he had taken so for granted in the Rectory study—a general "want of love," as he expressed it later—and, with it all, and worse than all, a suspicion, angered and poignant, that for all these people he was, for some strange reason, a little oddly conspicuous—a laugh now and then, a turn of the head, the raising of an eyebrow, and his nerves would prick to the consciousness, as it were, of his Louth tailor and his Lincolnshire boots; a pang, for the moment, to be back at Somersby with his mother and his sisters, or walking in the lanes round Harrington Hall, where he was known—where they all knew, surely, that he was very remarkable. And then, from the depths of his strangely dual nature, the glint of the steel which lay buried deep within him: the canine lift of the upper lip which so startled the later pilgrims to Farringford. What did it matter? They would be glad one day, they would *all* be glad, to have been at Trinity with Alfred Tennyson. "Arthur," he had said to a young brother before leaving Somersby, "Arthur, I *mean* to be famous." And sixty years later, on reading in *Henry the VIIIth* that ambition was the sin by which the angels fell, he banged the table with his fist. "Shakespeare," he thundered, "never wrote that. I know it, I know it, I know it." And again he banged the table.

So in those early Trinity days the head would be held a little higher, with the backward toss of its mane, and the eyes would flash defiance at the astonished young men who met him striding on the way to Chapel. And later, after Hall, he would come back to his rooms at Rose Crescent and think of Somersby, with a dull longing for the "hollies and the yews of home." Such moods would come upon him even in his later terms at Cambridge, even when, with the help of the Apostles, he had secured a definite label and function. There is, for instance, an invective against Sunderland, a decorative Trinity undergraduate with his sleek hair and lack-lustre eyes, which appears in the collected edition under the title of *A Character*. The lines do not seem to have disturbed Sunderland unduly: when told of them and that their author was Tennyson, he "smoothed his chin and sleek'd his hair" and said "Oh! Which Tennyson? The slovenly one?" But later, on leaving Cambridge, Sunderland became insane, and ceased further to trouble the poet with his polished indifferences. There is also the more general diatribe against Cambridge which is quoted in his son's biography, and, as more specifically reflecting the despondency of those first weeks the following letter to his aunt, Mrs. Russell of Tealby:—

"I am sitting owl-like and solitary in my rooms (nothing between me and the stars but a stratum of tiles). The hoof of the steed, the roll of the wheel, the shouts of drunken Gown and drunken Town come up from below with a sea-like murmur. I wish to heaven

I had Prince Hussain's fairy carpet to transport me along the deeps of air to your coterie. Nay, I would even take up with his brother Abdul-something's glass for the mere pleasure of a peep. What a pity it is that the golden days of Faerie are over! What a misery not to be able to consolidate our gossamer dreams into reality! When, my dearest Aunt, may I hope to see you again? I know not how it is, but I feel isolated here in the midst of society. The country is so disgustingly level, the revelry of the place so monotonous, the studies of the University so uninteresting, so much matter of fact. None but dry-headed, calculating, angular little gentlemen can take much delight in them."

In sombre, sober colours therefore his first term at Cambridge drew to a close. Easter found him back at Somersby, rejoicing in the gradual spread of spring, the little green buds in the quick-set hedge, the violets among the ash-roots. In June he returned to Trinity with firmer courage; and gradually, in spite of his shy aloofness, his almost morbid sensitiveness, he began to make friends and to create interests. It would have been surprising indeed if he had failed to make some impression. The stature of him, in the first place: the firm-set, leonine head and the dark complexion; those fierce and heavy-lidded eyes; the great brown hands, with their long, square-tipped fingers. From the first we hear of the effect created by his actual physique. Thompson, who noticed him one evening in his first term striding, long-haired and defiant, into Hall, murmured below his breath: "That man there must be a poet." And FitzGerald, who at Cambridge knew him only by sight, recorded later: "I remember him well: a sort of Hyperion."

Gradually the circle, the famous Trinity circle, was forming itself. And into this circle, almost against his will, Tennyson was shortly to be drawn. We find him leaving the little top-floor rooms in Rose Crescent, and moving to King's Parade, to No. 57 Corpus Buildings. We find him purchasing a pet snake and sitting there in clouds of tobacco "watching its sinuosities upon the carpet." We find him getting to understand, to respect, actually to like, his tutor Whewell, known to the under-graduates as "Billy Whistle." We find him meeting Trench, Alford, Blakesley, Brookfield and Spedding.

We find him meeting Arthur Hallam.

## II

Arthur Henry Hallam, the "light of those dawn-golden times," the "prime passion" of Tennyson's whole existence, the inheritor of so much renown, vicarious as well as unfulfilled, had been born in Bedford Place, London, on February 1, 1811. He was thus a year and a half the poet's junior. "His childhood," says Mrs. Brookfield, "was not like that of others. The scope and capacity of his mind was so prodigious and so early evident that his parents, themselves of the highest culture, were startled by it, and when they realised how prodigally he was endowed, became almost afraid to contemplate or speak of his gifts." At nine years of age we hear of him writing dramatic poetry, at fourteen translating Dante's *Ugolino* into Greek Iambics, while "all his youthful hours were employed in learning foreign tongues."

From a private school at Putney he proceeded to Eton, where he joined W. E. Gladstone under the tuition of Dr. Keate. A close and fervent friendship sprang up between them: they shared a study; Hallam addressed to Gladstone some verses inscribed "to my bosom friend"; they both contributed to the "Eton Miscellany"; and when they separated, Gladstone going to Oxford and Hallam to Trinity, the intimacy was maintained. It was maintained so closely that Tennyson appears to have shown signs of jealousy: the following verses figure among Hallam's all too scanty literary remains:—

### "To A. T.

"Oh, last in time, but worthy to be first
　Of friends in rank, had not the father of good
　On my early spring one perfect gem bestowed,
　A friend, with whom to share the best and worst,
Him will I shut close to my heart for aye;
　There's not a fibre quivers there but is
　His own, his heritage for woe or bliss.

Thou would'st not have me such a charge betray,
　Surely, if I be knit in brotherhood
　So tender to that chief of all my love
With thee I shall not loyalty eschew,
　And well I ween, not time with ill or good
　Shall thine affection e'er from mine remove,
Thou yearner for all fair things and true."

This affection was, we are given to understand, warmly
reciprocated by Mr. Gladstone; and in the latter's "Glean-
ings from Past Years" (Vol. II. p. 136) we can read his
reminiscence of this, his own Hallam period:—

"The writer was more than half a century ago in a
condition to say:—

" 'I marked him
As a far Alp; and loved to watch the sunrise
Dawn on his ample brow.'

There perhaps was no one among those who were
blessed with his friendship, nay, as we see, not even
Mr. Tennyson, who did not feel at once bound closely
to him by commanding affection, and left far behind
by the rapid, full and rich development of his ever-
searching mind."

And indeed the chorus of approval, of hope and disappointment is unanimous.

It was in Tennyson's second term, in June 1828, that

Hallam came to Trinity. Owing doubtless to the Academic prestige of his father, he was at once allotted rooms in college, No. 3G in the New Court, which had then only just been completed. His success with his contemporaries was immediate: they were charmed and overawed. Backed by his Eton reputation, this chubby, red-faced, blue-eyed, voluble young man, with the bumpy forehead and the protruding underlip, had become at once the hero of his College. In a "tumult of acclaim" they lauded his genius and his Italian accent, his wit and his gentleness, his oratory and his theological opinions. They predicted a rich and meteoric future; they were not quite sure what that future was to be, certain only that it would be rich and meteoric. Some said he was to be the poet of the age. Tennyson himself did not agree with this forecast; for him Hallam was to be the supreme statesman of the nineteenth century: "the life in civic action warm," "the potent voice of Parliament." With this conception it was Gladstone who disagreed: for him it was as a writer in theological and religious subjects that Hallam would fulfil his destiny. But on the main point —on the point of eventual and blazing success—their agreement was remarkable.

It is unprofitable, perhaps, and ungracious for us to consider whether there was any serious exaggeration in all this worship. We must discount, of course, the addiction of the age, of Cambridge in particular, of the Trinity set especially, to a peculiarly determined and propagandist form of hero-worship. We must admit the inadequate quality of the little that Hallam left in the form of literary remains. We must remember that he tried and failed three times to secure the Chancellor's medal; that he failed to secure a degree; that he failed to make any serious impression with his journalistic work; that his legal studies after 1832 were admittedly "irregular and unpunctual." We may suspect the actual diffuseness of his intelligence (which they took for universality), his incapacity for concentration (which they excused as versatility), his undoubted, if intermittent,

laziness (which was part of his charm), his fluency, his
bounce, his bursts of hectic energy and his impulsiveness.
But we must set against these disparagements, which are
purely hypercritical, the basic fact that the best minds of
his age and throughout their lives looked back on Hallam
as the real phœnix of the century; and that Gladstone, who
at any rate was a good judge of men, maintained his original conviction unqualified. Even for us, who can only ap-
prehend Hallam indirectly, there remains a very distinct
impression of a compelling personality, a quick, flickering
intelligence, an immense kindliness, and a rather bustling,
rather breathless, and at the same time rather dilettante
charm. Even the fact that he got considerably into debt
at Cambridge, and that Brookfield, that useful man, was
obliged to square his creditors, has a pleasant, unapostolic
flavour. And we can read with sympathy, with conviction
and with a feeling of intimate regret the personal touches
which humanise the stanzas of *In Memoriam*—

> "Thy converse drew us with delight,
>     The men of rathe and riper years:
>     The feeble soul, a haunt of fears,
> Forgot his weakness in thy sight.
>
> On thee the loyal-hearted hung,
>     The proud was half disarm'd of pride,
>     Nor cared the serpent at thy side
> To flicker with his double tongue.
>
> The stern were mild when thou wert by,
>     The flippant put himself to school
>     And heard thee, and the brazen fool
> Was soften'd, and he knew not why;
>
> While, I, thy nearest, sat apart,
>     And felt thy triumph was as mine,
>     And loved them more, that they were thine,
> The graceful tact, the Christian art;

Nor mine the sweetness or the skill,
    But mine the love that will not tire,
    And, born of love, the vague desire
That spurs an imitative will."

One passes from these reflections to the more practical
consideration of the effect upon Tennyson of this "comet
of an age": the immediate effect produced by the brilliant,
courted Etonian, upon the lone, listless, home-bred, home-
sick Lincolnshire undergraduate; upon that strange com-
pound of wold and Rectory garden, of ploughland and mus-
lin, of force and daintiness.

And, since one cannot but have a glow of sympathy for
the shy, unhappy Tennyson of 1828, for that "Virgin's spirit
in a Titan's form," one emerges with a feeling of frank and
kindled gratitude towards Hallam; a desire to shake him
by the hand; a desire to express to him how very intelligent
we consider him to have been in dragging Tennyson by
force out of Rose Crescent; in being kind and voluble to
him; in calling him "old Alfred"; in telling him not to write
jocular poetry; in telling him that his temperament was akin
to Titian and not to Rubens; in taking him abroad; in
fussing Moxon about him; in going to stay at Somersby;
in getting engaged to his sister Emily, and generally start-
ing Tennyson and the Tennyson legend promisingly upon
their way.

And in the warmth of our gratitude we can forgive the
other things. The fact that his adulation and encouragement were so very undiscriminating; that he pronounced
*The Darling Room* to be "mighty pleasant." The fact that
he did not weed out the 1830 and the 1832 volumes. The
fact that he dragged Tennyson off on the Torrijos expedition and killed thereby a quite healthy romanticism. The
fact, finally, that he introduced him into the circle of the
Apostles.

But whatever may, at this later date, be our own feelings
about Hallam, there can be no doubt, no possible doubt I

think, as to the amazed and tremulous feelings with which he inspired Tennyson.

### III

It must be realised, in the first place, that Tennyson had been expecting—nay, was anxiously awaiting—the advent of some such Messiah; that Hallam appeared upon the scene, and took the necessary initiative of friendliness and persistence, at a time when Alfred considered himself, rightly or wrongly, to be "in disgrace with fortune and men's eyes." The first dazzled acceptance of Hallam was thus inevitable; but the causes of the deepening and perpetuation of his influence must be sought for among the more recondite tissues of Tennyson's temperament.

Not that the fairy prince element in Hallam was for Tennyson a merely secondary emotion. Even in retrospect, even in *In Memoriam*, the sense of the actual privilege of Hallam's friendship is abundantly apparent: there is more than one picture of Tennyson sitting silent in his corner thrilled with an almost possessive joy at Arthur's meteorics. In the 60th section of *In Memoriam* there is a very precise definition of their relation from this point of view:—

"He past; a soul of nobler tone:
My spirit loved and loves him yet,
Like some poor girl whose heart is set
On one whose rank exceeds her own.

He mixing with his proper sphere,
She finds the baseness of her lot,
Half jealous of she knows not what,
And envying all that meet him there. . . .

. . . . .

The foolish neighbours come and go,
And tease her till the day draws by:
At night she weeps, 'How vain am I!
How should he love a thing so low!'"

It was not only the gentleness of Hallam, the fact that he was the "sweetest soul that ever looked with human eyes"; not only his kindly judgment and authoritative tact, his "likeness to the wise below his kindred with the great of old"; the actual daily enlightenment of an intercourse:—

> "When one that loves but knows not, reaps
> A truth from one that loves and knows."

It was more than all this. It was that Tennyson was lonely, morbid, and above all afraid: he was afraid of life; he was afraid of death; predominantly and persistently he was afraid of the life after death. Nor was this any intellectual process of the mind which can be analysed or explained. Its roots, obscure and terrible, thrust down into the depths of Tennyson's nature, and fed on the black blood that flowed obscurely in his veins. And on all such subjects he was, and remained, completely neurasthenic; and as the hypochondriac will clutch eagerly at comfort and assurance, only, in the sad hour before the dawn, to be assailed again by the old doubts and suspicions, so was Tennyson in a sense hypochondriac about faith and doubt, about the immortality of the soul. And it was Hallam, in the years from 1828 to 1830, in the first bitter crisis of this neurosis, who gave him courage. I do not think that one can question the predominance of this element: it was this that inspired what to his own generation was most helpful in all Tennyson's work; nor do I see how one can read the 50th section of *In Memoriam* and doubt any longer that here we have the real Tennyson crying in agony across the grave to what had been to him the essential Hallam:

> "Be near me when my light is low,
>     When the blood creeps, and the nerves prick
>     And tingle, and the heart is sick,
> And all the wheels of Being slow.
>
> Be near me when the sensuous frame
>     Is rack'd with pangs that conquer trust,

And Time, a maniac scattering dust,
And Life, a Fury slinging flame.

Be near me when my faith is dry,
     And men the flies of latter spring,
     That lay their eggs, and sting and sing,
And weave their petty cells and die.

Be near me when I fade away,
     To point the term of human strife,
     And on the low dark verge of life
The twilight of eternal day."

There is a sonnet (incidentally one of the finest among Tennyson's few sonnets), written evidently when he was with Hallam in the Pyrenees, which reflects this aspect of their relationship even more convincingly:—

"If I were loved, as I desire to be,
 What is there in the great sphere of the earth,
 And range of evil between death and birth,
 That I should fear—if I were loved by thee?
 All the inner, all the outer world of pain
 Clear Love would pierce and cleave, if thou wert mine,
 As I have heard that, somewhere in the main,
 Fresh-water springs come up through bitter brine.
 'Twere joy, not fear, claspt hand-in-hand with thee,
 To wait for death—mute—careless of all ills,
 Apart upon a mountain, tho' the surge
 Of some new deluge from a thousand hills
 Flung leagues of roaring foam into the gorge
 Below us, as far on as eye could see."

The deep and lasting affection with which Hallam inspired Tennyson appears to have been quite warmly returned. Tennyson's own letters to Hallam were destroyed by the latter's father at the end of 1833. "It may be as well," says the present Lord Tennyson in the Memoir, "to say here that all the letters from my father to Arthur Hallam were destroyed by his father after Arthur's death; a great loss, as these particular letters probably revealed his inner self more truly than anything outside his poems." But some of Hallam's own letters to and about Tennyson have been preserved. We find him explaining Tennyson to his friends; writing, for instance, to Trench in 1832: "His nervous temperament and habits of solitude give an appearance of affectation to his manner"; sending "Poems by Two Brothers" to Leigh Hunt with the following: "You will, if you peruse the book, be surprised and delighted to find a new prophet of those true principles of Art, etc. . . ." He adds that neither of the two brothers is likely to be popular with the great public, that they addressed "the elect church of Urania, which we know to be small and in tribulation." We find him encouraging Tennyson more directly: telling him that in fifty years Somersby would become a Mecca of literary pilgrims; writing reviews of his poetry in the *Englishman's Magazine,* of which more hereafter; reading the proofs of the 1832 volume and hinting that the notes were a little too copious.

For those who care for such things, there are more precise indications of Tennysonian parallelisms in the posthumous edition of Hallam's work: a reference to the "abysmal secrets of personality"; a hint of evolution, here and there; an expression of man's insignificance in Space and Time; a dislike of abrupt revolution; an expansion of the doctrine of "God is love"—that "solemn idea which alone solves the enigma of our feelings, and while it supplies a meaning to conscience, explains the destination of man." Which last is very recognisably Tennysonian.

In spite of it all, however, and the good sense of much of it ("Poems," he wrote to Tennyson in 1832, "are good things, but flesh and blood is better"), Hallam shares with the Cambridge of 1830 in general, and the Apostles in particular, the blame, if blame there is, of instilling into Tennyson those convictions as to the applied purposes of poetry, as to his "message" or his "mission," which played such havoc with his later compositions. We find him writing to the young poet: "You say pathetically, 'Alas for me! I have more of the beautiful than the good!' Remember to your comfort that God has given you to see the difference. Many a poet has gone on blindly in his artist pride."

But apart from this sort of thing, Hallam, unlike the other Apostles, was not essentially a prig.


IV

The "Cambridge Conversazione Society," known to its contemporaries and to posterity as "The Apostles," had begun life as a comparatively unpretentious debating club in St. John's College. By the year 1824 it had fallen under the control of John Sterling and Frederick Denison Maurice, those two earnest, puzzle-headed young men, and had been transferred to the wider field of Trinity, taking upon itself in the process a troubled, militant, masonic atmosphere, as of some secret society which was to reform the world. The wide responsibility of their mission weighed sombrely upon the spirits of the earlier Apostles: the sense of predestination, the sense that there was so little time to lose—"so many worlds, so much to do"—united them with a close co-operative bond which outlasted their mere residence at the University. They would congregate in after years for Apostolic dinners in Cambridge, or at the "Star and Garter"; they founded the Sterling Club in London; they bought the *Athenæum;* they reviewed each other's books in terms which could leave no doubt in the minds of a backward English people that some new force had come to shake the world; they promoted an abortive, bloody and apparently quite unnecessary insurrection in Spain; they unearthed Shelley's *Adonais* at Pisa and had it republished in Cambridge: and they imbued Tennyson with a deep and perfectly modest conviction that it was his function, his privilege and his duty "to teach":—

"And bravely furnish'd all abroad to fling
    The winged shafts of truth,
To throng with stately blooms the breathing spring
    Of Hope and Youth.

So many minds did gird their orbs with beams
    Tho' one did fling the fire.
Heaven flow'd upon the soul in many dreams
    Of high desire.

Thus truth was multiplied on truth, the world
    Like one great garden show'd,
And thro' the wreaths of floating dark upcurl'd
    Rare sunrise flow'd."

Nor was any relapse from the strict Apostolic doctrine allowed to pass unnoticed. They eyed each other's careers with anxious and rather inquisitorial expectancy; they were determined, it appears, to keep each other up to the mark. "Hallam," writes Blakesley to Thompson in 1830, "has gone back to Cambridge. He was not well while he was in London; moreover he was submitting himself to the influences of the outer world more than (I think) a man of his genius ought to do." And Arthur Hallam, at the date when this letter was written, was only nineteen years of age.

"Our common bond," writes Dean Merivale, who had been one of the Apostles in Tennyson's period, "had been a common intellectual taste, common studies, common literary aspirations, and we have all felt, I suppose, the support of mutual regard and perhaps some mutual flattery. We soon grew, as such youthful coteries generally do, into immense self-conceit. We began to think that we had a mission to enlighten the world upon things intellectual and spiritual. We held established principles, especially in poetry and metaphysics, and set up certain ideas for our worship. Coleridge and Wordsworth were our special divinities, and Hare and Thirlwall were regarded as their prophets;

or rather, in this celestial hierarchy, I should have put Shakespeare at the top of all, and I should have found a lofty pedestal for Kant and Goethe. It was with a vague idea that it should be our function to interpret the oracles of transcendental wisdom to the world of Philistines, or Stumpfs, as we designated them, and from time to time to call forth from this world the few souls who might be found capable of sympathising with them, that we piqued ourselves on the name of the 'Apostles'—a name given us, we were sometimes told, by the envious and jeering vulgar, but to which we presumed we had a legitimate claim, and gladly accepted it."

There is a letter of Hallam to Gladstone written on the subject of F. D. Maurice in the year 1830. "The effect," he said, "which he has produced on the minds of many at Cambridge by the single creation of that Society of Apostles (for the spirit, though not the form, was created by him) is far greater than I can dare (*sic*) to calculate, and will be felt, both directly and indirectly, in the age that is upon us."

The Apostles would meet on Saturday evenings behind locked doors, and there would be coffee and anchovy toast and tobacco, and one of their number would read, for subsequent discussion, an essay upon such subjects as the Origin of Evil, or the Derivation of Moral Sentiments, or Prayer and the Personality of God, or Have Shelley's Poems an Immoral Tendency? And Tennyson, in the corner with his pipe, would say very little; and Hallam, with his cup of coffee, would say a great deal; and Jack Kemble would announce that the world was one great thought, "and he was thinking it"; and Venables would express surprise at their privilege and good fortune. "I often wonder," he remarked, "what we have done to deserve being gifted as we are so much above those cursed idiotic oxford brutes."

For, in fact, oxford (they spelt it with a small "o") was a point of disquiet (sympathetic disquiet, but still disquiet) for the Apostles. And there is that strange story of the mission undertaken by Hallam, Milnes and Sunderland for the purpose of enlightening Oxford as to the importance of Shelley, and how Oxford knew nothing of Shelley, thought they had said "Shenstone," thought, alternatively, that he was the man who kept the ponies in the Park; and how brilliant and impressive Sunderland and Milnes and Hallam had all of them been, and how they had returned to Cambridge satisfied and triumphant. All of which story is, of course, nonsense; for Oxford knew and cared just as much about Shelley as did the Apostles. For had not Beddoes been there as early as 1820? And had not he and Procter in 1823 raised a subscription between them to publish the Posthumous Poems? And had not this edition actually been issued in 1824, only to be suppressed by the action of Mrs. Shelley and Sir Timothy? But the Apostles knew nothing of all this, and their pleasure at what they had been able to do for oxford was unimpaired.

The actual date of Tennyson and Hallam's entry into this select circle was January 24, 1830. Tennyson had, the previous June, secured the Chancellor's medal for his prize poem, *Timbuctoo*, and he thus appeared among the Apostles with the function and label of a poet, or rather of *the* poet, or, more accurately, of *their* poet. For it was in this capacity that he was to justify his membership and "shake the world." But in actual fact, in actual everyday contemporaneous fact, he does not seem to have been a great success as an Apostle: he recorded his vote, of course, at the conclusion of each debate, he lent a willing ear to Hallam's "rapt oration flowing free," and watched with love and admiration "the God within him light his face" and the "azure orbits heavenly-wise"; but for all personal or positive part in the debate he was a failure. In fact, when his own turn came to read an essay, he let the Apostles down badly: the subject was "Ghosts," and when the eleven arrived at Corpus Buildings they found Tennyson in a mood of obstinate embarrassment; he had torn up his essay before their arrival; the evening was a disaster. And, according to Leslie

Stephen, Tennyson ceased from that day to be counted among the elect.

And indeed it is a melancholy circumstance that of the original band it was only the less Apostolic among them who achieved undoubted eminence. For Blakesley, the "clear-headed friend," whom Tennyson had marked out, "if aught of prophecy be mine," to be Lord Chancellor, got no further than the Deanery of Lincoln; Merivale than the Deanery of Ely; Alford than the Deanery of Canterbury. Venables failed to achieve distinction; the success of the two Lushingtons was personal and academic; Thompson became Master of Trinity; Spedding, after deciding that the Colonial Office was "no place for the indulgence of individual genius," retired to Lincoln's Inn and devoted his life to the rehabilitation of Francis Bacon; Kemble became an authority on Anglo-Saxon; Sunderland died insane; the short life of Sterling was a succession of unhappy failures; even the deep and disturbing influence of F. D. Maurice himself was of a dissolving rather than a constructive character; and Charles Buller, before whom a brilliant parliamentary career had already opened, died suddenly before he could justify his early promise. Trench alone actually became an Archbishop, and Trench had never quite liked the Apostles, "the whole band," he called them, "of Platonic-Wordsworthian-Coleridgean-anti-utilitarians." Even Richard Monckton Milnes, whose inclusion among the Apostles had been decided only after heated controversy as to his worthiness (for, as Mrs. Brookfield so pertinently remarks in this connection, "it was not the wont of the early Apostles to choose their associates on account of any mirthfulness of disposition"); even Dicky Milnes, that "bird of paradox," as Mrs. Norton rated him, was more successful, according to his lights, than any of his more prophetic fellows. For did not Milnes, that "bland-smiling, semi-quizzical, affectionate, high-bred, Italianised little man," as Carlyle called him—did not Milnes, who "might have won the Poet's name," decide to do nothing of the sort, but to succeed to the mantle of Rogers as the purveyor of historic breakfast parties? And was he not welcome in whatever drawing-room flourished between such diverse triangular points as Holland, Lansdowne and Gore Houses? And does he not live and flourish in the memoirs, in all the memoirs of the day? And did not Sidney Smith spend much trouble in priming him with epigrams—in calling him "In-I-go Jones," and "London assurance," and "Cool of the evening"? And did he not entertain the most diverse and thrilling people at Fryston and at 26 Pall Mall? And was he not made Baron Houghton? And did he not edit the "Life and Letters of Keats," and write occasional verses, some of which are in the "Oxford Book of English Verse," and charm Carlyle, and patronise Guizot, and leave behind him a vast circle of friends in his own generation, and a vivid impression of charm for their successors? But, then, Milnes, that cheerful man, did not, unlike the other Apostles, take himself at all seriously, as is witnessed by this letter of his to Macartney of October 15, 1857. "I was thinking to-day that the thing I was intended for by nature is a German woman. I have just that mixture of *Häusliche Thätigkeit* and *Sentimentalität* that characterises that category of Nature. I think Goethe would have fallen in love with me; and I am not sure that Platen didn't." None other of the Apostles, even in 1857, could have written as buoyantly as that. And so one dwells rather lovingly on Milnes, and not wholly irrelevantly, since he serves to soften one's inevitable dislike of the Apostles, and to indicate that, in him at least, they must have had some point of connection with an exterior and more human world.

For there was such a world, even at Cambridge in 1830. In type at least there were Arthur Pendennis and his friend Foker. Not that the Apostles approved of them; but they were there. They are there to-day. They were there when Tennyson came back to Trinity five years later, after Hallam's death—a gloomy, morbid visitation—and passed up the staircase at 3G New Court, and paused outside by the door there where they put those tin-covered plates, and heard the sound of young men within who "crash'd the glass and beat the floor."

They were there, in their many variations, from 1828 to 1832; and the Apostles disapproved of them—disapproved mildly of the great majority of the harmless whose friendship was mere "fellowship of sluggish moods"; disapproved terribly of those others, who, being of

> "coarsest Satyr-shape,
> Had bruis'd the herb and crush'd the grape,
> And bask'd and batten'd in the woods."

And somewhere, at that time and among these different categories of ordinary and unknowable mortals, could have been found, if the Apostles had desired, Kinglake and Edward FitzGerald and William Makepeace Thackeray.

But they did not so desire.


## V

His connection with the Apostles, and through them with John Sterling, led Tennyson in the summer of 1830 into a very remarkable and uncharacteristic venture. It will be remembered that King Ferdinand of Spain, the sly-faced Prince of the Asturias of the Goya portraits, had in 1823 finally broken all the constitutional oaths and undertakings which the Cortes and successive pronunciamientos had previously extracted from him, and had re-established the Inquisition and a quite successful form of personal despotism. The leading Liberals had escaped to London, where, to the number of some sixty or seventy, they could be seen smoking on the pavement in Euston Square, muffled in their native capes and in a general "tragic condition, as of caged Numidian lions." And indeed the vivid picture which Carlyle has left us in his Life of Sterling can be no very exaggerated presentment of the effect which these exotic figures produced on London during the years ending in 1830. Their leader, General Torrijos, had himself arrived in Euston Square in 1824. His adherents had been able to support themselves precariously by giving Spanish lessons; but Torrijos himself was a man of wider education: he could speak English fluently; he was a man of the world; he was a guest at the tables of happy English Liberals, and, among other houses, he visited the home of John Sterling's parents in South Place. It happened that this meeting with John Sterling synchronised with a crisis in that earnest young man's psychological development. For Sterling was beginning to tire of transcendentalism, to tire of "Coleridgean moonshine," and a visit to the flabby old prophet up at Highgate had not revived his waning enthusiasm. It was on the crest of this reaction that Torrijos became an intimate; that the adherents of Torrijos became a cause; that the cause became a conspiracy; that the conspiracy led by rapid degrees to an insurrection.

The main difficulty, however, was that of money. For a time Sterling confined himself to imposing Spanish lessons upon his wide circle of young lady friends; but that was not enough; what was necessary, in order thoroughly to clear one's head of transcendental moonshine, was to finance, and even to direct, an insurrection. By an unfortunate coincidence a cousin of Sterling's, a certain Lieutenant Robert Boyd, had recently thrown up his commission in the Indian Army, was adventurous and at a loose end, and, what was more important, possessed an available capital of some £5000. Sterling succeeded in inspiring him with enthusiasm for the cause; Torrijos undertook that when the insurrection was over he should be given the colonelcy of a Spanish regiment; all that was needed was that Torrijos should actually land in Spain, when the whole country would rise as a man to his support. What was also needed was a brig to take them there, and arms and munitions sufficient to force a landing. Boyd bought the brig. It was at once embargoed by the Port of London authority, who had been warned by the Spanish Legation. But Sterling's enthusiasm was not damped by this misadventure: without delay he embarked his conspirators for St. Valéry, on the French coast; he even went down to Dover to see them off; and then he returned to South Place, feeling exhausted but relieved.

Torrijos, Boyd and their party reached Gibraltar in the summer of 1830. They remained there for eighteen months, the hospitality of the British authorities becoming less and less exuberant as the time wore on. Finally, on November 30, 1831, they were told to leave, and Torrijos, Boyd and fifty-five companions crowded into a small felucca and set sail for Spain. They were at once seen and chased by a Spanish man-of-war; the felucca was run ashore at Fuengirola. For a few hours they were able to defend themselves in a farm-house; eventually they were surrounded. A few days later they were shot in a row on the Esplanade at Malaga. But by then Sterling had given up radicalism and was planting sugar-cane in the West Indies.

The date at which Tennyson himself became so incongruously involved in this episode was the summer of 1830. It appears that there was to be a diversion in the north of Spain to synchronise with Torrijos' landing in the south. It was necessary for money and secret instructions to be sent by some sure hand to Ojeda, the leader of the northern insurrectionaries. And Sterling, who had dragged the resident Apostles into his venture, allotted this particular task to Arthur Hallam. The latter invited Tennyson to go with him; they left together in August for the Pyrenees.

And it was in this way that *Mariana in the South* came to be written in the diligence between Narbonne and Perpignan; that the scenery of Cauteretz became the background of *Oenone,* and of many later poems; that the message and the money were delivered to Ojeda; and that, thirty-one years later, Tennyson wrote *All Along the Valley.*

They returned early in September 1830 by the packet *Leeds* from Bordeaux to Dublin. The Misses Harden were on board, with their father, and there exist two drawings by the latter of the party on deck, the ladies in their poke bonnets and the men in capes and top hats, and Hallam, sprawling on a mattress, reading aloud a novel by Sir Walter Scott.

Eventually they all arrived in London. Old Hallam was not at all enthusiastic about their expedition. "I cannot find," writes Arthur to Tennyson, "that my adventures have produced quite the favourable impression on my father's mind that his letter gave me to expect. . . . He does not seem quite to comprehend that, after helping to revolutionise kingdoms, one is still less inclined than before to trouble one's head about scholarships, degrees, and such gear."

Tennyson's own comments on the adventure are practically non-existent. Indeed it was not an episode to which he would subsequently refer. As his son puts it in the Memoir: "No further information on this business has been preserved." And yet, a deep and quite definite impression had been made, an impression which was to last him for over sixty years—an impression of rocks and waterfalls and meadow-ledges and pines. An inexhaustible reservoir for future Alpine passages.

And for the rest—"I am struck," he wrote, "on returning from France with the look of good sense in the London people."

## VI

In dealing with the three years which Tennyson spent at Trinity—the years, that is, from February 1828 to February 1831—I have concentrated upon those elements and influences which produced, in my opinion, the most permanent and recognisable impression upon his poetry. It will be thought perhaps that I have exaggerated his uncouth and unhappy isolation on arrival; that I have visualised this a little too conjecturally in order to bring out the high lights, to give the necessary relief to the figure of Hallam—a figure curiously legendary and elusive. This may be so. When one looks back on one's own undergraduate days, they stretch out coloured but uniform in the spring haze, marked only by the gentle recurrence of unimportant accidents and diversified by no emergent landmark. But I am dealing not with Tennyson as an undergraduate, not wholly with Tennyson as a man, but primarily with Tennyson as a poet. And from this point of view only two things really happened to him at Cambridge: the first was Hallam; the second was the Apostolic doctrine.

For we can, I think, exclude for the moment "the Schoolmiss Alfred" category, the category of those poems which recur from time to time in all his volumes, from the Album verses in the 1830 volume, through *The Darling Room* and *The May Queen* of the 1832 volume, down to *Charity* in the posthumous volume of 1892. We are then left with a residue which falls into the two general if arbitrary categories of lyric and didactic. And, to my mind at least, the lyrical poems, which are a permanent possession, would have been less valuable, or at least different, had it not been for Hallam; while the didactic poems, which are already dead to us, would have been less didactic—might never have happened at all—but for the Apostles.

And indeed the essential note of Tennyson's lyricism, the note of frightened agony, as of some wild creature caught in a trap at night-time, might well, but for the glow, the Titianesque glow, of his love for Hallam living and for Hallam dead, have degenerated into the charnel-house morbidity of Beddoes, into the intricate sentimentality of the spasmodics, or have passed unheard as a cry of weakness upon the storm. And I am convinced that all that is greatest in Tennyson's poetry—and there is much which is very great indeed—was enhanced by his love for Hallam, and the fact that at the essential crisis of his life he was mastered by no enervating influence, but by this all-absorbing, persistent and intensely emotional stimulus.

So much for the essential Tennyson, the Somersby Tennyson, the Titian Tennyson, the poet of the half-light and the glooming flats, the Tennyson who will survive. And conversely, the other Tennyson, the Isle of Wight Tennyson, can be traced in no small degree to the Apostles—can be traced, that is, to the idea which they implanted so firmly in his mind, that one must labour with a "conscience and an aim"; to their insistence on the poet as prophet; to the almost civic responsibility which they laid upon him of his "mission" and his "message"; to the way in which the seed they had sown was nursed and propagated in the later 'fifties, until even Tennyson himself became convinced that he was a great and authoritative thinker, that his views on doubt and faith were not only helpful, but profound.

It was all very well for Tennyson to exclaim

> "I do but sing because I must,
> And pipe but as the linnets sing."

Only on rare occasions—only on very rare, Hallam-inspired occasions—was this true. Deep within him, as a canker in the rose, was a quite other conception of the poet's function:—

> "The boundless yearning of the Prophet's heart—
> Could *that* stand forth, and, like a statue rear'd
> To some great citizen, win all praise from all
> Who past it, saying 'That was he.'"

And for all this we must, in the first instance, blame the Apostles; and in the second, though less virulently, their long line of successors, Woolner and Bradley, and Palgrave and Mrs. Tennyson, and his sons and even Jowett.

But though I have foreshortened, and indeed altered, the apparent proportions of the Cambridge period, there are certain subsidiary facts of his undergraduate years which can scarcely be omitted. Mention, for instance, must at least be made of the reform agitation which swept over England in the year 1831, and the agricultural disturbance by which it was attended. Mention must also be made of the early mutterings of the theological storm which in the coming decade was to cause such havoc in academic and domestic circles. The effect of these two movements upon Tennyson will be referred to in the subsequent sections devoted to his views on politics and religion, but we may remark that the Reform Bill agitation lives only in his convinced horror of excess (a horror strengthened by the Torrijos episode), and in scattered references to rick-burning in *The Princess* and in his lines to Mary Boyle. Finally, it must be pointed out that from a strictly academic point of view his residence at Cambridge was not successful. Whereas his brother Charles secured a Bell scholarship, Alfred failed even to obtain his degree. We read even in a letter from Charles Merivale to John Frere of his "trying to make his eyes bad enough" to qualify for an honorary pass on the score of ill-health or, more technically, an "aegrotat." But at the very date when this letter was written, in the early spring of 1831, Tennyson's father died suddenly at Somersby, and the poet need have bothered himself no further about academic distinctions.

It is pleasant moreover to realise that in the single public honour which Alfred secured at Cambridge—and it was important enough—his father had taken a definite and preponderating share. For the prize poem set for the year 1829 was on the subject of Timbuctoo, and although Alfred had naturally hesitated to compete on so unpromising a theme, the Rector had insisted on his doing so, had even encouraged him to touch up an old poem called *Armageddon* for the purpose.

Hallam and others of the set contributed to the competition. Thackeray also wrote his poem, but not, we fear, for the eye of the examiners:—

"In Africa—a quarter of the world—
Men's skins are black, their hair is crisped and curled.
And somewhere there, unknown to public view,
A mighty city lies, called Timbuctoo. . . .

> I see her tribes the hill of glory mount,
> And sell their sugars on their own account;
> While round her throne the prostrate nations come,
> Sue for her rice, and barter for her rum."

And indeed Tennyson's composition is not, in essence, very dissimilar from that of Thackeray. "It is not," says Stopford Brooke, "at all like a prize poem." To my mind that eminent critic is mistaken: *Timbuctoo* is very like a prize poem indeed. Not so bad as the generality, not so good as Dean Stanley's; but still an obvious academic exercise, and, as such, not of much importance.

The theme is simple enough. Tennyson finds himself alone on the rocks of Gibraltar, and is visited by a seraph who turns out to be the spirit of Fable. She shows him the legendary city of Timbuctoo:—

> "Her gardens fragrant with the stately palm,
> Her pagods hung with music of sweet bells
> Her obelisks of ranged chrysolite."

and proceeds to regret that this dream-city must soon render its mystery:—

> "To keen discovery: soon your brilliant towers
> Shall darken with the waving of her wand;
> Darken and shrink and shiver into huts,
> Black specks amid a waste of dreary sand,
> Low-built, mud-wall'd, barbarian settlements."

Upon which she leaves him:—

> "Thus far the Spirit:
> Then parted heavenward on the wing; and I
> Was left alone on Calpe, and the moon
> Had fallen from the night, and all was dark."

A touch of Tennyson here and there in the poem, as in the two concluding lines, and the repetition of "darken"

above quoted, but not, on the whole, a poem which need
be frequently re-read. Its originality consisted in the fact
that it broke with established tradition by being written in
blank verse, in place of the traditional rhymed couplet. In
fact his contemporaries were surprised that the examiners
should have approved such hardihood; it was even whispered that the first examiner had marked the lines "V.Q."
which had impressed the second examiner as signifying
"Very good," and not, as intended, "Very queer." But the
fact remains that the Chancellor's medal was accorded to
Tennyson; that the poem was read in public at Commence-
ment in 1829 by Merivale, since the author was too timid
to appear himself; that it was published in "Prolusiones
Academicæ" for 1829; that his friends greeted it with a
"tumult of acclaim"; and that the London *Athenæum,* an
Apostolic organ at that time, reviewed it in terms forecast-
ing—"a first-rate poetical genius."

## VII

For the rest, if one desires to fill in the details, the general atmosphere of the Trinity period, one can read, the
prelude to *The Princess,* or the sketch of the poet "Everard
Hall" in the prologue to the *Morte d'Arthur,* or even *The
Gardener's Daughter,* with the picture of Eustace and his
"solemn gibe." Nor are there absent other undergraduate
touches: the charades, the riddles and the theatricals;
Tennyson in the part of Malvolio; the game called "Tale
from mouth to mouth"; the usual threadbare references to
proctors and climbing through the college railings; or even
the following ditty:—

> "Sweet Kitty Sandilands,
> The daughter of the doctor,
> We drest her in the Proctor's bands
> And past her for the Proctor . . .

Up the street we took her
    As far as the castle,
Jauntily sat the Proctor's cap,
    And from it hung the tassel," etc., etc.

And, behind it all, the familiar regret which must ever
figure in after years:—

"And never yet
Had heaven appeared so blue, nor earth so green."

or, more importantly:—

"And all we met was fair and good,
    And all was good that Time could bring,
    And all the secret of the Spring
Moved in the chambers of the blood.

And many an old philosophy
    On Argive heights divinely sang,
    And round us all the thicket rang
To many a flute of Arcady."

Yes, for all its "moments of unutterable misery," he was
not to forget Cambridge in the after years—the years that
followed on that February evening of 1831 when he gave
a farewell supper in his rooms at Corpus Buildings, and
they all danced together a parting quadrille, and he drove
off in the coach with a last impression of "Thompson's handsome face under the light of the street lamp."

But, in spite of this, it must be admitted that his purely
academic unsuccess at Cambridge did at times lead him
to a reaction against that institution and its system, and to
certain subsequent diatribes which neither in intention nor
execution were very well conceived. Nor when, in after
years, he came to stay at Balliol, can he have failed to notice a certain contrast, if only in the personal stimulus with
which Jowett launched his favoured undergraduates upon
their studies and their careers. And yet, in the after period,

in those ten grey nomadic years particularly after Hallam's death—the tavern years of Tennyson's existence—the memory of Cambridge would recur to him, would recur when he was alone with his port and tobacco in some inn, and when:—

> "The gas-light wavers dimmer
>     And softly, thro' a vinous mist,
>         My college friendships glimmer."

And, more than all this—more than the mere picture of Thompson's handsome face under the street lamp; more than the sound of Blakesley's laughter at Brookfield's jokes; more than the soft aroma of mulled claret, or Spedding's forehead glimmering through the smoke—more than all this, something more poignant than these pleasant regrets: a stab to the very heart of reminiscence. The way that Arthur would burst in when one was reading Paley, and talk so brilliantly, so fluently, about the derivation of moral sentiments; the way that he would let his hand fall gently upon one's shoulder; the way that on Sunday afternoons he would join one on the Grantchester round. And his views, his helpful, optimistic, convincing views, about the immortality of the soul. And the Valley of Cauteretz; and the plans for the long vacation; and his reading Dante on the floor at Corpus Buildings; and the first day that he came to Somersby; and the evenings on the lawn; and the cherries by the Drachenfels.

And oh! the way he would take one's arm, on summer evenings, under the limes!

# CHAPTER FOUR

# THE 1830 AND 1832 VOLUMES

## I

It is not to be imagined that during his three years' residence at Trinity Tennyson's poetical activity was restricted to the composition of *Timbuctoo*. FitzGerald, who, although not in his set, was only just outside it, speaks of the circulation and recitation of several poems, notably one on *Sir Launce-lot and Queen Guinevere*, among Tennyson's private friends. In the Memoir certain additional and unpublished verses are ascribed to this period, notably a long poem in irregular stanzas entitled *Anacaona*. Nor is this particular poem without interest: in the first place, it represents the con-tinuance of the "exotic" series in the "Poems by Two Brothers," a manner never employed by Tennyson, except perhaps in the contemporary *Recollections of the Arabian Nights*, with any memorable success; and, in the second place, the verses, which with their curious Gauguin effect, are interesting in themselves, are prefaced by an explana-tory note on the part of Hallam Tennyson which is very illuminating.

For the verses run on in the following strain:—

> "A dark Indian maiden
>     Warbling in the bloom'd liana,

> Stepping lightly, flower-laden,
>     By the crimson-eyed anana,
> Wantoning in orange groves,
>     Naked and dark-limb'd and gay,
> Bathing in the slumbrous coves,
> In the cocoa-shadow'd coves
>     Of sunlit Xaraguay,
> Who so happy as Anacaona,
>     The beauty of Espagnola,
>     The golden flower of Hayti?"

And the note by Hallam Tennyson is as follows: "My father liked this poem, but did not publish it, because the natural history and the rhymes did not satisfy him. He evidently chose words which sounded well, and gave a tropical air to the whole, and *he did not then care, as in his later poems, for absolute accuracy.*" (The italics are mine.)

But, in any case, the main monument of Tennyson's literary activity at Cambridge—and it is substantial enough —consists in the two important collections known respectively as the 1830 and the 1832 volumes.

"Poems chiefly Lyrical," by Alfred Tennyson, were issued by Effingham Wilson, Royal Exchange, Cornhill, towards the end of June 1830. In the previous March, his brother Charles had already published a volume entitled "Sonnets and Fugitive Pieces," which achieved, with Wordsworth at least, a greater success than Alfred's own verses. It was originally intended that some of Hallam's poems should be included in the 1830 volume, which would then have appeared as "Poems by Two Undergraduates." But Henry Hallam intervened, and Arthur's participation in the venture was forbidden. Tennyson therefore launched the volume under his own name and alone. He received at the time the sum of eleven pounds for the copyright.

Of the fifty-six pieces included in this volume, twenty-three were subsequently rejected by Tennyson and never appeared again in any authorised edition during his lifetime.

They can now be read in a convenient form in the Every-man volumes. Four more, including that interesting poem *The Kraken*, were suppressed until their appearance in the Library Edition of 1872; two more (*Leonine Elegiacs* and the *Supposed Confessions*), whose exclusion for so long is curious, were only republished as late as 1884; *The Deserted House* and *The Sea Fairies* turned up again, the one in 1848, the other in 1853; *The National Song*, somewhat modified, was included as a chorus in *The Foresters* of 1892, and the remaining twenty-four, considerably trimmed and polished, joined with the smaller residue of the 1832 publication to swell the first part of the two volumes of 1842.

Nor is this process of progressive sifting to which the volume was subsequently subjected by its author without interest, for it bears on the much-vexed question of the extent of Tennyson's deference to public opinion. That he was morbidly and childishly sensitive to criticism is indubitable, and will be abundantly apparent in the course of this volume. But until recently it was taken almost as an axiom by writers on Tennyson that the secret of his literary development is to be found in a study of contemporary criticism, and that it was the critics who drove and pestered him into certain avenues of expression which were unnatural, or at least unessential to him, and who frightened his timid soul away from the more rugged heights where his genius could have enjoyed an ampler freedom. It remained for Professor Lounsbury to disprove, or at least to modify, this theory. In his brilliant and delightful book, which was unfortunately unfinished at the time of his death, he has shown with great urbanity, based on an amazing industry of research, that this convenient hypothesis is misleading; and by his premature death he has left it open to other and far inferior critics to discover some more substantial and organic solution of the Tennyson problem, and to indicate, if not to prove, why a man who wrote, say, *The*

*Two Voices,* could also have written, and even published, let us say, *Sea Dreams.*

And indeed, although there can be no question that the virulent attacks of the early critics produced a deep impression upon Tennyson's nerves and temper, and, as in the years between 1832 and 1842, profoundly affected the outward circumstances of his literary career; and although we may suspect that his subsequent popularity with the middle and purchasing public, coupled with the necessity of maintaining a certain rather fortuitously worldly style and position, tempted him to exploit unduly those particular qualities of his poetic temperament which eventually drove the little green Macmillan books into edition after edition, yet it would be unfair and unintelligent to attribute to such superficial, even though concomitant, causes, the whole explanation of Tennyson's shortcomings, or to contend that he wrote *The Lord of Burleigh* merely because Christopher North had disapproved of *The Dying Swan.*

It is not my intention to trace in very great detail the alleged tergiversations of Tennyson before the slings and arrows of nineteenth-century criticism. As I have said, the thing has been done once and for all, has been done supremely well, by Professor Lounsbury. But in order to illustrate the danger of the pre-Lounsbury theory, some confrontation of the Christopher North review with the rejections and reprints in the 1830 volume may well be useful.

I shall deal with the review itself in a later section. It will suffice here to say that Christopher North singled out seventeen of the fifty-six poems for particular vituperation. Of these seventeen, Tennyson did, it is true, suppress eight; but he also suppressed fifteen more which had not been noticed and abused by Christopher North or other critics. And he deliberately retained and republished nine of the seventeen poems which had especially aroused the sarcasms of "Maga." Whether he was well advised to retain all these particular nine poems, is another question. He retained the two poems on the Owl, which are obviously ridiculous; he retained the two pieces entitled respectively *Nothing will Die* and *All Things will Die*, which might well have been allowed to disappear; he retained *The Merman* and *The Mermaid* (so excellently parodied in the "Bon Gaultier Ballads"), which, in spite of Charles Dickens' admiration, are at least questionable achievements; he retained *The Poet's Mind*, which we should have been sorry to lose; and he republished in 1853 *The Sea Fairies*, which is valuable to us if only for the real Tennysonian movement of the two opening lines:—

"Slow sail'd the weary mariners and saw,
  Betwixt the green brink and the running foam."

And finally he eventually republished *The Kraken* and *The Dying Swan*. And in this, at least, Tennyson was right, and Christopher North abundantly wrong.

## II

The main interest, to the admirer of Tennyson, of the 1830 volume lies in its obviously transitional character. It contains some verses which are as bad as any in the "Poems by Two Brothers"; it contains others which are certainly among the most beautiful that Tennyson ever achieved. And between these two extremes are several intermediate compositions of a neutral quality, interesting only as containing the seeds of future development.

There are, in the first place, a series of Keepsake verses in the parlour manner, so dear to the early nineteenth century,—the Claribels, Lilians, Adelines, Madelines, Isabels, and Sainted Juliets. There are other juvenilia, such as the two poems on the Owl, the lines on the Grasshopper, and the remarkable *Ode to Memory,* in which Somersby and Mablethorpe are so lovingly depicted in the manner of Coleridge. There are some slight if decorative pieces, such as *The Merman* and *The Mermaid* and *The Burial of Love;* some boyish verses on the mutability of human destiny;

such as *The How and the Why* and *Nothing will Die*, with
its companion piece, *All Things will Die;* there is a series of
completely meaningless amatory poems, such as *Hero to
Leander* and *Love and Sorrow;* there is the poem called
*The Sea Fairies*, with its two fine Mablethorpe lines already quoted, and there is the *Recollection of the Arabian
Nights*. It is this last which figures most prominently in the
juvenilia category of the 1830 volume; and, except perhaps
for the jaunty and recurrent jingle of the concluding lines
to each stanza, it is indeed a beautiful poem, with a
movement, a "carrying-through" movement, reminiscent of
Keats:—

> "Far off, and where the lemon-grove
>  In closest coverture upsprung,
>  The living airs of middle night
>  Died round the bulbul as he sung;
>  Not he: but something which possess'd
>  The darkness of the world, delight,
>  Life, anguish, death, immortal love,
>  Ceasing not, mingled, unrepress'd,
>      Apart from place, withholding time,
>      But flattering the golden prime
>          Of good Haroun Alraschid."

One would have preferred, perhaps, some arrangement
by which the nightingale would have replaced the bulbul,
and the exclusion of the final jingle; but it is surprising that
the critics, for all their general approval, did not fix more
pertinently upon the stanzas of this poem as showing that
something new and unmistakably important had occurred.

The second aspect of this Janus-like volume, the aspect
which predicts the future Tennyson, his faults and his virtues, is generally apparent. There are two very characteristic patriotic songs, a type of composition in which Tennyson so often blustered and became foolish; nor are the
following either better or worse than his occasional later
outbursts of jingoism:—

NAME

| | DATE | DEPART. DATE | ROOM NO. |
|---|---|---|---|
| 1205 MAN | 10-31 | 11-2 | 514 |

★ PLEASE READ . . . IMPORTANT ★

**PARKING:** This slip entitles Nassau Inn residents to free use of the designated parking area. **Note:** overnight parking on the streets of Princeton is prohibited.

**DEPARTURE TIME:** Our check-out time is 2:00 p.m. — should you desire to extend your reservation beyond the departure date indicated above, please consult with the front desk to determine if it will be possible. We regret that it will be necessary to charge for an additional night's lodging should a late check-out occur.

**BILLING:** In order to avoid billing confusion, please stop at the front desk when leaving.

**NASSAU INN** on Palmer Sq., Princeton, N. J.

> "Shout for England!
> Ho! for England!
> George for England!
> Merry England!
> England for aye!"

or again (and at least metrically preferable):—

> "There is no land like England
>     Where'er the light of day be;
> There are no hearts like English hearts
>     Such hearts of oak as they be.
> There is no land like England
>     Where'er the light of day be;
> There are no men like Englishmen,
>     So tall and bold as they be.
>
> *Chorus:* For the French the Pope may shrive 'em
>     For a devil a whit we need 'em:
>     As for the French, God speed 'em
>         Unto their hearts' desire,
>     And the merry devil drive 'em
>         Through the water and the fire."

And indeed, in all Tennyson's considerations on foreign policy there is this tinge of prejudice against our Gallic neighbours.

But there are other, and more important, verses in the 1830 volume which indicate how early was the development of his subsequent manner and characteristics. There is an experiment in late classical metre, and at least in the first line a very successful experiment, called *Leonine Elegiacs;* there are two dedicatory sonnets, addressed respectively to Blakesley and Kemble, which augur his later perfection in this urbane style; there are the first indications of theological doubt in the *Supposed Confessions* and *hoi reontes,* the first signs of sensitiveness to criticism in *The Poet's Mind* and, more indirectly, in *A Character;* there is the strange grotesque note of *The Kraken;* the magnificent grey gloom of *The Dying Swan.* And finally, there are the lines entitled *The Poet,* lines beautiful in themselves, and important as showing that the Apostolic doctrine of a "mission" had, for better or worse, already eaten into his soul:—

> "The poet in a golden clime was born,
>     With golden stars above;
> Dower'd with the hate of hate, the scorn of scorn,
>     The love of love.
>
> He saw thro' life and death, thro' good and ill,
>     He saw thro' his own soul.
> The marvel of the everlasting will,
>     An open scroll
>
> Before him lay."

After likening the mission of the Apostles, of their particular poet, the effect of their fruitful propagating devotion in the cause of human enlightenment, to the seeds of the dandelion, Tennyson proceeds to speak of Freedom, with "No blood upon her maiden robes" shaking "hoar anarchies":—

>                       "No sword
>     Of wrath her right arm whirl'd,
> But one poor poet's scroll, and with *his* word
>     She shook the world."

In subsequent editions he altered "hoar anarchies" to "all evil dreams of power"; but he kept the passage about her bloodless robes, he kept the passage about the poet's scroll, and he kept throughout his life the conviction that it was his business to guide and to teach.

I have dealt in a summary and perhaps unconvincing manner with these poems, since, although it is necessary to mention them at this stage, they are not sufficiently mature to necessitate more elaborate treatment. But there are four outstanding pieces in the collection which I have reserved for separate consideration. The first is the poem entitled *Supposed Confessions of a Second-rate Sensitive Mind not in Unity with Itself,* in which the whole of Tennyson's later philosophy, if it can be so styled, is clearly adumbrated. For in this composition he has, in the first place, employed, as so often in his later poems, the device of an alias—the vehicle, that is, of an imaginary character, a character who, if need be, could be dissociated from himself; could even, if necessary, be repudiated. And he has employed this method to illustrate the theological conflict which had already arisen within him, and which, more acutely, but not with any essential difference, was to disturb and puzzle him all his life. And with it all—with all the familiar Tennyson formulæ on faith and doubt, on love and conscience, on death and the immortality of the soul— is a faint echo here and there of the curious Calvinistic moods of the "Poems by Two Brothers." If we exclude this element, this spiritual abasement and the fear of hell, the *Confessions* of the 1830 volume are but little different in substance from the agonised perplexities of his later theological manner. There is, in the first place, the defence of doubt:—

> "It is man's privilege to doubt,
>  If so be that from doubt at length,
>  Truth may stand forth unmoved of change."

But on the heels of this defiance, a defiance derived possibly at Trinity from Niebuhr, Hare and Connop Thirlwall, we find the quick pang of terror at such presumption—the terror of the lengths, the dark and sinister lengths, to which inquiry may lead; the dread that it may lead to doubts not doctrinal merely, but actually essential; the dread that it may lead to doubts as to the immortality of the soul. And with this realisation comes the reaction, the familiar reaction which, in after years, would lead Tennyson to rant and scream and asseverate. In the present poem he is merely

conscience-stricken and afraid: he yearns to get back to
the old easy days in Somersby church, to his early heaven
and his childhood's views:—

> "Thrice happy state again to be
> The trustful infant on the knee!
> Who lets his waxen fingers play
> About his mother's neck, and knows
> Nothing beyond his mother's eyes."

Better even to be the beast of the field, "with placid lows
unfearing," than to be tortured by this terror of eternal
death, to be launched helpless upon an angry sea:—

> "Unpiloted in the echoing dance
> Of reboant whirlwinds, stooping low
> Unto the death."

And the poem ends with an appeal for the wider knowledge, and a cry of misery at the perplexities of human
doubt:—

> "Oh teach me yet
> Somewhat before the heavy clod
> Weighs on me, and the busy fret
> Of that sharp-headed worm begins
> In the gross blackness underneath.
>
> Oh weary life! Oh weary death!
> Oh spirit and heart made desolate!
> Oh damned vacillating state!"

It is a fine poem, conceived and written with that sinister
twilight effect of which Tennyson was so supreme a master,
an effect of the tempter whispering in the dusk.

Of his religious poems and theories there will be much
to be said at a later stage and in a more comprehensive
manner. I have only dwelt on the *Supposed Confessions* in
order to show that the conflict between faith and doubt
which to so large an extent absorbed and obscured the

flame of his lyrical genius had already in 1830 begun to cloud and hamper him with its acrid, smoke-laden convolutions.

And in conclusion I must mention *Mariana* and *Oriana*, the two familiar ballads which, with their wide-swelling vowel sounds, the moaning dirge:—

> "When the long dun wolds are ribb'd with snow
> And loud the Norland whirlwinds blow,"

and the "weary," "dreary" iteration, their sense of impending catastrophe, are not excelled by any of the later poems. And finally I must quote the following familiar lines, possibly the most purely original passage in all Tennyson's Nature poetry:—

> "The air is damp, and hush'd, and close,
> As a sick man's room when he taketh repose
>     An hour before death;
> My very heart faints and my whole soul grieves
> At the moist rich smell of the rotting leaves,
>     And the breath
>     Of the fading edges of box beneath,
> And the year's last rose.
>
> Heavily hangs the broad sunflower
>     Over its grave i' the earth so chilly;
> Heavily hangs the hollyhock,
>     Heavily hangs the tiger lily."

For I do not see how, for the effect desired, observation and technique could go much further.

## III

The reception accorded to the 1830 volume by contemporary authorities and critics forms a curious chapter in Tennyson's literary history. Wordsworth, we are given to understand, preferred Charles' sonnets to the more ambitious compositions of the younger brother. Coleridge, up at Highgate, expounded an even more original opinion, an opinion which filled Professor Saintsbury with "a great awe," and almost persuaded him to abandon for ever the study of English prosody. "The misfortune is," he remarked, "that Mr. Tennyson has begun to write verses without very well understanding what metre is." He advised the young man to confine himself for a year or two to certain well-tried metres before entering on experiments. "As it is," he concluded, "I can scarcely scan his verses."

This criticism was repeated to Tennyson, and it rankled. He attributed it, however, to Coleridge's misunderstanding of the use made in the poems of unhyphenated double words, such as *goldennetted, sablesheeny,* and he relieved his mind by concluding that it was his own absurd antipathy for hyphens, and not any real metrical failing, which had thrown Coleridge out of step in scanning the verses.

In January 1831 there appeared an article on the poems in the *Westminster Review* which was unduly eulogistic in spirit; which compared the two companion pieces of *All Things will Die* and *Nothing will Die* to *Il Penseroso* and *L'Allegro;* which gave vent to a great many other foolish opinions, such as that the amatory poems spoke "not of heartless sensuality, nor of a sickly refinement, nor of fantastic devotion, but of manly love." This unfortunate pæan was followed in February by a series of laudatory articles which Hallam had induced Leigh Hunt to publish in the *Tatler* (February 24 and 26, March 1 and 3, 1831). "We have seen," he wrote, "no such poetical writing since the last volume of Mr. Keats." The comparison was provocative, and the older critics were further aroused by a review in the new *Monthly Magazine* for March 1831, in which the young poet was again lauded for his similarity to Keats.

But in the final event it was the exaggerated propaganda of the Apostles, and of Hallam in particular, that was to prove Tennyson's undoing.

For, as may well be supposed, the Apostles had from the

outset greeted the 1830 volume with a "tumult of acclaim." They went further. In April 1830 a monthly periodical had appeared under the title of the *Englishman's Magazine*. In August this periodical had been acquired by Moxon, the publisher, and in that same number Arthur Hallam published an article "On Some Characteristics of Modern Poetry and on the Lyrical Poems of Alfred Tennyson." In October the *Englishman's Magazine* collapsed—killed, according to Christopher North, by the "universal guffaw" raised by Hallam's article. And indeed the said article is sufficiently absurd. Hallam compares the 6th stanza of the *Recollections of the Arabian Nights* to Milton, and the 12th to Æschylus, and, as Leigh Hunt himself remarked, his quotations were remarkably badly selected. The whole tone of the review was one of almost hysterical panegyric. It was not surprising that the old guard were aroused.

The *Edinburgh* and the *Quarterly,* those ancient authorities, merely ignored the volume. The attack, when it came, was led by Christopher North (Professor Wilson) in *Blackwood*. It was delivered in two instalments. The first was depreciatory only, and not malignant: it occurred as a passage in the dialogue of "Noctes Ambrosianæ" for February 1832. There was some mention of Tennyson's genius and imagination, and some criticism of his affectation. But, on the whole, "I have good hopes," pronounced Christopher North, "of Alfred Tennyson. But the Cockneys are doing what they may to spoil him—and if he suffers them to put their bird-lime on his feet, he will stop all the days of his life in hedgerows, or leap fluttering about the bushes." This was harmless enough, a mere echo, and not ungratifying, of the old Keats controversy. But in May there was more to come. It appears that in the interval Wilson had read Hallam's unfortunate article in the *Englishman's Magazine,* and indeed his second review opens with a characteristic and full-blooded attack upon that "narcotic dose administered by a crazy charlatan." The article in the *Westminster Review* next comes under castigation, and is described as "the purest mere matter of moonshine ever mouthed by an idiot-lunatic, slavering in palsied dotage." By the time he reached the poems themselves and Alfred Tennyson, Christopher North was somewhat out of breath, and his vituperation became of a milder quality. Seventeen of the poems, as has been stated, were dismissed as being either "miserable" or "dismal drivel." But others, and notably the *Recollections of the Arabian Nights* and *Mariana,* were warmly commended, and the review concludes with the opinion that in spite of his "not infrequent silliness . . . Alfred Tennyson is a poet."

It must be observed that Wilson's attack in *Blackwood* was aimed, and with some justification, not so much at the volume itself, as at the "inspired" reviews which had treated it with such excessive adulation. In other words, it was aimed at Hallam rather than at Tennyson, and had the latter taken the attack with average dignity, its ultimate effect could only have reached to his advantage. In the face of criticism, however, Tennyson was neither dignified nor even averagely prudent, and in this particular instance he committed an error of taste and judgment which was to recoil on his head with devastating consequences.

For in his volume of 1832 he inserted, against the advice of Hallam, the following foolish and provocative epigram:—

> "*To Christopher North*
>
> "You did late review my lays,
>     Crusty Christopher;
> You did mingle blame and praise,
>     Rusty Christopher.
> When I learnt from whom it came,
> I forgave you all the blame,
>     Musty Christopher;
> I could *not* forgive the praise,
>     Fusty Christopher."

## IV

The 1830 volume, and the dust raised by the ground-swirl of critical controversy which it provoked, did much to render Tennyson's name familiar in circles outside the small band of Cambridge propagandists. But there were other means, more subtle insinuating means, by which a writer in those days could penetrate into the very heart of nineteenth-century England—could penetrate, that is, into the home.

There were the Annuals. And indeed the importance of these publications, their importance to nineteenth-century literature in general, their importance in particular to Tennyson, requires at this stage to be stated and underlined. For if we can trace the development of Tennyson's lyrical genius from a nervous and wistful childhood, through Hallam, to the urbane and confident manner of his later years; if we can attribute his didactic outbursts to the influence of the Apostles and other devotees working upon a mind naturally perplexed and inconclusive, we can to a large extent assign the third main category of his work—what has been called his "School-miss Alfred" or his "Keepsake" style—to the influence of that peculiar condition of public taste in which the Annuals prospered and multiplied, and to which they pandered.

It was not indeed that, in comparison with Landor, Bulwer or Disraeli, Tennyson figured very largely in the Annuals, or that the few poems which he contributed to them are very characteristic of his own Keepsake manner. There are three poems in the *Gem* of 1831, namely, *No More, Anacreontics* and *A Fragment;* there are sonnets in *Friendship's Offering* and the *Yorkshire Literary Annual;* and later, in 1836, there is *The Eve of St. Agnes* in the *Keepsake*, which was then edited by Lady E. Stuart-Wortley, and finally there are the famous lines *O that 'twere Possible* in the *Tribute* of 1837.

That he actually intended in 1831 to become a more regular contributor to these Annuals can be gauged from Hallam's letter to Merivale which I have already quoted; that he did not carry out that intention, may be due perhaps to the lack of enthusiasm on the part of editors to pay for—nay, even to accept—the contributions of so young and comparatively unknown a writer. A further cause may have been a reference in the *Literary Gazette* to his contributions to the *Gem* as being but "silly sooth." And, in any case, we know that after Lockhart's review of the 1832 volume he desired only to hide his head in shame and anger. And thus we find him writing in 1836 as follows: "Provoked by the incivility of Editors, I swore an oath that I would never again have to do with these vapid books." And vapid they were, enough so to merit Charles Lamb's condemnation of their "ostentatious trumpery" and "their combinations of show and emptiness."

The importance of the Annuals in Tennyson's literary development does not therefore lie in the actual number or quality of the poems which he composed for, or inserted in, these publications. It lies in the fact that the Annuals are at the same time an indication and a cause of a change in the angle of public taste, more precisely a change of literary audience. And this change is important; for the young poet between 1823 and 1850 found himself writing with the picture of a very definite audience before him, an audience of young ladies. It is true, of course, that this audience had for long been present in the minds of our English poets. "The Annuals," wrote Southey in 1828, "are now the only books bought for presents to young ladies, in which way poesies formerly had their chief vent." This is true enough. But the young lady of 1830 was already a different person from the young lady of 1820. In the first place, she was younger; in the second place, she was far more ladylike. She was positively thrilled by the Annuals. As Tennyson himself puts it:—

> "She left the novel half-uncut
>     Upon the rosewood shelf;
>   She left the new piano shut."

And thus we have *The Lord of Burleigh, Lady Clare* and their companions. All of which poems are merely topical in inspiration, and can, by the present admirers of Tennyson, be ignored.

The Annuals were intended to be given as Christmas presents, and were therefore published in the November preceding the year of their date. They were based on the German Taschenbuch model, which still, at least at Munich, survives and prospers. Originally the *Whittaker's Almanack* element predominated, and the pictures and stories were introduced but incidentally to enliven the dates and the statistics. In 1824, however, Alaric Alexander Watts produced the *Literary Souvenir, or Cabinet of Poetry and Romance,* 1825, which, from the fact that the calendar element was subsidiary to the literary and artistic, achieved a huge success. With the growth of competition, publishers began to specialise: there were religious annuals, such as the *Amulet* and the *Iris;* geographical annuals, missionary annuals, musical annuals, comic annuals. In 1826 Charles Heath brought out the *Keepsake,* the type and glory of all the Annuals, which figures in connection with the Hon. Percy Popjoy in "Pendennis." "The *Keepsake*," writes the *Literary Gazette* of October 1, 1831, "has the most aristocratic list of contributors—there are very few common names." But in spite of this, by 1840 the passion for Annuals began to decline: the editor of *Forget-me-not,* the pioneer of all the Annuals, in the preface to the 1842 volume, writes sadly as follows: "Certain it is that the Annuals, from especial favourites of the public, have come to be regarded almost with indifference."

But by 1842 they had done their work: they had done it very thoroughly.

## V

On leaving Trinity in February 1831 Tennyson had returned home to Somersby, bringing with him his Chancellor's medal and the 1830 volume, but no specifically academic honours. Nor do we find that he had made any serious plans for a future career: the Church loomed vaguely in the distance, and he left it at that. It was no use arguing with a grandfather incensed by one's having failed to take a degree, or with a father whose petulance had increased with declining health. For the Rector was by then very ill—was, in fact, within a few weeks to die. The local legend has it that he succumbed to typhoid, for there were no drains in the house. But from the Memoir it is evident that he died of some paralytic stroke, and was found, one March morning, leaning back in his study chair, "having passed peacefully away." And a week later, Tennyson, whose morbidity was streaked with a curiously hard vein of the macabre, slept in his father's bed in the hope of some ghostly visitation.

The immediate preoccupation, however, was whether the family would now be obliged to leave Somersby Rectory. Fortunately the incumbent of the living was still a minor, and an arrangement was made by which they could remain on in the house for the present, the services being conducted by a Rev. E. A. Robinson, a curate. And thus they lived in the little white house, at peace but still congested, until the year 1837, when they moved to Epping.

In the interval Alfred himself became increasingly restless and nomadic. Already, while at Cambridge, he had been with Hallam to London and had met Arthur's father, the old historian with the fierce eyes and the curiously unintelligible enunciation. And in this year, 1831, he goes again to No. 67 Wimpole Street, and we find him talking and smoking in Hallam's attic-study under the leads, and their deciding between them that in future they "will not lose hold of the Real in seeking the Ideal." We find him, also, reading *Oenone* to Hallam's father. Not the *Oenone* that we know so well, but the first rather hesitating version of the 1832 volume written in the Valley of Cauteretz. Nor does this particular recitation appear to have been a quite unqualified success. The old man "seemed to like Juno's speech, but was called away in the middle of Venus'." The reading was not resumed, nor can Tennyson have relished the part about the old man being called away. But he was to make up for all that later at Farringford and at Aldworth. No chance in those days, no possible chance, of anyone being called away.

And then, more importantly, Hallam would come to Somersby. He had been there first in the spring of 1830. And one day the Sellwood girls drove over from Horncastle, where their father, Harry Sellwood, was a solicitor, and lived in the square red-brick house which still looks upon the market place. And Arthur and Emily Sellwood went for a walk together in the Fairy Wood. "At a turn of the path," records Hallam Tennyson, "they came upon my father, who, at sight of the slender, beautiful girl of seventeen, in her simple grey dress . . . suddenly said to her: 'Are you a Dryad or an Oread wandering here?'" Nothing seems to have come of this observation at the moment, but the encounter was not without significance, since one June day, twenty years later, Tennyson married this eldest Sellwood daughter, at Shiplake Rectory, in the vicinity of Pangbourne.

It was during this first visit, apparently, that Hallam fell in love with Alfred's second sister, Emily, a brown-skinned, blue-eyed girl of nineteen, to whom he addressed sonnets as an "English maiden, English wife." They became engaged some time in February 1831. As was but natural, for Arthur was only twenty at the time, old Hallam did not approve of the engagement: he insisted, as the wise insist in such cases, that it should be kept secret for a year, that meanwhile they should correspond, but not meet. And in

February 1832, when the time of probation was up, Hallam flew to Somersby and the engagement became authorised and public. Tennyson, as may well be supposed, was ravished by this development. In the first place, it gave Hallam, who by then was studying for the Bar, an additional incitement to brave the congested discomforts at Somersby, and rendered him:—

> "Call'd to the bar, but ever call'd away
> By one low voice to one dear neighbourhood."

And, in the second place, it opened vistas of an even closer intimacy—of a domestic intimacy, of a time when Arthur and Emily's children would "babble 'Uncle' on his knee." And thus we have the identification with Arthur Hallam of the later Somersby, the lawn, the hillside and the distant woods; and the two mainsprings of his inspiration are fused into a poignant whole.

Of Emily Tennyson there is perhaps not very much to be said. The shock of Hallam's death for a while rendered her seriously ill. A period of widowhood, of the "perpetual maidenhood" prescribed for her by her brother, ensued; she was accorded a pension of £300 by the Hallam family; and finally, in the year 1842, she appalled them all by marrying a Lieutenant Jesse of the Royal Navy. From that date she rather drops out of the picture. It appears that Tennyson himself never wholly forgave her; the Memoir is silent, ominously silent, on the subject. She crops up for a moment in Paris during the disturbances of 1848; and finally she emerges again, reconciled to her brother, in a very welcome passage of the late Mrs. Warre Cornish's recent contributions to the *London Mercury*. The passage is worth quoting:—

> "The Tennysons' carriage met me on the Yarmouth pier: in it I found Miss Thackeray and a lady with her dog in her lap who was staying at Farringford. As we drove through the lanes a personal conversation which

had been interrupted by my arrival was resumed. The elder lady had a deep, serious voice, and she attracted me at once by her fine blue expressive eyes, which still gave forth light, though set in a deep-lined face. She had a well-cut profile: dark bandeaux of hair fell with delicate curves on each side of her brown face: they were streaked with grey. She had once been Arthur Hallam's fiancée, Emily Tennyson. To everything Anne Thackeray was saying in her gentle reflective way about life and its contradictions she replied with a strong Lincolnshire accent: 'I know that: I have felt that . . . I have felt averything; I know averything. I don't want any new emotion. I know what it is to feel like a stöanl"

For the rest, for what remains of these last months of their companionship together, there is but little to record of Alfred Tennyson and Arthur Hallam. We hear of them at Sheffield together, and, of course, there was the Rhine journey in the summer of 1832—the "summer belts of wheat and vine," and the picture of them eating cherries on the Drachenfels. But the real setting for their friendship was not the Rhine, but Somersby and the little room in the attic, where Arthur slept in Charles' bed and where they smoked together and talked theology. Yes, that was better than the Rhine:—

> "For I the Nonnenwerth have seen,
>   And Obenwenter's vineyards green,
>   Musical Lurlei: and between
> The hills to Bingen have I been,
> Bingen in Darmstadt, where the Rhene
> Curves towards Mentz, a woody scene.
>
> Yet never did there meet my sight
> In any town, to left or right,
> A little room so exquisite,
> With two such couches soft and white."

## VI

The second volume, entitled simply "Poems by Alfred Tennyson," was issued in foolscap octavo by Edward Moxon of 62 New Bond Street in December 1832, and bore on the title-page the date of 1833. It consists of thirty pieces of varying length and purport, and is fully representative of the different Tennysonian themes, classical, romantic, domestic and descriptive. Thus we have *The Lotos-Eaters*, *The Hesperides*, and *Oenone*; *The Lady of Shalott*, *Eleanore*, *The Sisters* and *Mariana in the South*; *The Miller's Daughter* and *The May Queen*; *The Palace of Art* and *A Dream of Fair Women*. We have also some Keepsake verses to Rosalind, Margaret and Kate; we have some good lines addressed to James Spedding on the death of his brother; and we have finally *The Darling Room* and the epigram on Christopher North. The theological element is absent, for one can scarcely force into that category the foolish little ditty, later omitted, which begins:—

> "Who can say
> Why To-day
> To-morrow will be Yesterday?"

The sense of a poetical mission is dormant, and lives only in the introductory sonnet (subsequently suppressed until it appeared in the Library Edition of 1872), with its lines:—

> "Mine be the Power which ever to its sway
> Will win the wise at once, and by degrees
> May into uncongenial spirits flow."

The contrast between the "wise" and the "uncongenial" irritated the reviewers considerably; nor, as a forecast of the progress of his literary reputation, are the lines very accurate.

With the 1832 volume we enter on the firm ground of an established literary manner. Tennyson was to develop this manner in several directions: even these very poems of 1832 were, by the time they came to be inserted into the 1842 volume, improved and modified in some cases, such as in that of *Oenone*, almost beyond recognition. For the moment, however, it is necessary only to mention the titles of the more outstanding and familiar poems, and to pass on to the important effect which the reception accorded to this volume produced upon his life and character.

For with the British public the volume of 1832 was not merely a failure: it was a disaster. The Cambridge circle alone approved of it, and we read of FitzGerald mumbling the assonances of *The Lady of Shalott* in the dawn while driving on the top of the coach from Cambridge to London. The Apostles were almost alone in their approval. Even before the reviewers had condemned the volume, the public had pronounced it "affected and obscure." Those few who had appreciated the 1830 collection were perplexed by its successor. And when the reviewers began on the latter volume, this perplexity changed into a convinced and vocal disappointment. On the crest of the reaction came the famous Lockhart review in the *Quarterly*, and with it Tennyson's reputation sank to zero. And, what was worse, he had become a subject of derision: he became a joke—he was not an author whom any intelligent young lady could be caught reading. For it must be remembered that at that date the *Quarterly* for most people was "second only to God's bible," and its opinions constituted an authority which no man or woman of culture could ignore. Thus by 1834 we find the *Oxford Magazine* expressing the view that "Alfred Tennyson is still more laughed at than wept over." And in September of that year the future Dean Stanley could write from Hurstmonceux and confess that Julius Hare has been reading "for instance (*tell it not in Gath*) Alfred Tennyson's poems." And Gath at that date was the whole reading public.

In that "universal guffaw," one man alone, John Stuart Mill, had the courage to raise his voice in protest. But his defence appeared in the *London Review* only in July 1835, and by then Tennyson and the Tennyson joke had both been temporarily forgotten. And of the eight hundred copies which Moxon had printed only three hundred had been sold by the spring of 1835.

Seldom indeed has the critical community been so unanimous in condemnation. The only favourable notice which has been unearthed was in the *Monthly Repository*, a Unitarian organ edited by W. J. Fox. For the rest he was attacked for his affectation, his use of far-fetched words and combinations, and for his "shallow metaphysics." The *Spectator* dubbed him "shadowy and obscure." The *Athenæum* abused him for compounding double words "after the German model." The *Literary Gazette* was even more vehement, accused him of belonging to the "Baa-Lamb" school, and advised him to retire into an asylum. And finally there was Lockhart[1] in the *Quarterly* for April 1833.

There can be little doubt that the peculiar virulence of this notorious review was due to the insertion in the 1832 volume of that foolish attack upon Christopher North. Wilson himself disdained to notice the poems in *Blackwood;* but he undoubtedly encouraged Lockhart, hoping thus to dispose of Tennyson vicariously and finally in the even more influential *Quarterly*. And this Lockhart proceeded to do with a malignity which, amusing as it is, fills one even to-day with a certain indignation. But, then, we happen to know the Tennyson of 1833 as a large, brown, lonely creature who felt any criticism as a burn upon the flesh, whereas to Lockhart he appeared only as a small, impudent and effeminate Cockney who deserved a drubbing; and this, I suppose, is sufficient justification. And finally Tennyson, to Lockhart's mind, was a disciple of Keats, and we know what both Croker and Lockhart thought of Keats.

His review of Tennyson's poems is thus from the first tinged with the bile of the former controversy, and opens

[1] See pages 310–11.

with a curiously tasteless snarl over the body of the last unfortunate victim. It then proceeds to deal with Tennyson as with "another and a brighter star of that galaxy or *Milky Way* of poetry of which the Lamented Keats was the harbinger." After pulling to pieces the introductory sonnet, in which Tennyson has spoken of his poetic mission, he proceeds to demolish the second poem in the volume, the lines which begin: "All good things have not kept aloof." This poem is interesting to us to-day as one of the early instances of Tennyson's characteristic Nature poetry, the "poetry of observation."

This is how Lockhart deals with it:—

> "The next piece is a kind of testamentary paper addressed 'To ——,' a friend, we presume, containing his wishes as to what his friend should do for him when he (the poet) shall be dead—not, as we shall see, that he quite thinks that such a poet can die outright.

> " 'Shake hands, my friend, across the brink
>         Of that deep grave to which I go.
>     Shake hands once more: I cannot sink
>         So far—far down, but I shall know
>         That voice and answer from below.'

> "Horace said 'non omnis moriar,' meaning that his fame should survive. Mr. Tennyson is still more vivacious, 'non *omnino* moriar'—'I will not die at all; my body shall be as immortal as my verse, and however *low I may go* I warrant you I shall keep all my wits about me,—therefore':—

> " 'When in the darkness over me
>         The four-handed mole shall scrape,
>     Plant thou no dusky cypress tree,
>         Nor wreathe thy cap with doleful crape,
>         But pledge me in the flowing grape.'

> "Observe how all ages become present to the mind of a great poet; and admire how naturally he com-

bines the funeral cypress of classical antiquity with the crape hatband of the modern undertaker.

"He proceeds:—

> "'And when the sappy field and wood
>>    Grow green beneath the *showery gray*
> And rugged barks begin to bud
>>    And through damp holts, new flushed
>>        with May,
>>        Ring sudden *laughters* of the jay.'

"Laughter, the philosophers tell us, is the peculiar attribute of man—but as Shakespeare found 'tongues in trees and sermons in stones,' this true poet endows Nature not merely with human sensibilities, but with human functions—the jay *laughs*, and we find, indeed, a little further on, that the woodpecker *laughs* also; but, to make the distinction between their merriment and that of men, both jays and woodpeckers laugh upon melancholy occasions. We are glad, moreover, to observe that Mr. Tennyson is prepared for, and therefore will not be disturbed by human laughter, if any silly reader should catch the infection from the woodpeckers and jays.

> "'Then let wise Nature work her will
>>    And on my clay her darnels grow,
> Come only when the days are still
>>    And at my headstone whisper low
>>    And tell me . . .'

"Now what would an ordinary bard wish to be told under such circumstances? Why, perhaps, how his sweetheart was, or his child, or his family, or how the Reform Bill worked, or whether the last edition of the poems had been sold—*papae!* our genuine poet's first wish is—

> "'And tell me—*if the woodbines blow!*'

"When, indeed, he shall have been thus satisfied as

to the *woodbines* (of the blowing of which in their due season he may, we think, feel pretty secure), he turns a passing thought to his friend, and another to his mother:—

> " 'If *thou* art blest, my *mother's* smile
> Undimmed';

but such inquiries, short as they are, seem too commonplace, and he immediately glides back into his curiosity as to the state of the weather, and the forwardness of the spring:—

> " 'If thou art blest—my mother's smile
> Undimmed—if *bees are on the wing?*'

"No, we believe the whole circle of poetry does not furnish such another instance of enthusiasm for the sights and sounds of the vernal season! The sorrows of a bereaved mother rank *after* the blossoms of the *woodbine* and just before the hummings of the *bee*; and this is *all* that he has any curiosity about; for he proceeds:—

> " 'Then cease, my friend, a little while,
> That I may . . .'

" 'Send my love to my mother,' or 'give some hints about bees which I have picked up from Aristaeus, in the Elysian Fields,' or 'tell you how I am situated as to my own personal comforts in the world below'? Oh no:—

> " 'That I may—hear the *throstle sing*
> His bridal song—the boast of Spring.
> Sweet as the noise, in parched plains,
> Of bubbling wells that fret the stones
> (*If any sense in me remains*)
> Thy words will be—thy cheerful tones
> As welcome to——my *crumbling bones.*'

*'If any sense in me remains.'* This doubt is inconsistent with the opening stanza of the piece, and, in fact, too modest; we take upon ourselves to reassure Mr. Tennyson, that even after he shall be dead and buried, as much *'sense'* will still remain as he has now the good fortune to possess."

I have quoted this at length to show the general tone and manner of a review which was to affect Tennyson's immediate future very profoundly. The remainder of the more important poems are dealt with in a similar style: in their turn *The Lady of Shalott, The Miller's Daughter, Oenone, The Hesperides, The Lotos-Eaters, The Palace of Art,* and *A Dream of Fair Women* are all ridiculed for faults real or imaginary, and Lockhart is able to profit by *The Darling Room* and the lines to Christopher North to end on a note of hilarity, and to dissolve into laughter whatever sympathy might in the course of the article have been growing for a young poet so cruelly vituperated.

Incidentally, also, Lockhart does manage to get the maximum fun out of *The Darling Room.* After quoting the first section of what he calls this "elegant and playful" piece, he continues:—

"We entreat our readers to note how, even in this little trifle, the singular taste and genius of Mr. Tennyson break forth. In such a dear *little* room a narrow-minded scribbler would have been content with *one* sofa, and that one he would probably have covered with black mohair, or red cloth, or a good striped chintz: how infinitely characteristic is white dimity! —'Tis as it were a type of the purity of the poet's mind."

Lockhart then passes to the second movement of *The Darling Room,* to the part about the Nonnenwerth, and concludes: "We have ourselves visited all these celebrated spots, and can testify, in corroboration of Mr. Tennyson, that we did not see in any of them anything like *this little room so exquisITE."* And after a sound trouncing over the Christopher North epigram, Lockhart leaves Tennyson for dead.

## VII

The Lockhart review has been given this prominence because it was undoubtedly one of the main causes of the silent and morose decade which was to follow. In a general way, therefore, in that it kept Tennyson from publication at the most vital years of a poet's life—that is, between the ages of twenty-three and thirty-three—the effect upon his literary development was all-important. But it would be an exaggeration to say that the subsequent rejections and alterations which Tennyson adopted were chosen in slavish obedience to the dictates of Lockhart. Indeed, of the fourteen poems which he did not allow to reappear in the reprint of 1842 only five had been actually mentioned by Lockhart; and, conversely, eight poems, including *The Lotos-Eaters* and *Oenone,* which had been attacked by Lockhart, were retained. It must be observed, however, that the expression "retained" is only relative: retained they were, but in a form very different from that in which they had originally outraged the *Quarterly.* And it cannot be denied that the lines which Lockhart particularly ridiculed were those to which the labour of the file was most rigorously applied: the "water rat" of *The Miller's Daughter* becomes a "trout"; the "stern" under which the Lady of Shalott's name was written on her funeral barge became "And round the prow they read her name"; the "sudden laughters of the jay" became eventually "sudden critches"; and in *The Lament of Iphigenia* the verses:—

> "One drew a sharp knife, thro' my tender throat
>     Slowly and nothing more."

became, under the gibe of Lockhart:—

"The bright death quiver'd at the victim's throat;
        Touched: and I knew no more."

Whereas, and perhaps more inevitably, the following
stanza in the 1832 *Palace of Art:—*

"Isaiah with fierce Ezekiel,
        Swart Moses by the Coptic sea,
Plato, Petrarca, Livy and Raphael,
        And eastern Confutzee,"

becomes in 1842 the less provocative:—

"Below was all mosaic choicely plann'd
        With cycles of the human tale
Of this wide world, the times of every land
        So wrought, they will not fail."

But, in contrast to all these obedient modifications, we
must point out that in *Oenone,* although twenty of the
twenty-six lines quoted by Lockhart were suppressed and
although the whole poem was practically re-written in the
years that followed, yet the main point of attack, namely
the iteration of "O Mother Ida," was completely ignored,
and this iteration occurs in the second version nineteen
times, compared to a bare sixteen in the 1832 volume.

In spite of these isolated evidences of courage and defiance, the effect of the Lockhart review upon Tennyson
himself was penetrating and prolonged. His first act was at
once to withdraw from the press *The Lover's Tale,* which
was then about to issue. We find him thinking of leaving
England altogether, of living abroad. We find him even
writing a frightened letter of apology to Christopher North
—not a very dignified letter, and one which strikes a strange
note in the first volume of the Memoir, a book which, as a
whole, has been so scrupulously edited. Nor, incidentally,
did this letter appease the heart of Wilson. It was left un-
answered. In 1836 we find Christopher North going quite
a long distance out of his way (he was reviewing Joanna

Baillie) to attack the Cambridge Debating Society for discussing whether Tennyson was a great poet. "The bare
imagination," he says, "of such a debate must bring the
blush of shame on the face of every man of common sense."
And then, after some patronising remarks on Alfred's imagination, "but oh!" he exclaims, "how feeble too often is his
Thought! Feeble because he is a wilful fribble—flattery had
made him so." And later, when people no longer laughed
at Tennyson, we find Wilson running a rival poet, "our new
contributor," under the name of "Archæus," otherwise
Sterling, and condemning the Tennyson coterie as the
"sumphs." Only by 1844 does the note change a little: by
then he has become the "great artist" from whom Miss
Barrett has drawn so much of her manner; we hear of the
"finished elegance of his style." Finally in 1849 the *Quarterly*, but not Christopher North, issued a general recanta-
tion. And he, that fierce old man, lived till 1854 to see *In
Memoriam* and the Laureateship and the dawn of the Isle
of Wight period. But he never, personally, forgave or forgot the squib of 1832, so that Tennyson's letter of apology
was in the end an unnecessary, as well as a regrettable,
episode in the whole unfortunate incident.

VIII

And thus by June 1833, at a date when Newman was
writing "Lead, kindly Light," on a sailing-ship between
Sicily and Marseilles, and Darwin was on board the *Beagle*
in the South Sea Islands, we find Alfred Tennyson struck
dumb by the shouts of derision which his enemies had
raised around him. "I gather," says Hallam Tennyson in
the Memoir, "from the letters of that time that there was a
strong current of depreciation of my father in certain literary quarters." There was. It carried Tennyson with it, a bewildered unhappy Tennyson, away from the early inspiration and out into the open sea. From now on he began to
think of other means of getting past the reviewers; he be-

gan "to base his poems on broad and common interests of the time and of universal humanity."

But luckily there was Arthur Hallam. In April he was with him in London, visiting "the Elgin marbles, the Tower and the Zoological Gardens." In July we find Tennyson alone in Scotland, and early in August he receives from Hallam the first news of his intended journey. The letter is dated July 31, 1833. "I do own," Hallam writes, "that I feel the want of you at some times more than at others: a sort of yearning for dear old Alfred comes upon me, and that without any apparent reason. . . . I should like much to hear your adventures (in Scotland), but I daresay it will be difficult to persuade you to write to Vienna, whither I am going on Saturday." On the receipt of this letter Tennyson returned at once to London. We hear of a supper at his lodgings, with Moxon, Leigh Hunt, Hallam and Tennant, and of Tennyson's reading to them *The Gardener's Daughter*.

The following day Hallam left with his father for the Tyrol, Salzburg and Buda Pest. By September they reached Vienna, and on the 6th of that month he writes his last letter to Tennyson. He speaks of Titian's Danäe: "I wish you could see his Danäe! Do you just write as perfect a Danäe."

A few days later Hallam had a slight touch of fever and kept to his room. He ordered the fire to be lighted and he lay down. His father, returning from his walk found Arthur apparently asleep and continued writing letters.

But the blow had fallen. Arthur Hallam, at the age of twenty-two, had burst a blood vessel, lying on a sofa in the bedroom of a Vienna hotel.

The news reached Somersby on October 1, 1833.

# CHAPTER FIVE

# THE TEN YEARS' SILENCE

## I

In the poem published but three years before his death, the Laureate issued to the world, for its enlightenment, and for the greater confusion of all subsequent biographers, his own metrical version of the life and literary development of Alfred Tennyson. The poem is entitled *Merlin and the Gleam*, and is, both in the Memoir and in the Eversley edition, accompanied by a loyal and painstaking commentary. But neither Tennyson's poem nor his son's commentary is very convincing in the way of chronological accuracy, and the biographical problem which they both raise centres particularly on the period with which we are now concerned.

For although we can readily identify and be satisfied with Tennyson's own record of his early development at Somersby, and although we can recognise as a description of the Farringford and Aldworth periods the section which begins:—

> "And broader and brighter
> The Gleam flying onward,
> Wed to the melody,
> Sang through the world";

yet, when we read the central passage relating to the years between 1832 and 1850, we are faced with what appears to be almost a deliberate act of mystification. For this is the version of these years which Tennyson gives to posterity:—

> "Once at the croak of a Raven who crost it,
>     A barbarous people,
>     Blind to the magic
>     And deaf to the melody,
>     Snarl'd at and curst me.
>     A demon vext me,
>     The light retreated,
>     The landskip darken'd,
>     The melody deaden'd,
>     The Master whisper'd
>     'Follow the gleam.'"

Now anyone with even a superficial knowledge of Tennyson's literary history will, and must, at once identify these lines as a very accurate and complete picture of what his biographers call the "ten years' silence"—the years, that is, which followed on Lockhart's review and Hallam's death, and which ended with the publication and success of the volume of 1842. This impression is fortified and confirmed by the fact that the poem passes on at once to describe the gradual return of "the gleam" and the emergence therefrom of a series of idyllic and romantic poems—obviously the volume of 1842. The conviction grows when we read the next section, which tells of an increasing interest in early romance centring gradually upon the figure of King Arthur. Having reached this point, we feel justifiably confident that we are somewhere about the year 1857. We read the next section:—

> "Clouds and darkness
>     Closed upon Camelot;
>     Arthur had vanish'd
>     I knew not whither,

The King who loved me,
And cannot die;
For out of the darkness,
Silent and slowly,
The Gleam, that had waned to a wintry glimmer
On icy fallow
And faded forest,
Drew to the valley
Named of the shadow,
And slowly brightening
Out of the glimmer,
And slowly moving again to a melody
Yearningly tender,
Fell on the shadow,
No longer a shadow,
But clothed with The Gleam."

And here we are suddenly, not in 1857, as we have been led to suppose, but back in 1833—back at the period of Hallam's death and the early stages of *In Memoriam*. And from all this results a very deliberate confusion. It is possible doubtless by a little straining to identify the "Raven," not with Lockhart, but with Christopher North; to ascribe the subsequent resumption of poetry to 1832, and not to 1842; to explain the reference to the Arthurian interest as applying to the epic which we know that Tennyson was considering about that date. I doubt whether such an explanation is satisfactory. The Christopher North review produced little effect upon the general public; even in Tennyson it awakened only an unfortunate burst of petulance: it can scarcely be described as having darkened his faculties, for between 1830 and 1832 he was writing hard all the time. And finally, although it is probable that he abandoned the idea of an Arthurian epic mainly owing to Hallam's death, he was also influenced by a well-timed article of Sterling's in which it was argued that a romantic epic would, by that date, make no possible appeal to the British reading public.

It may be thought that in criticising Tennyson's chronology I am making no allowance for poetical licence. But, in the first place, Tennyson was not himself, and perhaps regrettably, imbued with any conception of the privilege of poetical inaccuracy; and, in the second place, he stated definitely that the poem *Merlin and the Gleam* represented all that there was to be known about his literary development. It was intended as an historical document, and it is not, so far, at least, as I can ascertain, historical. One cannot but remain mystified by this discrepancy.

For indeed, from a biographical point of view, the whole meaning of Hallam's death is intensified, is illuminated, by a more lurid glow of tragedy when we realise that it synchronised with a grave neurotic crisis in the life of Tennyson. He had set much store by the 1832 volume: his friends would mouth the verses in a perfect ecstasy of acclaim; even Moxon was optimistic. And then suddenly he was faced, not by disparagement merely, but by yelping hostility, by shouts of malignant laughter, by disgrace. He was not only discouraged, he was not only dismayed: he was actually frightened. Never, never again would he expose himself to the coarse brutality of the English public. It was worse than Louth; it was worse, far worse, than the first term at Cambridge. He would go and live in Italy, as Byron had done and Shelley and Keats. There was only one role left to him—that of the indignant exile. So he went to Scotland. And then Hallam called him and he came to London, and Moxon came to supper, and after they had all gone Arthur and he walked back to Wimpole Street and went up to the attic and smoked and talked it over. And next day Arthur had gone to Vienna, but, after all, he would return in the late autumn. And Arthur *knew* that the 1832 volume was better than that of 1830, was in fact a very fine piece of work. Yes, there was always Arthur: his confidence in one; his unclouded, voluble confidence; and then his influence with the Press. Really people like Lockhart should be, *would be*, taught a lesson. And thus during that September up at Somersby the shattered, wounded nerves began to readjust themselves to thoughts of triumph, to thoughts even of revenge, to thoughts of Arthur over there in the Tyrol.

The first confusing crash of the news from Vienna is not to be gauged from *In Memoriam*. Although the elegies which compose the volume were written at intervals over seventeen years, and thus reflect the more sober moods of gradually retreating distances, yet some of them date actually from the first weeks of October 1833 and from the New Year following. And, curiously enough, these earliest elegies are among the least despairing in the whole volume, give the impression, indeed, of mere mechanic exercise as a narcotic to his grief. The earliest of them all was "Fair ship that from the Italian shore"; the second, "With trembling fingers did we weave"; the third, "When Lazarus left his charnel cave"; the fourth, "This truth came borne with bier and pall"; the fifth, "It draweth near the birth of Christ." And in none of these sections, beautiful as some of them are, is there any note of the real agony, the real spiritual catastrophe, that the shock had occasioned.

We must look elsewhere for a record of the emotion of those dark winter months: we must look to *Break, break, break,* composed, as we know, striding at night-time in the lanes near Somersby; and, above all, we must look to *The Two Voices*—one of the finest and least appreciated of all Tennyson's poems.

For in *The Two Voices* we have a definite and disturbing picture of Tennyson's panic-stricken bewilderment at the blow that had fallen; a picture of him gazing in an agony of despair at the ashes of the faith and fire which had once been his; a picture of a lonely, frightened spirit crouched broodingly over thoughts of death. The poem, which is cast in the form of a dialogue between his weaker and his stronger self, is composed in that curious minor key, that flickering half-light between the sane and the insane, which, as in *Maud*, constitutes Tennyson's most personal and poignant note. But, unlike *Maud*, in which the victim beats his head against a padded cell and cries aloud, the poem of *The Two Voices* is conceived in a grey and muffled mono-tone. The dialogue proceeds in the same sullen key through-out, varied only by the frequent and insinuating feminine stress given to the promptings of the weaker self which are thus made to beat upon the brain, faint, persistent and tor-menting; the whispered hints; the sighing despair; the faint moan of some vaster despair yet to come; the intent, deliberate hush of impending suicide.

> "A still small voice spake unto me,
> 'Thou art so full of misery
> Were it not better not to be?'"

And drop by drop the still small voice instills the poison of doubt—doubt firstly of the significance of life on earth com-pared to the vastness of the "hundred million spheres" of space; doubt of the significance of the human brain com-pared to the vastness of time:—

> "'Forerun thy peers, thy time, and let
> Thy feet, millenniums hence, be set
> In midst of knowledge, dream'd not yet.
>
> Thou hast not gained a real height,
> Nor art thou nearer to the light,
> Because the scale is infinite.
>
> 'Twere better not to breathe or speak,
> Than cry for strength, remaining weak,
> And seem to find, but still to seek'";

doubt as to the immortality of the human soul:—

> "'A life of nothings, nothing-worth,
> From that first nothing ere his birth
> To that last nothing under earth!'"

And with what arguments can the stronger self counter such insidious suggestions? As usual with Tennyson, he is more convincing when he constructs the fabric of doubt than when he endeavours to demolish this fabric with the tools of faith. As usual, at such moments he becomes a little vague and a little angry; he falls back, at first, upon conscience, upon intuitive theology, upon the "heat of inward evidence":—

> " 'Here sits he shaping wings to fly:
>      His heart forebodes a mystery:
>      He names the name Eternity.
>
> That type of Perfect in his mind
>      In Nature can he nowhere find.
>      He sows himself on every wind.
>
> He seems to hear a Heavenly Friend,
>      And thro' thick veils to apprehend
>      A labour working to an end.' "

He falls back upon a still more tentative theory of metempsychosis:—

> " 'Some vague emotion of delight.
>      In gazing up an Alpine height,
>      Some yearning towards the lamps of night.' "

And moreover:—

> " 'Moreover, something is or seems,
>      That touches me with mystic gleams,
>      Like glimpses of forgotten dreams—
>
> Of something felt, like something here;
>      Of something done, I know not where;
>      Such as no language may declare.'

> The still voice laugh'd. 'I talk,' said he,
> 'Not with thy dreams. Suffice it thee
> Thy pain is a reality.'"

And finally he falls back upon "A hidden hope"—the hope that "God is love":—

> "To feel, altho' no tongue can prove,
> That every cloud, that spreads above
> And veileth love, itself is love."

That he should have prefaced this conclusion by a passage about the Sabbath morn, will, for some, introduce a fatal note of bathos into the otherwise perfect symmetry of the poem. I do not defend the passage, I would observe only that if we are to be affected by Tennyson's bathos we shall lose our appreciation of all that is really valuable in his work. The only reasonable thing to do is to ignore these sudden relapses into the domestic. For which of us, of those who take an appreciative interest in Tennyson, can hesitate to blot out from his mind the epilogue to *In Memoriam*, the Crimean War passage in *Maud*, or even if you happen to like the rest of the poem, the last fatal line of *Enoch Arden*? And indeed bathos, like taste, is but a secondary criterion, a standard volatile and provisional. And the fact that Tennyson, of all poets, exposes himself most readily, almost with an engaging readiness, to the guffaw of the critical humorist, may well be the reason why, in our scavenger age, he is still in some unprogressive circles derided.

I have dwelt upon the central argument of *The Two Voices* because it shows how the death of Hallam was, as in the whole of *In Memoriam*, fused into his almost morbid perplexity about faith and doubt and immortality. But there is a more personal and immediate side to the poem. There is predominantly that pathetic passage in which he yearns after the old sense of his poetic mission, that glad conviction which had been trampled under foot by Lockhart:—

" 'Nay—rather yet that I could raise
One hope that warm'd me in the days
While still I yearn'd for human praise.

When, wide in soul and bold of tongue,
Among the tents I paused and sung,
The distant battle flash'd and rung.

I sung the joyful Pæan clear,
And, sitting, burnish'd without fear
The brand, the buckler, and the spear—

Waiting to strive a happy strife,
To war with falsehood to the knife,
And not to lose the good of life—

Some hidden principle to move.
To put together, part and prove,
And mete the bounds of hate and love—

As far as might be, to carve out
Free space for every human doubt,
That the whole mind might orb about—

To search thro' all I felt or saw,
The springs of life, the depths of awe,
And reach the law within the law.' "

There is an echo of that apprehensive soul-tormenting
gloom which had again descended upon him:—

" 'Sick art thou—a divided will
Still heaping on the fear of ill
The fear of men, a coward still.' "

A note also of the puzzle-headedness which came to him
from Maurice, and which descended upon all decent-
minded people in that serious unhappy age:—

> "'And that, in seeking to undo
>     One riddle, and to find it true,
>     I knit a hundred others new.'"

And finally, in the concluding cantos, a desire, a really stern-willed desire, to shake off the numbing misery which darkened his mind and clogged his faculties. It is this impetus —an impetus derived from the other Tennyson, the Tennyson who was eventually to triumph—which at this date was embodied in *Ulysses*. In the last section of *The Two Voices* he had cried:—

> "'Tis life, whereof our nerves are scant,
>     Oh life, not death, for which we pant;
>     More life, and fuller, that I want.'"

And in *Ulysses* this thought is echoed with the swing and courage, the strong-winged verse, of Tennyson at his best:—

> "Life piled on life
> Were all too little, and of one to me
> Little remains: but every hour is saved
> From that eternal silence, something more,
> A bringer of new things; and vile it were
> For some three suns to store and hoard myself,
> And this gray spirit yearning in desire
> To follow knowledge like a sinking star,
> Beyond the utmost bound of human thought."

And thus, although he also had:—

> "suffer'd greatly, both with those
> That loved me, and alone; on shore, and when
> Thro' scudding drifts the rainy Hyades
> Vext the dim sea";

yet it was his duty to "strive, to seek, to find, and not to yield." To launch out again upon the "dark broad seas":—

"The lights begin to twinkle from the rocks:
The long day wanes: the slow moon climbs: the deep
Moans round with many voices."

Yes, in spite of death and disappointment, it was not too late to seek a newer world, to begin again, as Arthur would have wished one to begin, to continue until that ultimate but certain reunion:—

"It may be that the gulfs will wash us down:
   It may be we shall touch the Happy Isles,
   And see the great Achilles, whom we knew."

## II

In such a mood, the glint of resolution flickering but intermittently through the mists of his despair, did he spend that winter of 1833 at Somersby. In order to distract his mind, and incidentally to deepen the "shallow metaphysics" which the reviewers had attacked, we find him prescribing for himself an exacting and definite course of study. The programme which he laid down has remained:—

| | |
|---|---|
| Monday | History, German. |
| Tuesday | Chemistry, German. |
| Wednesday | Botany, German. |
| Thursday | Electricity, German. |
| Friday | Animal physiology, German. |
| Saturday | Mechanics. |
| Sunday | Geology. |
| Next week | Italian in the afternoon. |
| Third week | Greek. |
| Evening | Poetry. |

The combination of the exact sciences with German transcendentalism is interesting; as regards the latter, Tennyson does not appear to have pushed his studies very far. His philosophy, as elaborated in the years that were to follow, was of a personal and, I suppose, of an amateurish order. But in the exacter sciences he made much progress. A forlorn period, those first sad months at Somersby.

October passed with the calm haze of later autumn, the heavy, spider-webbed dews upon the gorse, the sound only of the chestnut falling through the fading leaves. November came, and with it the west wind moaning over the fen, the whirl of the last dry leaf upon the trees, the rooks tumbling above the Somersby elms. And when Christmas approached, the sense of loss crept darkly among the little Rectory passages, as with trembling fingers they fixed the holly among the brown plaster ogives which enriched the hearth. For through it all their thoughts turned south to where Arthur's body was being brought home by sea, from Trieste and through the Mediterranean to the Severn. And in January they heard that he had arrived, that he lay in Clevedon church, near his mother's home, and "in the places of his youth":—

> "The Danube to the Severn gave
>     The darken'd heart that beat no more;
>     They laid him by the pleasant shore,
> And in the hearing of the wave.
>
> There twice a day the Severn fills;
>     The salt sea-water passes by,
>     And hushes half the babbling Wye,
> And makes a silence in the hills.
>
> The Wye is hush'd nor moved along,
>     And hush'd my deepest grief of all,
>     When fill'd with tears that cannot fall,
> I brim with sorrow drowning song."

For the rest, during the year 1834, and with the exception of a few days at Worthing with Heath, he spent his time either at Somersby or Mablethorpe.

It was the latter which was most akin to his temperament; he had loved it as a child:—

> "Here stood the infant Ilion of the mind
>     And here the Grecian ships did seem to me."

But now it seemed even more attuned to his deeper, more personal melancholy:—

"And here again I come and only find
    The drain-cut levels of the marshy lea—
Gray sand-banks and pale sunsets—dreary wind,
    Dim shores, dense rains, and heavy clouded sea."

The cottage in which he lived during those days is still extant—an orange-coloured little house, separated from the forty-foot dune by a sluice that, after creeping for a few yards with sluggish waters parallel to the sea, cuts under a bridge through the sandbank to lose itself upon the wide wet beach. And on the other side stretches the cropped level of the marsh, with the faint curve of the wolds upon the western sky-line. It was here that he would escape alone—escape even from Somersby and the dumb look in his sister's eyes; it was here that he began to write *In Memoriam*, *The Two Voices* and *Ulysses*; it is here finally that he had the courage to pick up his two previous volumes and embark on that process of careful, unremitting revision which was to take him seven years.

The Mablethorpe of those days has suffered alteration. The little orange cottage is now no longer desolate. There is a railway which runs from Louth and on to Boston and Spalding; there are hotels and lodging-houses which cater for the visitors from these places, and on the beach there are little green-and-white tents and automatic machines and ginger beer. It was otherwise in the days when Tennyson went there and began *In Memoriam*: there was only the sound then of the North Sea booming on the flat, wet sands, and the sighing of the dune grasses under the wide Lincolnshire sky.

And thus Tennyson for a space of months:—

"Vex'd with a morbid devil in his blood
    That veil'd the world with jaundice, hid his face
From all men, and communing with himself,
    He lost the sense that handles daily life."

The mood was, fortunately, not to last. In 1835 we find him selling the gold medal he had received from the Chancellor of Cambridge University, and proceeding, thus enriched, to stay with the Speddings at their home in the Lake district. We hear of him there, "very gruff and unmanageable," sitting indoors and reading poetry to Spedding and Fitz-Gerald, to the indignation of Spedding's father. And it was on this occasion that he first became intimate with Fitz-Gerald, whom he had not "known" at Trinity. It was on this occasion, also, that he refused to go over to Rydal Mount to see Wordsworth. His refusal irritated Spedding, who had always heard Tennyson speak warmly of the older poet. And it is satisfactory to think that the meeting delayed by the cantankerous mood of 1835 took place later at Hampstead, and again at a dinner-party of Moxon's, when Tennyson was able to conquer his shyness and blurt out some confused words of admiration, with which Wordsworth was pleased enough.

And then, in May of the next year, a faint glow of hope came to illumine his darkness. For in that year his brother Charles married Louisa Sellwood, and it fell to Alfred to conduct her elder sister, who acted as bridesmaid, to the church. It was only one of several previous meetings since that day four years ago when he found her walking with Arthur Hallam in the Fairy Wood. But on this occasion, as they stood there in the church behind the bridal pair, a "pleasant truth" descended upon Alfred:—

> "And all at once a pleasant truth I learn'd,
> For while the tender service made thee weep,
> I loved thee for the tear thou could'st not hide,
> And prest thy hand, and knew the press return'd,
> And thought, 'My life is sick of single sleep:
> O happy bridesmaid, make a happy bride!'"

And so the next year they became engaged. It was not a very impulsive engagement: it lasted for thirteen years, nor did they marry until Tennyson was forty-one and Emily was thirty-seven. There was nothing, so far as is known, to prevent their marrying except his lack of settled occupation; and he appears at the time to have taken no steps to secure such employment. It would not have been impossible in those days for a man like Monckton Milnes to have obtained him a sinecure: it would have been easier than the compassionate pension secured for him from Sir Robert Peel in 1845. Poetry is all very well, but "flesh and blood," as Arthur Hallam had warned him, "is better." And in these two necessary constituents Tennyson was strangely lacking. He was by temperament a mystic, and to that extent one can forgive his indifference to worldly things; but the pity of it was that he never allowed himself to be mystic enough. And so the engagement was broken off in 1840. "We must bear," wrote Tennyson to his fiancée, "or we must die. It is easier to die but infinitely less noble." And, for her part, Emily Sellwood remained unmarried and became seriously ill. And Tennyson for his part went mooning and moping about country inns, drinking heavy port and writing domestic idylls.

In this connection, it should be mentioned, perhaps, that in his book, *Memories of the Tennysons,* Canon Rawnsley states that Tennyson again proposed in 1847, "and this time was refused on the highest and noblest principles of self-abnegation by the woman who loved him. Emily Sellwood had grown to feel that they two moved in worlds of religious thought so different that the two would not 'make one music' as they moved."

It is not clear what led her to alter this opinion; unless it be that Tennyson convinced her by selections from the then almost completed *In Memoriam.*


III

By the year 1837 Frederick and Charles, the two elder brothers, had left Somersby, and the responsibility for looking after the family devolved upon Alfred.

For Frederick had thrown over his temporary appointment on the staff of the High Commissioner of the Ionian Islands, and had inherited some of the family property at Grimsby. He was thus able to live in comfort with a Sienese wife at Fiesole, to indulge his tastes for music and psychical research, and to sit in his hall surrounded by forty violinists. But then Frederick had always been very odd indeed; and finally, like his brother Horatio and his sister Emily, he became a Swedenborgian, retired to the Channel Islands, and died in 1898. And in the intervals of all this he published two volumes, in 1854 and 1890, which were well received; but for posterity, if he lives at all, he will live because of his unceasing correspondence with Edward FitzGerald.

With Charles things had gone differently. He had inherited some Turner money and added to his name accordingly: in 1836 he married Louisa Sellwood and led a quiet, gentle life as Vicar of Grasby, diversified only by his taste for curious apparel. And he too wrote sonnets from time to time, which in 1880, the year after his death, were published in a collected edition.

It was thus upon Alfred that the task fell in 1837 of moving the family from Somersby. For by that year the new Rector, the Rev. Langhorne Burton Burton, came into residence, and the Rectory was required for his use. The bitter wrench of this departure, the snapping of so many intimate associations, is familiar to us from Sections C to CIII of *In Memoriam,* nor is there any passage in the poems which indicates more clearly how extremely localised was Tennyson's love of Nature. And indeed, as I have said already, it was the peculiar oasis character of Somersby which gave so detailed a significance to every individual tree and flower, and which, coupled with his extreme short-sightedness, accounts for the tender, microscopic character of Tennyson's observation.

The family moved to Beech Hill House, High Beech, Epping, where a home had been prepared. "The furniture," we are told, "was pretty and inexpensive." The house had been chosen owing to Alfred's desire to be near London, and a study was allotted to him over the dining-room, "with a bay window, red curtains and a Clytie on a pedestal in the corner"; and in winter he could be seen skating in his blue coat on the pond. Even this did not make him care for Epping: he felt it too enclosed after the wide spaces of Lincolnshire. "Nothing," he commented, "but that muddy pond and those two sharp-barking little dogs." They must have been his mother's dogs: she cared for animals. But she did not care for Epping: she was frightened away from Somersby. And one night there was a thunderstorm. Alfred went to her and found her "grovelling on the floor in an extremity of fear." "Oh, I will leave this house," the poor lady sobbed; "the storms are very bad here."

And so in 1839 they moved to Tunbridge Wells: "a place," wrote Alfred, "which is my abomination." And thus, not unnaturally, they moved again—to Boxley, this time, near Maidstone.

## IV

In spite of the pond and the thunderstorms, and that general enclosed feeling, and the "absence of birds and men" (whatever that particular grumble may signify), there was one advantage which Epping offered which was not provided by Somersby, by Tunbridge Wells or by Maidstone. For Epping, at least, was very near to London; and if one could bear it all no longer, one had but to walk to the highroad and catch the evening mail; and there, in a few minutes only, above the stunted trees of Epping Forest, glowed the reflection of the lights of London, "flaring like a dreary dawn."

And during those years from 1837 to 1842 London meant a great deal to him—more than it had meant to him before and more than it was to mean to him later. Nor are we to conclude that he spent his whole time there pacing up and down Wimpole Street in the blank wet hours before

sunrise. He had other relaxations. It is a mistake to imagine
that during the later half of the "ten years' silence" he desired to shut himself off from human intercourse. He was
not, perhaps, very sociable—he never was—but at least he
went about in a sulky, slovenly, bohemian sort of way, and
he saw a great many men of interest and importance. And
sometimes even he was happy, and the gruff Lincolnshire
laugh would rattle the frosted glass, the cruets and the little tin covers at the Cock Tavern or at Bertolini's:—

> "You thought my heart too far diseased;
>     You wonder when my fancies play
>     To find me gay among the gay,
> Like one with any trifle pleased.
>
> The shade by which my life was crost,
>     Which makes a desert in the mind,
>     Has made me kindly with my kind. . . ."

One wonders, perhaps, whether his associates of those
days would fully have endorsed this urbane description of
himself at this period. We hear of him down at Torquay
in 1838, and going on to see Bernard Barton. "We have,"
writes his Quaker host, "had Alfred Tennyson here; very
droll and very wayward; and much sitting up at nights till
two or three in the morning with pipes in our mouths, at
which good hour we would get Alfred to give us some of
his magic music, which he does between growling and
smoking." We hear of him at the Cock Tavern with Spedding. The latter writes to Milnes: "We had two chops, one
pickle, two cheeses, one pint of stout, one pint of port, and
three cigars. When we had finished I had to take his regrets
to the Kembles; he could not go because he had the in-
fluenza." We see him, as in the portrait by Samuel Lawrence: the falling mass of untidy dark hair; the fine eyes and
forehead; the prominent nose; the curiously coarse, ill-
tempered mouth and chin which were, after 1857, to be
hidden by moustache and beard; the great size and bulk

and swarthiness—"the thews of Anakim, the pulses of a Titan's heart." We find him returning again and again to London in the years that follow: staying with Spedding, chiefly, at 60 Lincoln's Inn Fields; sometimes with Lushington in the Temple at 1 Mitre Court buildings; sometimes in lodgings of his own in Norfolk Street, Strand, the last house on the left; feeding at Bertolini's ("Dirtolini's," they called it), and more rarely having his port at the Cock Tavern. For it appears that the identification of this later resort with Tennyson's London period has been a little exaggerated. The legend springs, of course, from "Will Waterproof's" monologue, which is addressed to the head-waiter at that establishment. But we know from FitzGerald that he went there only on the more festive occasions, and Samuel Butler, who did not like legends which were not of his own contrivance, went so far as to question the said waiter, who denied all knowledge of Tennyson, or that he had ever been there.

To a date only slightly later than this period must belong a reminiscence which I have found in a magazine article by Mrs. Brookfield. For Mrs. Brookfield, with all her reverence for the later Tennyson, was too humorous a lady to have taken very seriously the querulous affectation of his middle manner. It is clear that she shares with Mrs. Cameron the distinction of being one of the few people who dared to criticise his behaviour. And that there was much to criticise is apparent from the following:—

"A very delightful and highly cultivated friend of ours, who belonged to a strictly conventional section of society, had gladly accepted an invitation to meet Tennyson at our house. She had read his poetry with great admiration, and was prepared to make his acquaintance with reverent enthusiasm. He was, however, as retiring as usual when with absolute strangers, and the graceful deference of our dear friend's demeanour towards him did not at first tend to dispel his shyness; later in the evening, however, when Alfred had realized that this lady was intimate friend of ours, and that we particularly wished that he should make himself agreeable to her, he went up to her with good-natured friendliness, saying, 'I could not find anything to say to you before dinner, but now that I have a bottle of port in me, I can talk as much as you like.' My friend was at first rather alarmed at this playful announcement, receiving it as a literal assertion. But she was soon reassured. . . ."

More important than all this was the Sterling Club, which had been founded, under the name of the "Anonymous Club," in 1838. It was here that he would meet Carlyle, Rogers, "Barry Cornwall," Thackeray, Dickens, Forster, Landor, Maclise, Leigh Hunt and others of his own and the preceding generation. And with Rogers and Carlyle at least he was to be on terms of intimacy. For the former, who left nothing to chance, went out of his way to cultivate the fierce young poet, even asked him to some of the historic breakfast-parties in 22 St. James' Place; even took his arm, sometimes, in walking down Bond Street. And it was thus that Tennyson met Tom Moore, and found that he had "a George the Fourth look"; and thus also that he became the recipient of a confidence on the part of Rogers which strikes us to-day as peculiarly salutary. "One day," records Tennyson, "we were walking arm in arm, and I spoke of what is called Immortality, and remarked how very few writers could be sure of it. Upon which Rogers squeezed my arm and said, 'I am sure of it.' " And for the rest, Tennyson rather liked the worldly old poet, with his regency anecdotes and his unwrinkled, apple-woman face; nor did he find his venom really malicious, and they would talk of their mutual infirmities, for by then Tennyson was entering his hypochondriac period, and would discuss the life after death till the "tears rolled down Rogers' cheeks."

With Carlyle his acquaintance, which after 1842 was to

develop into intimacy, was based upon more serious and more abiding elements. By 1839 Carlyle and his wife had already been five years in Cheyne Row, and *Sartor Resartus*, which, when it first appeared in *Fraser's Magazine*, had struck the critics as but "clotted nonsense," had been introduced to America by Emerson, and had but the year before dawned in volume form upon a public already seriously impressed by the "French Revolution" of 1837. Carlyle was thus at the outset of his prophetic career when Tennyson was first admitted to his intimacy, and his outright certitude on all those problems which disturbed and muddled the younger man acted as an immediate and very bracing stimulus. For indeed there is an essential similitude between the actual stuff of Carlyle's doctrine and the more nebulous and tentative theories with which Tennyson endeavoured to allay the doubts and anxieties of the Victorian mind. There is the same mistrust of logic, the same mistrust of mere soulless intelligence, the same belief in truth and virtue dominant and triumphant in face of the evidence of sense, in face of those two disturbing negatives—the infinity of space and the infinity of time. We have, more fundamentally, the same ultimate appeal to intuitive theology— to the "heat of inward evidence." For it is Carlyle, and not Tennyson, who writes: "The evidence to me of God—and the only evidence—is the feeling I have, deep down in the very bottom of my heart, of right and truth and justice. . . . Whoever looks into himself must be aware that at the centre of things is a mysterious Demiurgos—who is *God*, and who cannot in the least be adequately spoken of in any human words." And it is thus that Froude is able to link their names together as the exponents of a similar doctrine of hope and comfort. "In this condition," he writes, "the best and bravest of my own contemporaries determined to have done with insincerity, to find ground under their feet, to let the uncertain remain uncertain, to learn how much and what one could honestly regard as true, and believe that and live by it. Tennyson became the voice of this feeling in poetry, Carlyle in what was called prose."

It was on this mutual identity of thought, on this common attitude towards the doubts raised by the disturbing and intrusive progress of science and historical criticism, that the friendship between Tennyson and Carlyle was based. Without so firm a foundation, we doubt whether it would have prospered. For Carlyle did not treat Tennyson the poet with the same sympathy which he extended to Tennyson the man; nor was the latter generally given to cultivating the acquaintance of people who were outspoken in their criticism of his work. And Carlyle, with his broad Annandale accent, was very outspoken. He advised Tennyson to give up writing verses altogether; he advised him to put his thoughts into prose; he said that he was by nature a "lifeguardsman spoilt by making poetry"; he laughed at him for his sensitiveness to criticism. It is true that later he approved of the 1842 volume, that he expressed definite appreciation of *The Revenge*, and also that he had a weakness for *The May Queen*, which, in an unexpectedly nineteenth-century way, he considered "tender." But in spite of all this, their friendship was not based on a community of literary tastes, and we do not find Tennyson indulging Carlyle with recitations from *Maud* or *The Duke of Wellington*. Their companionship was of a more robust, and in truth of a more enduring character. They would take long walks at night together, and come back at ten o'clock for tea in Cheyne Row, and Jane Carlyle would puzzle as to how Tennyson had derived "that gypsy look"; and then they would go upstairs and smoke their tobacco. We have two portraits of Tennyson at this date drawn as only Carlyle can do such things. In spite of their familiarity, they must again be quoted. The first is in a letter to his brother dated September 1840:—

"Some weeks ago, one night, the poet Tennyson and Matthew Allen were discovered here sitting smoking in the garden. Tennyson had been here before, but was still new to Jane—who was alone for the first hour or two of it. A fine, large-featured, dim-eyed, bronze-coloured, shaggy-headed man is Alfred: dusty, smoky, free and easy: who swims, outwardly and inwardly, with great composure in an articulate element as of tranquil chaos and tobacco smoke; great now and then when he does emerge; a most restful, brotherly, solid-hearted man."

The next account is written somewhat later to Emerson in America:—

"Alfred is one of the few British and foreign figures (a not increasing number, I think) who are and remain beautiful to me, a true human soul, or some authentic approximation thereto, to whom your own soul can say 'Brother!' However, I doubt he will not come: he often skips me in these brief visits to town: skips everybody, indeed; being a man solitary and sad, as certain men are, dwelling in an element of gloom, carrying a bit of Chaos about him, in short, which he is manufacturing into Cosmos. . . . One of the finest-looking men in the world. A great shock of rough, dusky dark hair; bright, laughing, hazel eyes; massive aquiline face, most massive yet most delicate; of sallow brown complexion, almost Indian looking, clothes cynically loose, free and easy, smokes infinite tobacco. His voice is musical, metallic, fit for loud laughter and piercing wail, and all that may lie between: speech and speculation free and plenteous; I do not meet in these late decades such company over a pipe! We shall see what he will grow to."

But there were other friends besides Carlyle to stimulate Tennyson during this period. There was FitzGerald, whom he saw often in London, and FitzGerald, at that period, however tiresome he may have become later, was very encouraging, so encouraging that forty years after Tennyson still thought back with pleasure upon those "gracious times."

Not that FitzGerald can at any period have been much of a literary critic. It is true that he preferred Tennyson's earlier poems to those published in 1850 and after; he also disliked Euripides, Goethe, George Eliot and Victor Hugo; he expressed the opinion that "Crabbe will flourish, when Browning is dead and buried"; and he preferred *Audley Court* to *In Memoriam,* which he considered to be "machine made."

And then there was Richard Monckton Milnes, already with a cheerful eye fixed on the mantle of Samuel Rogers.

But although these "low beginnings of content" are indubitably noticeable during this period, they can easily be exaggerated. It is no use pretending that Tennyson was confident and happy again until his marriage in 1850. In the first place, he was considerably bothered by actual poverty. We find him writing in 1838: "Perhaps I am coming to the Lincolnshire coast, but I scarcely know. The journey is so expensive and I am so poor." And then he was troubled by his health, which had indeed suffered from the port and the tobacco and the irregular meals; and his eyesight, which had been defective since the Cambridge days, was also causing him anxiety. So that the periods of acute nervous depression would recur upon occasions, would descend upon him at night-time when he was alone listening to the rain upon the roof, and would drive him out into the cold dawn and up alone to Wimpole Street.

> "Then I rise, the eavedrops fall,
> And the yellow vapours choke
> The great city sounding wide;
> The day comes, a dull red ball
> Wrapt in drifts of lurid smoke
> On the misty river-tide.

Thro' the hubbub of the market
I steal, a wasted frame,
It crosses here, it crosses there,
Thro' all that crowd confused and loud,
The shadow still the same;
And on my heavy eyelids
My anguish hangs like shame."


## V


Although in the year 1842 Tennyson had in this way
entered into certain literary circles in London, it must be
remembered that he was in no way at home in the metropolis. He came there only as an occasional and rather
defiant visitor, and was never to become urbanised like
Thackeray, Browning or Matthew Arnold. There was no
daily Garrick, no familiar Athenæum even, for Tennyson.
And thus when in the middle 'seventies he would come up,
with his big cape and sombrero, from Farringford or Aldworth in connection with his plays, he could be seen shambling about the streets in a bewildered, short-sighted fashion, losing his way generally, helped over crossings by
kindly policemen, and gaped at in astonishment by the
nursery-maids in Kensington. Nor can it be said that, with
the exception of a few carefully chosen intimates, always
amenable and sometimes even distinguished, he had much
occasion in his later years to test his own intellectual development by the progress of other contemporary minds.
People who were asked to Farringford did not contradict
the Laureate; people who contradicted the Laureate were
not asked to Farringford. And the pity of it all is that it
would have done Tennyson a great deal of good to be contradicted, very flatly and very often, between the year 1840
and the year 1892.

He preferred the country; and as remote as possible. And
thus we find him in the years before 1850 returning, in
spite of the expense, again and again to Mablethorpe and

to the sound of the North Sea beyond the dune. It was the solitude that he liked: the flat beach, the flat marsh and the flat sky. "There is nothing here," he wrote, "but myself and two star-fish."

By the year 1841 the family had settled at Boxley, near Maidstone, and in the vicinity of Park House, the home of the Lushingtons, familiar to us as the scene of the prologue to *The Princess*. And here he had the occasion, had he wished to profit by it, to become intimate with new and stimulating people, such as Lear and the future Lord Kelvin —not, indeed, that the Lushingtons appear to have been very abreast of the times. For at Park House gathered a circle which the future Dean of Westminster has described as "a circle so wholly, so widely different from that which had gathered round Arnold at Rugby. . . . The questions that stirred so deeply our seniors and ourselves at Oxford, the position of J. H. Newman and his friends, the course of the 'Oxford Movement,' the whole Tractarian controversy, were scarcely mentioned, or, if mentioned, were spoken of as matters of secondary or remote interest." And at irregular intervals Tennyson would go off alone on those morose pilgrimages of his, to Devonshire in 1838, to Eastbourne and Killarney in 1842, to St. Leonards in 1843; and with him always would come the growing mass of manuscripts, and the long, thin ledger in which from time to time he would inscribe some completed elegy to Arthur Hallam, some section of the future *In Memoriam*.

Meanwhile his continued poverty had become acute. What was more galling, it was all largely his own fault. The story is a curious one. It appears that in the neighbourhood of Epping there was a private asylum in the charge of a certain Dr. Allen. Tennyson took a great liking to this Dr. Allen, who, if we can judge by the portrait of him inserted in *Sea Dreams*, was plausible enough, a "scoundrel of the supple-sliding knee." In those early Epping days Tennyson was possessed of a little fluid capital. He had received a small legacy from an aunt of Arthur Hallam's, and he had sold a small property in Lincolnshire which had come to him from his own family. Instead of marrying Emily Sellwood, he proceeded to invest this capital in a scheme of Dr. Allen's for making wood-carving by machinery. Mr. Ruskin, as Andrew Lang observes, "had only just begun to write, and wood-carving by machinery was still deemed an enterprise at once philanthropic and æsthetic." This may well be so; but, as an enterprise, it was evidently not remunerative. For a while Tennyson's capital:—

> "like the little thrift,
> Trembled in perilous places o'er the deep."

And then came the crash. It was discovered that he had not only lost his own small fortune, but had induced his mother and his sisters to invest their scanty funds in the same unlucky venture. Whereupon Dr. Allen disappeared for a while from Epping and Tennyson was very seriously perturbed:—

> "He is fled—I wish him dead—
> He that wrought my ruin—
> O the flattery and the craft
> Which were my undoing."

In the end Edmund Lushington was called in to assist, and insured a rediscovered Dr. Allen's life for part of the debt; and in January 1845 the doctor very considerately died.[1]

This disaster, coupled with irregularities of diet, had however, affected Tennyson's health. A nervous break-down followed. He was himself convinced that he was very seriously ill: there were moments of panic and despair. He went to Cheltenham to undergo Dr. Gully's water cure. He did not like Cheltenham, which seemed to him "a polka-parson-

---

[1] It is only fair to add that during the same period Dr. Allen was behaving with great kindness to an even more unfortunate poet, John Clare, who was at Fair Mead Asylum from July 1837 to July 1841.

worshipping place," but the cure did him good, and meanwhile his friends, as usual, were complaining of neglect. We find FitzGerald writing of him to Frederick Tennyson in 1844: "hydropathy has done its worst: he writes the name of his friends in water." Through all this he had not lost his taste for literature: we hear of him reading *Ellen Middleton;* and he writes from Cheltenham in November asking for *Modern Painters*—"another (book) I long very much to see is that on the superiority of the modern painters to the old ones, and the greatness of Turner as an artist, by an Oxford undergraduate [*sic*], I think."

Although during these years Tennyson appears to have forgotten his friends, his friends had certainly not forgotten him, nor were they indifferent to his state of penury. As early as 1843 Barry Cornwall had, on the death of Southey, caused Tennyson's candidature for the post of Poet Laureate to be submitted to Lord de la Warr, the Lord Chamberlain. It is unlikely that, at a date when the 1842 volume had not yet "got home," the application would have been very seriously considered; but by the time the suggestion reached Lord de la Warr the post had been offered to Wordsworth, and the question of Tennyson's qualifications did not, therefore, arise. The correspondence which Canon Rawnsley has produced on the subject is, however, significant, since it discloses the fact that Tennyson's state of poverty had been mentioned to Sir Robert Peel as early as 1843, and that the latter had suggested some "palliation of Mr. Tennyson's complaint." This palliation matured in 1846, when, owing to the representations of Milnes, egged on by Carlyle and backed by the more authoritative recommendation of Henry Hallam, Tennyson was accorded a civil list pension of £200 a year.

He was himself always a little embarrassed by the possible implications of this pension. "I have done," he wrote, "nothing slavish to get it; I never even solicited for it either by myself or through others. . . . Something in that word 'pension' sticks in my gizzard. . . . I feel the least bit possible Miss Martineauish about it. Meantime there is some meaning in having a gentleman and a Classic at the head of affairs."

And indeed it may well seem surprising that the pension should have been accorded to a man who was then comparatively young, comparatively healthy and—for the 1842 volume was next year to go into a fourth edition—undoubtedly successful. It surprised and angered some of his contemporaries that the allowance had not been settled upon some more aged and deserving literary character, such as Sheridan Knowles. And so on February 21, 1846, there appeared a poem in *Punch* entitled *The New Timon, a Romance of London*. The poem was anonymous, and indeed the impression was conveyed in a footnote that the writer was an Anglo-Indian official but lately returned from the East. But no one appears to have doubted for a moment that its real author was Lytton Bulwer. It was not a very kind poem: it spoke of Tennyson's "purfled prettiness of phrase"; it suggested that it would be better to:—

"Let Schoolmiss Alfred vent her chaste delight
    In darling little rooms so warm and bright";

it protested against a Government which could proceed in so curious and unsystematic a manner—could

"pension Tennyson while it starves a Knowles."

And, as a final sting, *The Darling Room* was quoted in its entirety in a footnote.

Tennyson was roused to instant fury, and sent to *Punch* (February 28, 1846) a reply, signed "Alcibiades," in which some of Bulwer's characteristics were attacked in a very spirited and trenchant manner:—

"We know him, out of SHAKESPEARE's art,
    And those fine curses which he spoke;
The old TIMON, with his noble heart,
    That, strongly, loathing, greatly broke.

The New Timon, and the Poets

So died the Old: here comes the New.
　　Regard him: a familiar face:
I *thought* we knew him: What, it's you,
　　The padded man—that wears the stays—


Who kiss'd the girls and thrill'd the boys,
　　With dandy pathos when you wrote,
A Lion, you, that made a noise,
　　And shook a mane en papillotes.


And once you tried the Muses too;
　　You fail'd, Sir: therefore now you turn,
You fall on those who are to you,
　　As Captain is to Subaltern.


But men of long-enduring hopes,
　　And careless what this hour may bring,
Can pardon little would-be POPES
　　And BRUMMELS, when they try to sting.


An artist, Sir, should rest in Art,
　　And waive a little of his claim;
To have the deep Poetic heart
　　Is more than all poetic fame.


But you, Sir, you are hard to please;
　　You never look but half content:
Nor like a gentleman at ease,
　　With moral breadth of temperament.


And what with spites and what with fears,
　　You cannot let a body be:
It's always ringing in your ears,
　　'They call this man as good as *me*.'

What profits now to understand
    The merits of a spotless shirt—
A dapper boot—a little hand—
    If half the little soul is dirt?

*You* talk of tinsel! why we see
    The old mark of rouge upon your cheeks.
*You* prate of Nature! you are he
    That spilt his life about the cliques.

A TIMON you! Nay, nay, for shame:
    It looks too arrogant a jest—
The fierce old man—to take *his* name
    You bandbox. Off, and let him rest."

I have quoted the poem at length, since it represents one of the few attempts on the part of the cautious Tennyson at personal invective. On seeing it in print, he was himself rather dismayed at his own hardihood. And in the next week's *Punch* there appeared a rather feeble palinode under the title of "Afterthought." Moreover, as he explained afterwards, it was Forster, and not he himself, who had sent the lines to *Punch*. And this, considering his caution, may well be true. "Surely," he says:—

                "Surely, after all,
    The noblest answer unto such
      Is perfect stillness when they brawl."

But the controversy had excited considerable attention, and for some time occasional poems on the subject would appear anonymously in the London Press. Here is an example:—

"THE NEW TIMON," AND ALFRED TENNYSON'S PENSION

"You've seen a lordly mastiff's port,
    Bearing in calm, contemptuous sort
    The snarls of some o'erpetted pup,
    Who grudges him his 'bit and sup':

So stands the bard of Locksley Hall,
While puny darts around him fall,
Tipp'd with what TIMON takes for venom;
He is the mastiff, TIM the Blenheim."

Although the grant of a pension had thus exposed Tennyson to some personal and unpleasant publicity, and had raised some rather awkward questions, it was not without practical advantage. It enabled him to go to Switzerland with Edward Moxon in 1846; it enabled him to visit the Rhine: "deck very hot," he notes, "Nonnenwerth and Drachenfels—sad recollection." It enabled him, when Moxon suggested that there were signs of incipient baldness, to afford, and at once, an expensive massage-treatment. It enabled him, when in London, to take rooms of his own, in Brompton first, and then at 42 Ebury Street, and there to entertain Brookfield and his delightful wife. In 1848 we find him visiting the Burns country, and later staying with Aubrey de Vere, Stephen Spring Rice and the Knight of Kerry in Ireland.

And finally, in those golden untaxed days, it enabled him to think seriously again of marriage.

## VI

I have thought it best to complete, in this sketchy, inconclusive way, the general picture of Tennyson's outward life and habits during the years between 1833 and 1850. It is not, I fear, a very satisfactory or inspiring picture. It shows a lack of temperamental grip, a lack of impulse. One can appreciate either of these two conflicting manifestations. One likes people, and poets especially, to have an ample, extravagant gesture between the ages of twenty-four and forty: it is their last chance. One can accept, with respect if not with sympathy, the alternative course of conduct—the capable, industrious, everyday alternative. But one is forced to conclude that Alfred Tennyson during those important seventeen years was neither adventurous nor capable: he fell between two stools. He became, on the one hand, cautious, pernickety and prim; he became, on the other hand, neurotic, inefficient and selfish. He drank just enough port to render himself hypochondriac: he never drank enough port to forget that he was writing for an audience of young ladies. He wrote *Ulysses* and yet he wrote *Lady Clara Vere de Vere;* he let himself go, for a delirious moment, in *Locksley Hall,* and then pulled himself together and composed *The Talking Oak.* He mooned about the cheaper taverns of the metropolis; he huddled on the outside of the coaches which bore him from village inn to village inn; and he left it to Milnes and Sir Robert Peel to devise the means for such subsistence.

And thus one looks back to Somersby, or forward to Aldworth, with a pang of irritated regret that one of the least defensible periods in Tennyson's life should have synchronised with the vital years of his early manhood.

We could esteem, and even venerate, the ten years' silence were we convinced that it could be attributed solely to the death of Arthur Hallam. We are not so convinced. We suspect, in spite of *Merlin and the Gleam,* that the real reason was Lockhart and the *Quarterly.* Nor is it the latter against whom our indignation can justly turn: his review was little more than an angry, rather patronising, rather jolly outburst. It is with Tennyson himself that we become impatient; and indeed genius should be made of sterner stuff. For if the poetic faculty has as its origin some rare propulsive force, it should carry with it a sense of surprise, solved, so soon as it has been awakened, by a sense of the inevitable. And for this effect, for the appropriate preparatory emotion to be awakened, it is essential that there should be a conviction of impulse. I admit that this requirement may be only of to-day, that our present insistence upon this necessary jet of initial emotion may be a little overdone; but it has this in it, at least, of permanent truth —namely, that in the end what counts is the intensity of a

poet's reaction to his particular emotion, not the skill and
polish with which, when the reaction had faded, he can
capture a faint outline of what he may, or may not, have
felt. And it is for this reason that we are disappointed after
1832 with the absence of what FitzGerald called the
"champagne flavour" of the earlier poems, and that we are
apt to regard the later compositions as having the faintly
vapid taste of the réchauffé, as showing a little too much
afterthought and revision.

It is inevitable, of course, that, if once this inherent blem-
ish has been apprehended, it should sully many of the quite
spontaneous poems. It cannot apply, of course, to the essentially lyrical pieces—to the songs, for instance in *The
Princess*—but I confess that in my weaker moments, when
the pulse is low, this suspicion of the machine can throw a
tinny flavour even over the most sincere sections of *In
Memoriam;* and that this should be so is very lamentable.
For herein lies the sinister danger of the variorum method
—the danger of any accurate or scholarly examination of
Tennyson and his works.

It is perhaps necessary to explain that the current term
of "the ten years' silence" applies to this period only as a
relative expression. For although during these years Tennyson abstained from publishing another volume of poetry,
yet he composed with the greatest assiduity, and even, from
time to time, ventured into print. In 1837, as I have said,
he contributed *St. Agnes* to the *Keepsake,* then edited by
Lady Emmeline Stuart-Wortley, and in the same year, on
the insistence of Monckton Milnes, for Lord Northampton's
*Tribute,* he provided the fine lyric *O that 'twere Possible,*
which was later to form the nucleus of *Maud.* And we
must remember finally that during those years he was writing the whole of *The Two Voices* and *In Memoriam;* that
he was carefully polishing and collecting his two former
volumes; and that he was evolving pieces as different as the
*Morte d'Arthur, Dora, Audley Court, St. Simeon Stylites,
The Talking Oak, Locksley Hall, Godiva, Ulysses, Amphion,*

*Will Waterproof's Monologue, Lady Clare, The Lord of Burleigh, The Vision of Sin* and *Sir Launcelot and Queen Guinevere.*

It is curious also to observe that after 1835, with John Stuart Mill's favourable article in the *London Review,* in which the 1832 volume, and especially *The Lady of Shalott* and *Mariana* were warmly commended, his literary reputation began slowly but increasingly surely to revive. Moreover his old Cambridge friends were gradually attaining positions of influence with the critical world. By 1836 we find the *Edinburgh Review,* which had till then ignored him, referring to him casually as the "best known of the young Cambridge poets." By 1837 the reviewers were beginning to accuse Miss Barrett of being one of his imitators. By 1838 we find an account of him appearing in a journal at Boston, Massachusetts, and three years later he was appalled to learn that his two previous volumes were to be reprinted, and without all those careful corrections, in the United States. We may well believe that it is to this menace, rather than to any other cause, that we have to attribute his renewed publication in the year 1842. For it was an age in which America was rather apt to discover for us our neglected prophets. Emerson had done it for *Sartor Resartus;* in a lesser degree he did it for Tennyson. And E. A. Poe, who was to die before Tennyson's reputation had become completely assured, was a warm devotee. We find him, in 1843, speaking of "an enthusiastic admiration—a reverence unbounded," and later, in a posthumous article, he expressed the surprising view that "in perfect sincerity" he regarded Tennyson as the "noblest poet that ever lived."

That Tennyson was increasingly read before 1842 is evident from the familiar passage in *Cranford,* and the fact that by 1840 the previous volumes were very difficult to obtain. Moreover in 1843 we find the Oriel Debating Society discussing whether or no Alfred Tennyson was the greatest poet of his age.

It must not be supposed, of course, that before the 1842 volume Tennyson had entered into the position which he was afterwards to acquire. He was not in these ten years by any means a household name, nor, as is sometimes forgotten, did success really come to him until his forty-first year. The *Quarterly* would still snarl at him from time to time. We find in a review of Milnes' poems for June 1839 a quite unnecessary lunge at "the fantastic shimmer of such baby idols as Mr. John Keats and Mr. Alfred Tennyson." Moreover in the later 'thirties *Fraser's Magazine* published a "Gallery of Literary Portraits" containing some seventy studies, in which Tennyson's name does not even figure. The same thing happened in January 1842, when an anthology of nineteenth-century poets, including some forty-three selections from different poets, contained no extract whatever from the works of Alfred Tennyson.

But with the publication of the 1842 volume, with *Locksley Hall* and the *Morte d'Arthur*, his reputation became assured. Even the reviewers were obliged to pay some attention. In 1847 came *The Princess*, which in spite of these same reviewers had an immense popularity. The Pre-Raphaelite Brotherhood, with the exception of Rossetti, hailed it as finer even than *Sordello*, and in the next year we find FitzGerald owning that he was considered a "great heretic" for not sharing this universal appreciation.

And finally, as we reach the year 1850, we find the critics urging him to do "something big." We find them all beginning to talk again of Tennyson's "Mission." And they continued talking in this strain for forty-two more years.

# CHAPTER SIX

# FARRINGFORD

## *1850–1872*

## I

The year 1850 forms the central point of Tennyson's life and literary career: it emerges dominantly to mark the dividing moment between the lonely uphill struggle of his youth and manhood and the easy, cushioned slope of his later age. For in this year 1850 three very important things happened: he married Emily Sellwood; he published *In Memoriam;* and he became Poet Laureate.

Of the three, it was his marriage, perhaps, which was the most important. Not that we can regard it as some passionate emotional adventure, as some sudden experience infusing a new glow into his genius. It was anything but that. For, in the first place, he was no longer young: he was over forty, an age at which Shakespeare had already become a grandfather. And, in the second place, the whole business has a rather deliberate, wholly domestic flavour which robs it of the more flaming colours of romance. Its effect lay rather in the slow and gradual means by which the wistful lady who became his wife was able, with little worsted strands, to bind what was most wild in him and most original, and by the persistent creation around him of an atmosphere of reverent adoration to build up, even for the Laureate himself, the legend of an infallible and prophetic thinker, the legend of a great emphatical force—the legend, in fact, of all that Tennyson most emphatically was not, of all that he should never have attempted to be.

"The Peace of God," he wrote later, "came into my life before the altar when I wedded her." We may well believe it; but a great many other quite significant things went out of his life from that moment. The sense of unrest left him, and gradually the feeling of the wolds and the North Sea, the feeling of "the thorns of life," the sense, even, of Arthur Hallam, became blurred and distant; and in the foreground, soothing and protective, appeared the tea-table at Farringford, and Emily there upon the sofa to write one's letters for one and to pass timid but appropriate criticisms upon some "tender little thing" which had been written that morning in the summer-house. And, what was even more to the point, his wife must be right. The things that made her cry the most, sold the most. And as the gentle, happy, remunerative years slipped by, and Moxon gave place to Strahan, and Strahan in his turn to Henry S. King, and King to Kegan Paul, and Kegan Paul finally to Macmillan, it became more and more evident that Mrs. Tennyson was right; that she had always been right; that she was a very tender and spiritual woman.

One adopts this view of Mrs. Tennyson: it is the only view which, with the material before one, it is legitimate to adopt. And yet I wonder sometimes whether the accepted picture of the sweet, spiritual, self-effacing lady in the shawl and the grey dress is wholly fair. There was something more positive in Mrs. Tennyson than the evanescent, wistful charm which is generally attributed to her. She loved her husband with an almost religious devotion. It became for her a labour of love to veil, in her fluttering, tactful way, the more rugged crudities of his discontented, self-centred nature. But on occasions, and notably in her voluminous correspondence with her confidant, Thomas Woolner, there appear little defiant touches of personality; little touches, here and there, of independence; little

touches, almost, of humour. It became her duty to manage
the house, the children and the servants; to see that no
jarring note should disturb the serene altitudes at which
alone the Laureate could commune with his muse; it was
her duty, also, to act as his secretary, to answer his correspondence and to keep the accounts. There was little time
for her to think of herself, or to trouble about her own
health, which was obviously breaking under the strain. It
was her duty in life to enable Alfred Tennyson to write his
poetry. It was worth it—oh, it was worth it a thousand
times! But in the intervals—in those long and anxious intervals—when her husband was *not*, somehow, inspired to
write, it all became rather exhausting. Was it her fault?
It must be her fault. She must go on trying. But it was
no good: Alfred only became moodier and moodier. "We
have," he wrote to Patmore in April 1854, "hardly seen a
human face, except the members of our household. Happy,
I certainly have not been. I entirely disagree with the saying you quote of happy men not writing poetry. Vexations
(particularly long vexations of a petty kind) are much
more destructive of the 'gay science'. . . ." And indeed
these vexations appear to have been galling enough.

The day would have begun badly because the house-
maid had removed a can of hot water which he had put out
for his own shaving after breakfast. It would be close on
eleven before the can had been retrieved, the maid rebuked
and a shaven but grumbling Laureate sent off, with one
of those pretty little manuscript books she would make for
him, to the summer-house. With a wistful sigh Mrs. Tennyson would settle down again to the day's work. In ten
minutes, there he would be back in the doorway, nagging
about that can. Patiently she would listen to it all, and at
the end suggest for him a nice brisk walk upon the downs;
the garden door would slam through the little house and
set the mask of Dante wobbling against the red wall; from
the garden would come the scream of the mowing-machine
driven with injured fury across the lawn. Suddenly, the

sound would stop; slowly, wistfully, Mrs. Tennyson would again lay down her pen: "About that can, Emily, you won't understand: *a*verything in this house. . . ."

"I wish," the poor lady wrote to Woolner in 1859, "you would give A. something to do. He is pretty well but for want of this." And again in 1860: "Beyond all price to me would be a worthy subject for A.—one which would fix him, whether he would or no." And thus appealed to, Woolner, that inventive man, produced "The Fisherman's Story," which became *Enoch Arden,* and the "Sermon," which became *Aylmer's Field.* And thus for a period the clock in the red drawing-room ticked undisturbed to the gentle scratching of Mrs. Tennyson's pen.

Not, incidentally, that she felt that either of Woolner's suggested themes was worthy of Alfred's ethical mission. "I hope," she writes to Woolner, "that you think he has given your stories well. I wish he could give me mine now, and do the 'Sangreal' for me,—not but that I heartily *adopt* Enoch Arden." And later: "I wish," she writes, "that he would write a set of songs in lyrical metres, for since Burns he is almost the only poet who has been able to do a song."

This last suggestion makes one regret that Mrs. Tennyson had not the strength or audacity to urge her advice a little more forcibly upon her husband. For there were certain things which she appears to have seen with greater clarity than others of his immediate circle. We find her, for instance, in 1864 implying that some of the poems, at least, might be given to the world at a price less extravagant than that hitherto exacted. "Do you like," she writes, "the idea of the selections in sixpenny parts for the working man? And I wonder whether you would approve of my notion of having headings and tail-pieces . . . made out of flowers emblematic of the Colonies by way of telling the world that one considers that the Colonies too are among the people of England? Each colony, I think, ought to have its flower or tree emblem, but so far as I can make (out) it has not: so all that could be done would be to have kinds of typical plants—cotton, coffee, eucalyptus, acacia, rice, maize, vine, wheat, etc., bread-fruit tree, fern-tree, etc. . . ."

But it mattered little what Woolner or Mrs. Tennyson might devise between them; for Tennyson himself, it must be remembered, was a very excellent man of business.

As I have said, the engagement had lasted off and on for some fourteen years. We are told that the reason for the long delay was predominantly lack of funds; we may further, if we wish, read into a passage in *Edwin Morris* a possible biographical reference:—

> ". . . . a thought or two,
> That like a purple beech among the greens
> Looks out of place: 'tis from no want in her:
> It is my shyness, or my self-distrust,
> Or something of wayward modern mind
> Dissecting passion. Time will set me right."

Conversely, if we prefer it, we can apply a passage from *The Ring*:—

> "Two lovers parted by no scurrilous tale—
> Mere want of gold—and still for twenty years
> Bound by the golden cord of their first love."

We are not, perhaps, concerned with all this: what alone is certain is that time did set him right; what is also certain is that in his old age he addressed to her two dedicatory poems of remarkable beauty. He wrote the *Roses on the Terrace*, and he wrote *June Bracken and Heather*:—

> "There on the top of the down,
> The wild heather round me and over me June's high blue,
> When I look'd at the bracken so bright and the heather so brown,
> I thought to myself I would offer this book to you,
> This, and my love together,
> To you that are seventy-seven,

> With a faith as clear as the heights of the June-blue
> heaven,
> And a fancy as summer-new
> As the green of the bracken amid the gloom of the
> heather."

And, after all, a poem such as this must silence all questionings.

They were married at Shiplake on June 13, 1850, and
left at once for Weston-super-Mare. From there they proceeded to Arthur Hallam's grave at Clevedon—"It seemed
a kind of consecration to go there"—and finally to the Lakes.
But their real honeymoon was to be deferred till the summer of 1851, when they left for Italy, and the record of
their journey remains for us in the poem, with its original
and charming cadence, which appeared, under the title of
*The Daisy*, in the "Maud" volume of 1855.

> "O Love, what hours were thine and mine,
> In lands of palm and southern pine;
> In lands of palm, of orange-blossom,
> Of olive, aloe, and maize and vine. . . .
>
> What slender campanili grew
> By bays, the peacock's neck in hue;
> Where, here and there, on sandy beaches,
> A milky-bell'd amaryllis blew. . . .
>
> What more? We took our last adieu,
> And up the snowy Splugen drew,
> But ere we reach'd the highest summit
> I pluck'd a daisy, I gave it you.
>
> It told of England then to me,
> And now it tells of Italy.
> O love we two shall go no longer
> To lands of summer across the sea."

Their first home was a farmhouse at Warninglid in Sussex, but one night a storm blew down the wall in their

bedroom, and they discovered that the dining-room had
been a Roman Catholic chapel and that a baby had been
buried on the premises. They decided, therefore, that the
house was too "uncanny and uncomfortable," and so they
migrated, Tennyson pulling his wife in a bath-chair as far
as Cuckfield, to Chapel House, Montpelier Row, Twickenham, where they were to remain till 1853. In the vicinity
of Twickenham was Kneller Hall, a training college for
workhouse school teachers, of which Temple of Balliol was
at that time the director, and Jowett an occasional visitor.
And, in addition, other older friends would drive down from
London: Miss Thackeray, for one, who recalls the bene-
dictory statue of a bishop in the hall; and another afternoon
old Hallam and his niece, Mrs. Brookfield, arrived together,
to find Tennyson weeding in the garden, and the historian
was given a tin of sugared pineapple, which he finished in
the carriage going home. And finally, in the summer of
1853, they discovered the Isle of Wight and Farringford,
which they leased at once with the option of purchase, and
which was to become their permanent home.


II


As we know, Tennyson had been writing *In Memoriam*
since the early days of October 1833. Scattered throughout the records of those seventeen intervening years we find
isolated reports of progress. In 1841, for instance, we find
Lushington recording that "the number of the memorial
poems has rapidly increased"; in a letter to FitzGerald of
1848 the poet himself makes mention of "the elegies"; writing again to Aubrey de Vere in 1849 he announces his intention of printing twenty-five copies only for private circulation. Already in March 1850 these elegies, containing
ten sections less than the first published edition, had been
set up in type and withdrawn for revision. At the end of
that month we find William Rossetti recording that Patmore had in his possession "one out of some half-dozen of

Tennyson's Elegies that have been printed strictly for private perusal." It may be concluded that this early and privately printed edition was little more than a trial proof in book form, for the actual first edition was issued in June 1850 by Moxon in deep purple cloth boards with gilt lettering. Five thousand copies of this edition were printed. The author's name did not appear, although Moxon took good care to see that the real authorship was very generally known. Second and third editions were called for the same year, and fourth and fifth editions were issued in 1851. In subsequent issues the anonymity, which had ceased to delude anyone, was discarded; but some, at least, of the reviewers were at first deceived, and it is to this misunderstanding that we owe the famous commentary: "these touching lines evidently come from the full heart of the widow of a military man."

At first the reviewers were generally unfavourable, and it was only later, when the huge popularity of the book, not only with the general public, but also with the outstanding thinkers of the day, had been abundantly emphasised, that they altered their tone to one of deference. It should be remarked, however, that more than a year after publication, on November 28, 1851, *The Times* attacked the volume in terms of unexpected violence, the effect of which was only increased by the fact that the then Laureate was throughout mentioned as the author of the poem. This review begins, rather surprisingly even for 1851, by characterising Tennyson as being a spoilt child of the critics, with the result that he has become "the most resolute mannerist in England, except Mr. Carlyle." "His faults," the reviewer continued, "of taste and language are stereotyped, and he now writes his affectations in capitals." After commenting on the "enormous exaggeration" of the grief depicted in *In Memoriam*, an exaggeration which had led the poem to be "not a memorial but a myth," the reviewer proceeds: "A second defect which has painfully come out as often as we take up the volume is the tone of—may we say so?—

amatory tenderness. . . . Shakespeare may be considered the founder of this style in English. In classical and Oriental poetry it is unpleasantly familiar. We object to a Cantab being styled a 'rose' under any conditions. . . . We can appreciate the meditative rapture of Burns, who saw his 'Jean' in the flower under the hedge; but the taste is displeased when every expression of fondness is sighed out, and the only figure within our view is Amaryllis of the Chancery Bar." While objecting also to his use of archaic words such as "burgeons," and while insisting that the poem as a whole is much too long, *The Times* directed the central portion of its attack upon Tennyson's obscurity and lack of meaning. Thus, while admitting that much of this obscurity "is the result of the illimitable expanse of mystery over which the Poet sweeps," it concludes that the fault is not to be explained or forgiven for any depth of thought. "Sometimes," the reviewer says, "he is difficult, not from excess, but from want, of meaning," and he instances the concluding lines of Section XXVI:—

> "That shadow waiting with the keys
>     To cloak me from my proper scorn."

"That a shadow," says *The Times*, "should hold keys at all is a noticeable circumstance; but that it should wait with a cloak ready to throw over a gentleman in difficulties, is absolutely amazing." And so in subsequent editions the word "cloak" was altered to "shroud."

But in spite of *The Times*, it was *In Memoriam* which first placed Tennyson upon the pedestal which was to isolate and enhance him for over forty years; and it was *In Memoriam* which, we are told, decided the Prince Consort to secure for him the appointment of Poet Laureate.

### III

It will be recalled that so far back as 1843, when the post of Laureate fell vacant on the death of Southey, Ten-

nyson's name was put forward rather diffidently by his
friends as that of a possible successor. The popularity of
the 1842 volume had, during the seven years that followed,
rendered it inevitable that when the vacancy again occurred his candidature should be pressed in less restricted
circles. Even by 1845 we find him in the "Bon Gaultier
Ballads" exclaiming to the tune of *The Merman:*—

> "Who would not be
>     The Laureate bold
> With his butt of sherry
> To keep him merry,
> And nothing to do but to pocket his gold.
> 'Tis I would be the Laureate bold."

And on the death of Wordsworth in April 1850 his name
figured prominently in the controversy which then arose.
For the occasion, it should be noted, gave rise to a great
deal of controversy. There were many who contended that
the death of Wordsworth offered a suitable occasion to ter-
minate, with befitting dignity and on a reverent note, a cus-
tom which had but little relation to progressive and utilitar-
ian conditions. There were others who maintained that even
as a woman now sat upon the throne of England, so also
should a woman now wear the official crown of English
poetry, and that the Laureate should therefore be Mrs.
Browning. There were a few who canvassed the claims of
Rogers, who was then eighty-seven; there were others who
cast their votes for Leigh Hunt, for Henry Taylor and for
Sheridan Knowles. The dispute raged with no little publicity for six months, and in the interval *In Memoriam* had
been published and had reached its third edition. By 1850
there can have been little doubt that Tennyson was the
most popular candidate. Rogers, it appears, had already
signified that he was too old for the appointment; the name
of Browning himself had not been mentioned in any serious
quarter; it was questionable whether, after all, they would
really like Leigh Hunt very much at Osborne; there was

Henry Taylor, of course, and Henry Taylor had many useful friends; and then there was Sheridan Knowles; but he,
perhaps, could be discounted. The field seemed clear
enough.

But when the names were actually submitted to the sovereign by Lord J. Russell, Tennyson's figured only fourth
on the list, and in front of him came Leigh Hunt, Knowles
and Taylor. According to some authorities it was the Prince
Consort who, after reading *In Memoriam*, persuaded the
Queen to disregard the suggestions of Lord John Russell
and to pass over the first three candidates on his list. Mr.
George Napier, however, gives a different account, in which
*The Miller's Daughter* is represented as the deciding factor. "Our Queen," he writes, "was so much touched by its
simple strains, that when death removed the Laureate's
crown

> "from the brows
> Of him that uttered nothing base"

it was the recollection of this bucolic idyll which decided
Her Majesty, in face of all opposition, to confer the much
coveted wreath on its author."

Tennyson himself, during these six months, was, we are
told, wholly unconscious that his name had ever been mentioned. The offer of the appointment came to him, it appears, as an overwhelming surprise. "My father," says
Hallam Tennyson in the Memoir, "my father, as he assured
me, had not any expectation of the Laureateship or any
thought upon the subject. It seemed to him therefore a very
curious coincidence that the night before the offer reached
him he dreamt that Prince Albert came and kissed him on
the cheek, and that he said in his dream, 'Very kind, but
very German.'"

It was indeed a very curious coincidence. On the following morning a letter from the Queen's Private Secretary offering him the appointment was brought to his bedroom.
After hesitating for a day he decided to accept, and the

appointment was published, not without protest in some quarters, on November 19, 1850.

There can be no doubt, I think, that Tennyson, during his forty-two years' tenure of the post, executed his functions with very notable tact and dignity. He appears to have determined from the outset that he would not suffer it to affect, either positively or negatively, his poetical production, and in the proof of his Dedication to the Queen, which he prefixed to the seventh edition of the poems in 1851, there occurs a definite intimation to this effect:—

> "Nor should I dare to flatter state,
>      Nor such a lay would you receive
>      Were I to shape it, who believe
> Your nature true as you are great."

Although these lines were suppressed in the published version, and although his invectives of 1852 against Napoleon III (*The Third of February 1852, Hands all Round,* and *Britons Guard your Own*) were published anonymously for fear of causing offence at Osborne, yet *Maud* was issued defiantly in 1855, and *Enoch Arden,* with its unpleasant savour of bigamy, in 1864, in spite of possible disapprobation. Nor were the more positive duties of his position wholly uncongenial. He rather liked writing congratulatory poems to newly-wed maidens; he rather liked taking a domestic, almost a matriarchal, view of the British Empire; he had no hesitation whatsoever in celebrating the interest and importance of Indian and Colonial produce. His longer Laureate poems are equally sincere. His dedications to the Prince Consort and to the Queen herself have no shade about them of the perfunctory; and the Wellington ode, so strangely unappreciated by his contemporaries, is admittedly one of the finest in the language.

From the material point of view also, his appointment as Laureate was not without advantages. Although the direct emoluments were but slight, the indirect effect upon the sale of his poetry was very remarkable. For he had ceased as from that November 19, 1850, to be just a Mr. Tennyson, a poet: he became *the* poet, the Poet Laureate. And in that disciplined and Germanised age they liked the sound and the authority of the thing; they liked the certainty, the official certainty, of a title at once so decorative and so unique. It was nice to feel, when everybody was becoming so very variable and perplexing, that here at least one could be *sure;* to feel, without anxiety, that what was sanctioned at Osborne could be read at home; to know that, without appearing either paradoxical or affected, one could even quote the poems now and then; that, however distressing might be the universal growth of unbelief, however disturbing all this talk of science, of evolution, and of historical criticism, the Laureate had, in *In Memoriam,* solved these problems for one courageously and for all time. And so they bought, they all bought, the poems. And the Tennysons, for their part, bought Farringford.

We find the following entry in Mrs. Tennyson's diary for April 24, 1856, the day on which the purchase had been completed. "This ivied home among the pine trees is ours. Went to our withy holt. Such beautiful blue hyacinths, orchises, primroses, daisies, marsh marigolds and cuckoo flowers. Wild cherry trees too with single snowy blossom and the hawthorns white with their pearls of May. The park has for many days been rich with cowslips and furze in bloom. The elms are a golden wreath at the foot of the down. To the north of the house the mespilus and horse chestnuts are in flower and the apple trees are covered with rosy buds.

"A. dug the bed ready for the rhododendrons. . . ."

IV

I have divided the last forty years of Tennyson's life into two periods of equal proportion: the Farringford period from 1850 to 1870, and the Aldworth period from 1870 to 1892. This division is convenient rather than precise. Tennyson did not actually settle at Farringford till November 1853; on the other hand, even after 1869, when Aldworth was completed, he would return every winter to his Isle of Wight home. But in other ways the distinction between these two periods is legitimate enough. It is not that anything very startling can be recorded to differentiate the one period from the other. It might be said, indeed, that after 1850 nothing important happened to Tennyson at all: these forty years are but little variegated, a mere monochrome of adulation and success. It is rather that one can observe in this monochrome a slight variation in the shade and intensity of the said success and adulation, a more confident tincture in the second period, a more mottled surface in the first. And when one considers the subtle gradations by which the rather slovenly Bohemian, the swarthy, melo-dramatic, dirty-linened figure of 1849, passed through his early querulous, frock-coated Laureate period, to become the loose-tweeded, voluminous and shambling bear of the middle 'eighties, one realises that the progress was one from the puzzled simplicity of his middle youth, through a short and equally puzzled period of affectation, back to the serene simplicity of his later age. And thus, as one derides Farringford, one can venerate Aldworth.

To neither period does the chronological method lend itself with any hope of clarity or enlightenment. One considers the years from 1850 to 1870, and there echoes as an undertone to the domestic idyll of Farringford the distant flux and reflux of the growing tide of popularity. By 1851 Oxford had caught the enthusiasm from Cambridge; by 1853 it is the undergraduates of Edinburgh who ask him, but in vain, to stand for the Rectorship, and as early as 1852 Woolner had heard two Australian miners discussing *The May Queen* under a eucalyptus. *The Charge of the Light Brigade* in 1854 gave him, at a single stroke, a reputation in circles which were anything but literary, a reputation which remained unaffected by the perturbation of the critics at the publication of *Maud* in 1855. In 1859 came

the four first *Idylls of the King,* in 1864 the *Enoch Arden*
volume, and in 1870 *The Holy Grail.* And already by the
middle 'sixties the letters from the Colonies were encum-
bering the tables at Farringford and the tourists from the
United States were dotting the downs and hedgerows of
the Isle of Wight.

As a foreground to all this there is simply Farringford:—

> "Where, far from noise and smoke of town,
>    I watch the twilight falling brown
>       All round a careless order'd garden
>    Close to the ridge of a noble down. . . ."

A dip in the downs merely around Freshwater Bay; the
thick green overgrowth of the Isle of Wight clustering into
the valley and hiding the secretive little house, jumbled into
the damp hollow among its cedars and chestnut trees, with
the ivy and the magnolia leaves outlined against the wooden
ogives of the eighteenth-century Gothic windows.

How familiar to us has become the description of the
life at Farringford! The regularity and the method of it
all; the settled habits becoming, as it were, the etiquette
of the house, an etiquette, in later years, almost regal in
its rigidity. The honoured but apprehensive guest arriving
before sunset in a cab from Yarmouth pier; the momentary
glimpse of the poet over the hedge mowing the lawn in
spectacles and black sombrero, and hiding, as one approached, behind the juniper; the parlour-maid and the
very late Gothic of the drawing-room window; the evening
sun upon the cedar outside; the mask of Dante glimmering from the dark red walls and the engraving of Sebastiano
del Piombo's Lazarus above the mantelpiece; Mrs. Tennyson rising, gentle and nervous, towards one from the sofa, in
her grey gown; the anxious, expectant pause; the sense of
unbearable imminence—and then, slowly framed in the
doorway, the dark bulk of the Laureate. In an awful silence
he would advance into the room, a book held close to his,
by then, unspectacled eyes. An evanescent introduction

from Mrs. Tennyson, and those fierce eyes would be turned upon one in a penetrating myopic scrutiny, and a deep growl of acknowledgment, if not of greeting, would proceed from the mass of tangled mane and beard. Another aching pause, and in a crisis of embarrassment one would pass into the dining-room. It was six-thirty by the clock there; how long could all this be possibly expected to last? There was salt beef and carrots and side dishes on the table. The Laureate would begin to carve. A little fluttering conversation about Yarmouth pier from Mrs. Tennyson; a second sudden growl from the Laureate: "I like my meat in wedges," and the subject of Yarmouth pier would flutter down to another prolonged and awful silence. And then gradually in the appropriate and vacant expectancy thus created, the Laureate would embark with grunt and growl upon some broad Lincolnshire story, a story so broad and so North Country that one would wonder tremulously how much one understood, how much, with Mrs. Tennyson there, one could rightly be expected to understand; and with the conclusion would come from the Laureate a loud appropriate guffaw, in contrast to which one's own accordant laughter appeared but a slight and timorous cachinnation. Gradually under hammer-blows like this the ice would melt, and with the port a certain geniality, heartening but still very insecure, would descend upon the occasion. But there were worse trials to come. At eight one would be taken to the attic room for a pipe; still apprehensive, one would enter, and from a basket the Laureate would choose a pipe and transfer it, already lighted, to one's lips. And then there would be a growl or two about some recent review in an obscure periodical; and more stories; and one would sit there in the smoke, wondering why he was so different from what one had expected—wondering why he called a novel "a novéll," why he pronounced knowledge with a long "o," why he gave to the word "too" a thinness of vowel sound which was cockney rather than Lincolnshire; why he spoke of a pageant as a "paygeant";

why, finally, he sat there, as Mr. Gosse has told us in his inimitably vivid way, "a gaunt, black, touzled man, rough in speech, brooding like an old gypsy over his inch of clay pipe stuffed with shag and sucking in port wine with gusto."

And then one would descend to the drawing-room, where the curtains had been drawn and the lamps lit; and there was a table in the recessed window, with Mrs. Tennyson flickering over the tea-urn and the fruit. And more port. And then the reading would begin.

We have heard a great deal about this reading. It has been described very entertainingly by Mrs. Asquith; it has inspired what is perhaps the best of many wonderful passages in Henry James' "Middle Years." It figures prominently in all the endless references to these palpitating visits. He would sometimes read the *Idylls;* more often he would choose the *Ode to the Duke of Wellington*, lengthening the vowels into:—

"Bury the greaaat Duke with an empire's lamentaaation."

Or into:—

"To the nooise of the moourning of a mighty naaation."

Sometimes, and quite incomprehensibly, he would embark upon *The Northern Farmer,* and at other times he would startle his audience with a very metrical rendering of *The Battle of Brunanburh*. He would never consent to read *In Memoriam:* "I cannot," he said, "it breaks me down so." But it was *Maud* that was his favourite. "Come and let me read you *Maud*," he said to J. T. Fields; "you'll never forget it." On occasions, even, he would read German with a strong English accent.

But that he would read one something was a certainty:—

"and the poet, little urged,
But with some prelude of disparagement
Read, mouthing out his hollow oes and aes
Deep-chested music."

And thus one would sit there in the red drawing-room, conscious, as Henry James says, "of the heaviest pressure" one
"had doubtless ever known the romantic situations bring
to bear," watching the large brown hand rippling to the
movement of the verse, and from time to time clenched
with whitening knuckles on the arm of the chair. And
through it all the deep bucolic voice would continue, booming and chanting with sudden lifts and with disconcerting
hisses and whispers, and, if one's attention wandered for
a moment into thoughts of how exactly to phrase the situation in some eventual article or memoir, one would be suddenly pinioned and exposed by a break and a question:
"How exactly do you understand that?"

    The eventual comments, when all was over, were facili-
tated by the fact that Tennyson would generally make them
himself. "There's a wonderful touch!" he would say. "That's
very tender!" "How beautiful that is!" All that was expected of the audience during the recitation was their rapt
attention, and if, at the end, any comment was exacted, it
was easy to evade the point by becoming "broken down."
Take this, for instance, from Bayard Taylor:—

>     "I spoke of the Idyll of Guinevere as being perhaps
> his finest poem, and said that I could not read it aloud
> without my voice breaking down at certain passages.
> 'Why, I can read it and keep my voice!' he exclaimed
> triumphantly. This I doubted, and he agreed to try,
> after we went down to our wives. But the first thing
> he did was to produce a magnum of wonderful sherry.
> . . . We had two glasses apiece, when he said, 'To-
> night you shall help me to drink one of the few bottles
> of my Waterloo—1815.' The bottle was brought, and
> after another glass all round, Tennyson took up the
> *Idylls of the King*. His reading is a strange, monoto-
> nous chant, with unexpected falling inflexions, which
> I cannot describe, but can imitate exactly. It was very
> impressive. In spite of myself I became very much ex-

cited as he went on. Finally, when Arthur forgives the Queen, Tennyson's voice broke. I found tears on my cheeks, and Mr. and Mrs. Tennyson were crying, one on either side of me. He made an effort and went on to the end, closing grandly. 'How can you say,' I asked (referring to the previous conversations), 'that you have no surety of permanent fame? This poem will only die with the language in which it is written.' Mrs. Tennyson started up from her couch. 'It is true!' she exclaimed; 'I have told Alfred the same thing.'"

I have been informed that there exists somewhere, probably at Farringford, a gramophone record of Tennyson reciting *The Charge of the Light Brigade*. I have been unable to secure it. But it has been my privilege, on a very curious and decorative occasion, to edge Miss Ellen Terry into a corner of the Throne Room of Buckingham Palace and to insist, in return for a cup of coffee, on an exact imitation of the Laureate's recitation. The words, I said, did not matter: what I wanted was the tune. She was very gracious; she boomed off at once into the trochaics of *Locksley Hall*, swaying increasingly upon the red settee to the motion of the verses, stamping finally with her little feet until the cup upset upon her dress. It was a black dress with sequins, and the situation, though interrupted, was redeemed.

And by then I knew exactly how Tennyson recited *Locksley Hall*.

## V

In the year 1857 there occurred an interesting variation in the successive editions of the poems which Moxon was by then issuing in tens of thousands for the needs of an appreciative public. It had occurred to Moxon that an illustrated edition would now be welcome. He left the choice of the artist or artists to Tennyson himself, and the latter, who was but slightly versed in contemporary artistic movements, referred to Millais, whom he happened to know, who had, in fact, been down at Farringford in 1854. It was then fully seven years since the first publication of the *Germ*. It was but natural that Millais should have suggested himself and his brother Pre-Raphaelites. The Laureate had no objection: after all, it was really Moxon's business; but could not they get Maclise to join them? And there must be some other Academicians who would co-operate? Millais and Moxon promised to see to it, and by the end of the year there appeared a stout volume in blue cloth with a gilt urn upon the cover and enriched by over fifty engravings.

Maclise had chosen the *Morte d'Arthur;* there were other engravings by T. Creswick, R.A., and C. Stanfield, R.A.; *The May Queen* was depicted by J. C. Horsley; to Mulready fell the illustration of *The Goose*. Of the other poems, Millais himself had selected *Mariana, The Miller's Daughter, The Sisters, A Dream of Fair Women, Dora, The Talking Oak, Locksley Hall, St. Agnes' Eve, The Day Dream, Edward Gray* and *The Lord of Burleigh*. His depiction of the personages and incidents in these poems was, with the exception of *Mariana,* in complete harmony with the poet's intention. The same cannot be said of Holman Hunt and Rossetti. The former's engraving of *The Lady of Shalott* distressed Tennyson considerably. "My dear Hunt," he expostulated, "I never said that the young woman's hair was flying all over the shop." "No," replied Hunt, "but you never said it wasn't." Even more daring was Hunt's illustration of *The Beggar Maid*. "I never said," complained the Laureate, "that there were a lot of steps: I only meant one or two." "But," explained Hunt, "the old ballad says there was a flight of them." "I daresay it does," remonstrated Tennyson, "but I never said I got it from the old ballad." "Well, but," retorted Hunt, "the flight of steps does not contradict your account—you merely say: 'in robe and crown the King stept down.'" The Laureate was not appeased, he continued to grumble that he had only meant "two steps at the outside."

Rossetti, for his part, had been so dilatory about the business that the main design for *The Lady of Shalott*, which he had hoped to execute, was assigned to Holman Hunt before Rossetti had communicated his preferences. He fell back rather sulkily on a tail-piece for *The Lady of Shalott*, on a small engraving of *Sir Galahad*, and two beautiful drawings for *The Palace of Art*. It is the first of these two engravings which excites our curiosity. The passage illustrated is the following:—

> "Or in a clear wall'd city on the sea,
>     Near gilded organ pipes, her hair
> Wound with white roses, slept St. Cecily;
>     An angel look'd at her."

The perplexing thing about Rossetti's illustration is that, although the organ pipes are there, and the white roses in St. Cecily's hair, yet the angel is not an angel at all, but something far more sinister, and he is represented as biting St. Cecily very hard upon the forehead. It is fortunate, perhaps, that the Laureate was too indifferent to the arts and too short-sighted to notice the variation. Holman Hunt's inaccuracies had been bad enough: we dare not conjecture what, if he had observed it, would have been his view of Rossetti's licence. He did not observe it. He was unaware, until there appeared that unpleasant and perplexing volume by "little Swinburne" in 1866, that something very serious and very disturbing was happening to the taste and manners of the English people.

## VI

These twenty years at Farringford between 1850 and 1870 were varied for Tennyson by a series of foreign tours undertaken generally in the months of July and August. In 1858, for instance, he visited Norway, and the following

summer he proceeded to Portugal in the steam yacht *Vectis*
of the Peninsular and Oriental Company. His companion
was F. T. Palgrave, a very serviceable friend. They visited
Cintra, which the Laureate found "cockney," and at Lisbon
they attended the harmless Portuguese version of a bull-
fight. "We could not but feel that that which makes it a
more humane sport deprives it of reality." It had been their
intention to proceed to Seville, Gibraltar and Tangier, but
"the heat and the flies and the fleas and one thing and
another" decided them to return at once to Southampton.
The expedition had not been an unqualified success. "I
made some pleasant acquaintances," Tennyson records,
"but could not escape the autograph hunters." So the next
year, with Palgrave, Holman Hunt and Woolner, he went
to Cornwall. In 1865, accompanied by Mrs. Tennyson and
his two sons, Hallam and Lionel, then thirteen and eleven
respectively, he travelled via Brussels, Waterloo, Coblentz
and Eisenach to Weimar. They visited the Palace, the
Fürstengruft, the Schillerhaus and the Gartenhaus. With
some difficulty they obtained admission to Goethe's home
in the town. "Went," records Mrs. Tennyson in her diary,
"with Mr. Marshall—secretary to the Grand Duchess—to
Goethe's town house. No key there for the rooms. The old
woman said that she was alone in the house and could not
possibly go and fetch it. A. was touched by seeing the
'Salve' on the door-mat, and all Goethe's old boots at the
entrance." But eventually the Director was summoned and
they saw inside.

More interesting perhaps is the expedition, made in 1861,
to the Auvergne and the Pyrenees. His two boys accompanied him, and with them came "little Dakyns," their tutor. The latter has left behind him some reminiscences of
their journey which are not without a certain illustrative
significance.

"I remember," he records, "an instance of my own
audacity, at which I almost shudder now. We were

riding into a French town. It was the evening of a
fête and the whole population seemed to be capering
about with the most preposterous antics. It struck a
jarring note, and the Poet said to me, 'I can't understand them; it's enough to make one weep.' Somehow
I couldn't help answering—but can you imagine the
audacity? I assure you I trembled myself as I did so—
"Tears, idle tears, I know not what they mean.' And
he took it, he took it! He did indeed."

Here is another, and more poignant, reminiscence (it is a
friend of Dakyns, Miss Stawell, who supplies the record):—

"But the sweetest of our memories was, I think, the
memory of the valley of Cauteretz, sacred to Tennyson because of Arthur Hallam. I heard Mr. Dakyns
speak of that the first time he was at our house. My
mother chanced to ask him what he did after taking
his degree, and he said, 'I was with the Tennysons as
tutor to their boys, and we went to the Pyrenees.' The
name, and something in his tone, made me start. 'Oh,'
I said, 'were you with them at Cauteretz?' He turned
to me with his smile: 'Yes, I was, and if I had not
already a family motto of which I am very proud, I
should take for my legend *Dakyns isn't a fool*' (the
last phrase in a gruffly tender voice). And then he told
us: 'There was a fairly large party of us, the Tennysons, Clough and myself, some walking and some driving. Tennyson walked and I, being the young man
of the company, was the great man's walking-stick.
When we came to the valley—I knew it was a sacred
place—I dropped behind to let him go through it alone.
Clough told me afterwards I had done well. He had
noticed it, and the Poet said—and it was quite enough
—"Dakyns isn't a fool." ' "

And it was thus that on returning to the inn the Laureate
was enabled to write:—

"All along the valley, stream that flashest white,
  Deepening thy voice with the deepening of the night,
  All along the valley, where thy waters flow,
  I walk'd with one I loved two and thirty years ago.
  All along the valley, while I walk'd to-day,
  The two and thirty years were a mist that rolls away;
  For all along the valley, down thy rocky bed,
  Thy living voice to me was as the voice of the dead,
  And all along the valley, by rock and cave and tree,
  The voice of the dead was a living voice to me."

It was only after this poem had been published that Tennyson discovered that it had all happened thirty-one, and not thirty-two years ago. "As late," says Hallam Tennyson in the Memoir, "as 1892 he wished to alter it, since he hated inaccuracy. . . . I persuaded him to let his first reading stand, for the public had learnt to love the poem in its present form: and, besides, 'two and thirty' was more melodious."

Apart from these journeys during July and August, Tennyson would remain at Farringford, soothed by the gentle, undeviating routine of his home. He would not willingly visit the houses of his friends. Jowett had once in 1855 forced him to join one of Lady Ashburton's famous gatherings at the Grange. The Carlyles were there and the Brookfields. The occasion is historical in that it is the first recorded instance of a reading from *Maud*. I quote Mrs. Brookfield:—

"There was a large party staying in the house, where, to our great joy, Alfred Tennyson also arrived and, I think, only the next day the first copy of his latest poem *Maud* was forwarded to him. We were, all of us, of course, eager to hear his new poem read aloud by himself, and he most kindly agreed to gratify us. But there were difficulties to be got over. Carlyle and his wife were amongst the guests, and it was well known that he could not endure to listen to anyone reading aloud—not even to Alfred Tennyson.

"Carlyle was accustomed to take an early walk daily, and to be accompanied by an appreciative companion. What was to be done? All the visitors in the house were personally anxious to listen to Tennyson's delightful reading. Lord and Lady Ashburton were kept waiting, chairs had been arranged in a quiet sitting-room; the visitors (ourselves amongst the number) were taking their places. Alfred was ready. So was Carlyle—in the hall, waiting for a companion in his walk—and evidently he would not stir without one. It was quite an anxious moment. We each probably wondered which of us would volunteer to leap into the gulf, as it were, like Quintus Curtius of old. At length, to our great relief, Mr. Goldwin Smith generously stepped forward and joined the philosopher, whilst we remained to listen with enthralled attention to the new words of the poet."

Such excursions were not often indulged in. Only for the convenience of the thing would he stay sometimes with the Prinseps at Little Holland House. He preferred in general that those who were admitted to the presence should be admitted only at Farringford. Jowett was a regular guest; in 1860 we find the Duke of Argyll there and Lord Dufferin; in 1861 the Bensons and the Bradleys. Such visits were frequent enough. Frequent also, and to an increasing extent, became the appearance at the lodge gates of little groups of uninvited pilgrims, who would stand there patiently hoping to view the author of *In Memoriam*. They were on no account admitted. All that they could do was to walk a few yards down the road, turn to the right, and wait for some "chance glimpse" of the Laureate in the lane of elms. They were not often disappointed, and indeed, for one so sensitive to the pointing finger of publicity, Tennyson appears to have been unlucky in the frequency, the punctuality almost, with which these chance glimpses were afforded. And how majestically, with his big blue cape and his big black hat, did he surpass their expectations! But although, in this way, it was a very easy matter to *see* the poet, it was very difficult—nay, even impossible—to draw him into conversation. On one occasion a family had come all the way from Boston, Mass., in the hope of telling the Laureate how much they had liked *Maud*. On landing in England, they proceeded at once to Freshwater, and reached the gate, which barred their further progress. They were told that in no circumstances could they be granted an audience. As a great privilege, however, and in consideration of the fact that their pilgrimage had been long and arduous, they were allowed to walk up the drive to the point where the Colorado Pine screened the front door of Farringford from the eyes of the vulgar. As they crept with gingerly reverence up the gravel, a large black figure loomed suddenly upon them round the bend. "Mr. Tennyson," faltered the leader of the party, "we have come four thousand miles in order to tell you. . . ." But he got no further. "It cannot be," thundered the Laureate, as he swung round upon his heel. And then, I suppose, they all went back to Boston.

But the more authorised pilgrims were not always, in this abrupt manner, excluded. We hear of Lewis Carroll being there in 1861; of the Longfellows coming to Freshwater in 1868 "with a party of ten, very English"; and as early as 1858 we read: "Young Swinburne called here the other day with a college friend of his, and we asked him to dinner, and I thought him a very modest and intelligent young fellow. I read him (*Maud*), but what I particularly admired in him was that he did not press upon me any verses of his own."

As the Laureate's fame became universal, distinguished visitors would come to Farringford from abroad. In the spring of 1864 Garibaldi arrived in a carriage. Mrs. Tennyson chronicled the visit in her diary:—

"A. and I and the boys were in the portico awaiting his arrival. A. and he went up to A.'s study together, and they talked on politics, A. advising the general not to talk politics in England. They repeated Italian poetry to each other. . . . Mrs. Cameron wanted to photograph Garibaldi and dropped down on her knees before him, and held up her black hands, covered with chemicals. He evidently thought that she was a beggar until we had explained who she was. Then we went to plant the Wellingtonia. . . ."

And next week there was a full-page picture of this visit in the *Illustrated London News*.

In the following autumn the hospitality of Farringford was again offered to a visitor from overseas. The entry in Mrs. Tennyson's journal for September 28, 1865, runs as follows:—

"*Sept. 28. Farringford.* Queen Emma of the Sandwich Islands arrived, Major Hopkins and a huge native, Mr. Hoapili, in attendance. Aunt Franklin came. The Queen's maid and her luggage lost on the road: they arrived at midnight. We had had a throne chair made out of our ilex wood. It was first used by the Queen. She, poor lady, wanted to stay quietly here, but she had to go to banquets, etc., about the Island. I collected money for the projected cathedral at Honolulu. . . . Mr. and Mrs. Hoapili sang Hawaiian songs. They sat on the ground and acted the song while they sang."

This visit lasted three days, and on October 2nd the Queen took her departure:—

"A. gave her two large magnolia blossoms on her leaving.

"She has an affectionate nature: something very pathetic about her."

And finally for July 18, 1868, we find the following entry:—

> "Poor little Alamayne, King Theodore of Abyssinia's son, came with Captain Speedy."

Apart from such visitors, there were, of course, the Isle of Wight neighbours. It appears that in the first year of the Tennysons' arrival at Farringford the Island families had showed a certain reserve. But in 1856, at the very moment when the van of furniture had arrived from Twickenham, Prince Albert rode over to call upon them, and the social position of the Tennysons was thereafter assured. The subsequent advances of the neighbours were not encouraged; the poet would, in those early Farringford years, spend most of his time geologising in Alum Bay with Granville Bradley; but during the years that followed three very intimate and helpful friendships emerged. The first of these Isle of Wight friends was Sir J. Simeon, the second W. G. Ward and the third Mrs. Cameron.

Sir John Simeon of Swainston, that "Prince of Courtesy," shares with Hallam and Henry Lushington the distinction of being one of the three most intimate of Tennyson's friends:—

> "Two dead men have I known
>   In courtesy like to thee:
> Two dead men have I loved
>     With a love that ever will be:
>     Three dead men have I loved and thou art last
>       of the three."

"The only man on earth," Tennyson said of him later, "I verily believe, to whom I could, and have more than once, opened my whole heart." A genial, generous, warm-hearted gentleman, a man of a magnificent presence, as is shown by the Watts portrait, Sir J. Simeon became, as Mrs. Tennyson said, "a brother to us." The relations between Swainston, in the garden of which *Maud* was partly written, and Farringford were intimate and constant; and as a supreme mark of affection Tennyson gave to his friend the manuscript of *In Memoriam*. Upon Sir J. Simeon's death in 1870, Tennyson appears to have asked that the manuscript should be returned to him, in order that he might, by adding an inscription on the fly-leaf, safeguard its ultimate destination. There is a footnote in the volume entitled "Tennyson and his Friends," edited by the present Lord Tennyson in 1911, which says that the manuscript was "given back to Tennyson at his request after Sir J. Simeon's death, and after his death presented by his son and Catherine Lady Simeon to the Library of Trinity College, Cambridge." The whole incident is obscure, nor is the correspondence which throws light on how or why the Tennyson family came to repossess themselves of the manuscript available for publication. The manuscript, as bound together by Sir J. Simeon, is now in a show case at Trinity, opened at a page innocent of erasures or various readings. Moreover a procedure has been devised under the terms of the gift sufficiently elaborate to protect it from the heartless investigations of future critics and bibliophils. Which are what Tennyson himself would so fervently have disliked.

Another, although a later, friend of these years was W. G. Ward, referred to by the Laureate as "most generous of all ultramontanes." For Ward had been the *enfant terrible* of the Oxford Movement; had, in his passionate outspokenness, driven Arnold to his bed and Newman to Littlemore; had, by his tumultuous theology, shaken the harmony of Balliol Common Room to its very foundations, and caused Jowett many anxious questionings as to how far, with a friend so violent and so convinced, loyalty (adequate loyalty) should, after all, oblige one to go; and thus, after having thrown the whole academic and religious world into a turmoil, after having been "disgraced" by Convocation, become a Catholic, and seen the "Tractarian impulse," according to Jowett, "subside" from the shock of his own subsequent marriage, Ward had settled at Freshwater, and could be seen there on summer evenings walking with the poet upon the downs. A curiously ill-assorted pair. Ward, fat, ungainly, ultramontane, indifferent to poetry and quite passionately truthful; Tennyson, gaunt, grumbling and theistic. But there they would walk together, with the dogs and the children and the Jesuit chaplain following behind; and the Bard would twit Ward merrily upon the many and patent absurdities of the Church of Rome.

And finally there was Mrs. Cameron. For Mrs. Cameron was one of the few people who were not in the least frightened of the Laureate: she would burst in upon Farringford at any hour; she thought "Alfred's entourage too serious"; she would bustle and hustle him about, and tell him that Sir Henry Taylor was the greatest living poet, and other unpleasant things, and to make up would give him little painted ivory figures from Ceylon for his birthday, and leave her shawls about the drawing-room, and interrupt his guests, and take photographs of them, and arrange charades, and be generally bracing and irreverent. For Mrs. Cameron was a privileged person—a friend of the old Prinsep days; and often the Laureate, with his dogs and his great blue cape flapping under the black hat, would walk over to Dimbola, and there would be much rough-and-tumble banter, and Mrs. Cameron's husband would blink about with his white hair and purple dressing-gown, and finally Tennyson would go home, rather wistfully perhaps, with the scent of sweet-briar and chemicals in his nostrils—home to the red drawing-room and to Mrs. Tennyson upon the sofa.

And on such occasions, let us suppose, he would murmur, in the laburnam-scented lanes of Freshwater:—

"Sweet were the days when I was all unknown."

## VII

It is recorded that one evening the Laureate entered the drawing-room at Farringford and, as was his wont, stood poised and magnificent for a moment in the doorway glowering across at a group of his family clustered round a seated figure in a bonnet and many shawls. Suddenly a look of startled reverence was observed to flash into his face. Bowing low, he hastened across the room towards so unexpected, so miraculous a visitor. "This is indeed——" he began. But it was not Queen Victoria: it was only Mrs. Cameron in an unfamiliar garb.

Queen Victoria never came to Farringford. It was the Laureate who in March 1862 was summoned to Osborne. For the Queen had been deeply moved by the *Dedication* [to the Prince Consort] which prefaced the third edition of the *Idylls* at the beginning of that year; nor indeed could so difficult a task have been better accomplished, nor, with certain obvious reservations, could a more frank or beautiful testimony have been conceived to one whom we are only now beginning to appreciate and to understand. The whole incident is sincere and touching, bringing out, as it does, the deep ultimate simplicity of both their characters. It is prefaced by a charming letter from Tennyson to the Duke of Argyll:—

*March 26, 1862.*

"MY DEAR DUKE,

"I am a shy beast and like to keep in my burrow. Two questions, what sort of salutation to make on entering Her private room? And whether to retreat backward: or sidle out as I may? . . .

"Yours ever
"A. TENNYSON."

The interview itself is recorded in a note written down by Mrs. Tennyson immediately after her husband's return from Osborne:—

"A. was much affected by his interview with the Queen. He said that she stood pale and statue-like before him, speaking in a quiet, unutterably sad voice. 'There was a kind of stately innocence about her.' She said many kind things to him, such as 'Next to the Bible *In Memoriam* is my comfort.' She talked of the Prince, and of Hallam, and of Macaulay, and of Goethe, and of Schiller in connection with him, and said that the Prince was so like the picture of Arthur Hallam in *In Memoriam*, even to his blue eyes. . . . A. said, 'We all grieve with your Majesty,' and the Queen replied, 'The country has been kind to me and I am thankful.'"

Here is Tennyson's own account:—

"I was conscious of having spoken with considerable emotion to the Queen, but I have a very imperfect recollection of what I did say. Nor indeed—which perhaps you will think less excusable—do I very well recollect what Her Majesty said to me; but I loved the voice that spoke, for being very blind I am much led by the voice, and blind as I am, and as I told Her I was, I could yet dimly perceive so great an expression of sweetness in Her countenance as made me wroth with those imperfect cartes de visite of H.M. which Mayall once sent me. . . . I was charmed with Princess Alice. She seemed to me what Goethe calls *eine Natur* . . . and the little Beatrice with her long tresses was very captivating."

The next year Mrs. Tennyson and the boys were sent for to Osborne, and the relations thus established between Tennyson and his sovereign, the romantic and quite unembarrassed confidence with which he regarded her, were maintained by correspondence and occasional interviews until his death. And indeed this unaffected esteem and loyalty forms one of the more attractive passages in Tennyson's later biography.

Nor were the public slow to note, to appreciate, and to embroider the connection which had thus been established, over *In Memoriam* and the *Dedication,* between their sovereign and the Laureate. The type of legend which arose is illustrated by a curious article which appeared in the Berlin periodical, the *Gartenlaube.* I may be permitted, perhaps, as a conclusion to this chapter, to reproduce this article at some length, since it illustrates the quality of mind to which, in the later 'sixties, a portion of Tennyson's work appealed in England and scarcely less in Germany; and since, with all its obvious inaccuracies, it furnishes a better picture of all that Farringford was supposed to signify than can be conveyed by a more direct description.

I give a translation of the article as follows:—

"Queen Victoria is one of the most ardent admirers of Tennyson's poems, and shortly after *Enoch Arden* had appeared, she heard that Tennyson's enemies and enviers charged that poem with being immoral and a glorification of concubinage. She applied to an eminent clergyman, and learned from him that cases of bigamy, it was true, were not very rare, and those whom such a misfortune befell might, perhaps, be pardoned by the Lord on the day of judgment, for the mercy of the God of Heaven and Earth knows no bounds; but that it indicated an alarming confusion on the part of the poet to represent in a kind of halo a man who tolerated the continuance of such a sinful relationship between man and woman. This was what Enoch Arden was doing. Instead of appearing before his wife in order to resume his position as her husband, he lay down and died.

"The Queen was not a little disquieted on hearing this. It was true she was well aware that some of the High Church dignitaries were not very favourably disposed towards Tennyson. His open letter to a rector named Maurice, who had been removed from his cure, had not been forgotten. But, since her husband's death, the Queen had accustomed herself more and more to attach a higher importance to the voice of her surroundings than to her own opinions, and thus she was, for a while, unable to decide whether *Enoch Arden* really deserved the harshness with which it had been criticised or not. Finally, she thought she had better consult somebody else on the subject, and she happened to apply to a person who censured Tennyson's poem with still greater severity. . . .

"After this two-fold condemnation of *Enoch Arden*, whose wonderful success had meanwhile fallen in a thousand echoes upon her ears, the Queen thought it would be best for her to speak with the poet himself on the subject which he had treated of in *Enoch Arden*. She therefore extended her drive along the seashore that very afternoon beyond its usual length, and ordered the coachman to drive further west. Osborne, the Queen's country seat on the Isle of Wight, is rather distant from the house of the poet, who lives likewise on that island; but no distance is very considerable there, and the roads all over the island are excellent. She soon after saw the poet's house, which lies in the middle of a small grove of pine and firs, peering forth between the verdure and foliage around it. The Queen was accompanied by two of her daughters. When she perceived Tennyson's form in the garden—his long hair and full beard caused her to recognise him at a glance—she entrusted her sketch-book and the metal box in which she gathered flowers and plants for her herbarium to the princesses, and walked alone to the low garden gate, whither Tennyson had already hastened to meet her. She did not want to enter his house, but, walking with him along the shore, she explained to him what disquieted her in regard to his poem, on the beauties of which she dwelt with

that refined appreciation which is said to be peculiar
to her. . . .

"'Tell me, Mr. Tennyson, what have you to reply
to all those objections which I mentioned to you
before?'

"'Very little, Your Majesty.'

"'What?'

"'I should be sorry, Your Majesty, if the little girl
yonder had to bear the stain of illegitimate descent.'

"'What little girl?'

"'The little girl disappearing just now behind the
hawthorn hedge, Your Majesty; I mean the child
carrying the bundle of faggots.'

"'And what has that girl to do with your poem?'

"'A great deal, for if the Bishop of N. had had his
way, little Anna, yonder, would be considered a child
born in illicit wedlock.'

"The Queen had stood still.

"'You do not mean to say, Mr. Tennyson,' she replied, 'that on our little island here an event such as
you related in your *Enoch Arden* has really happened?'

"And, as Tennyson was silent for a moment, she
continued: 'Oh, I know you do not like to answer such
questions. But tell me now: did Enoch Arden live
here? And is he perhaps even buried underneath that
tombstone?'

"'Your Majesty,' said Tennyson, 'there occur among
the lowly and poor many traits of heroism, for which
historians might envy the quiet observer of the people.
Happy he who can contemplate and comprehend such
traits with an unbiassed mind; happy he who is enabled to relate them in his poems without spoiling their
simple originality too much; happy, above all, he of
whom poets can tell such traits. His memory dissemi-
nates heavenly seed.'

"The Queen had walked across the lawn to the
tombstone and laid her hand on its moss-grown edge.

She stood there a long while in silence, her eyes fixed on the spot where Enoch had found his last resting-place. At length she drew herself up, and, turning to go home, she said, 'God bless him! He did right, after all.'"

# CHAPTER SEVEN

# ALDWORTH

## *1870–1892*

### I

By the later 'sixties Freshwater Bay, at first but a little gap
in the cliffs, was showing symptoms of becoming a gay
and very promising seaside resort, while Freshwater itself,
over the hill, had blossomed out into an hotel, with pink
geraniums hanging in cork baskets on the balconies, and tin
tables and bottles of aerated lemonade and char-a-bancs.
The amenities of Farringford were seriously threatened.
"Yonder," exclaimed the Laureate in the æsthetic 'eighties,
"yonder," he expostulated:—

> "Yonder lies our young sea-village—Art and Grace are
>      less and less:
>   Science grows and Beauty dwindles—roofs of slated
>      hideousness"

Moreover Mrs. Tennyson, never a very strong woman, had
begun to feel the effect of the soft and steaming summers
of the Isle of Wight. And, what was far more important, the
Laureate himself was becoming seriously angry with the
tourists.

For they would come upon him, these tourists, with their
char-a-bancs, in some laburnum-scented lane, and they
would stare and gape and point, and he would turn an

embarrassed back to them—a black hat and an expanse of
alpaca coat were all they saw; a big brown hand prodding
viciously at the roadside grass; and then the white chalk
dust would settle down again upon the sombrero, and an
indignant Laureate would slouch on up the road inveighing
against the penalties of fame. And sometimes they would
peep and pry over the hedges of Farringford itself, penetrating importunately into the garden, tearing souvenirs
from the walls of the summer-house which he had built and
decorated with his own hands, picking daffodils, climbing
even, in an ecstasy of veneration, into the trees to watch
the Laureate playing battledore and shuttlecock upon the
lawn. And even on the downs, on *his* down, the improbous
tourist would follow, marking him down from a great distance, and cutting off his retreat. On one such occasion the
Laureate, on debouching from the little lane which led from
his garden to the downs, was perplexed to observe against
the distant horizon a tall figure voluminous in a dark cape,
the large sombrero outlined unmistakably against the sky,
and the surrounding strategical points picketed, as was customary, by groups of expectant tourists, with their opera-
glasses already fixed upon that other provoking and impertinent figure. Immediate inquiries were instituted. The
man was identified as the taxidermist of Freshwater. And
everybody agreed that he had shown remarkably bad taste.

Nor was it only the tourists who were to blame. I quote
from Rawnsley:—

"The next day I went for a morning walk with him
upon the down. As we went through the little wicket
gate that let us out from the seclusion of the garden
grove into the lane, I noticed that a rogue had written
in chalk upon it beneath the word 'Private' these other
words, 'Old Tennyson is a fool.' I half hoped the old
poet would not see it, but his eye caught sight of it,
and he said in a sort of cheery way, 'The boy's about

right: we are all of us fools, if we only knew it. We
are but at the beginning of wisdom.' "

Obviously it was time to leave the district: to discover,
for the summer months at least, some wilder and more
salubrious retreat, some corner hidden from the haunts of
tourists, some isolated district immune to the vulgarities of
a residential neighbourhood. The Tennysons decided therefore to migrate to Surrey.

They had already been to Hindhead in the spring of
1867, when Hallam Tennyson was recovering from an attack of pneumonia which he had contracted at Marl-
borough. In June of that year they had visited Blackdown,
near Haslemere, and had purchased a plot of land at Blackdown copse. They decided at once to build; the foundation
stone was laid in April 1868, and in August of the following
year they entered into possession. The architect of this new
residence, which was designed as a "free treatment of domestic Gothic of the Tudor period," was Mr. (afterwards
Sir James) Knowles, subsequently editor of the *Nineteenth
Century*. Tennyson had met him one day in 1867 at
Haslemere railway station, and, having heard that he was
an architect as well as a man of culture, had made the
proposal. Knowles agreed, but very courteously refused to
accept a fee for so distinguished a commission. The Tennysons, for their part, had not at first contemplated anything
quite so ambitious as Aldworth: their idea, really, had
been, more or less, a little bungalow on the top of the down,
which was to be called "Greenhill." Sir James Knowles soon
disposed of this pathetic fallacy. "The plans," he records,
"for a four-roomed cottage gave way somewhat as I talked
the matter over with Mr. and Mrs. Tennyson . . . and presently I went to Farringford with designs for a less unimportant dwelling. It grew and grew as it was talked over and
considered. . . ." It did. "At last," Sir James continues, "one
day, when I brought sketches for an arcaded porch to complete the design, he put his foot down and said he would

have nothing to do with it, that he would have no more additions, that it would ruin him and could not be entertained for a moment. He walked to and fro, coming back from time to time to the table where the drawing lay and looking at it. He admitted that he liked it more and more the more he looked at it, but presently cried out with simulated fury, 'Get thee behind me, Satan,' and ran out of the room. Then I knew that the porch was won."

In the end Tennyson became very fond of Aldworth, of the Gothic porch above mentioned, of the terrace hanging over the weald of Sussex with the red geraniums against the blue distance, and of the "hot-water bath"—that astonishing novelty—in which he would at first indulge four or five times a day, sitting therein and "reading about little birds." And gradually, although they discovered, to their regret, that the residents and the tourists at Haslemere became, as the years passed, quite as numerous and persistent as those of Freshwater, it was Aldworth and not Farringford that grew to be the official home, and where the distinguished guests, Boyd-Carpenter, Gladstone, Argyll, Dufferin, Bradley, Jowett, would pace up and down the terrace admiring the poet's yuccas and the view over the weald of Sussex to where the gap in the South Downs showed a short grey bar of sea.

"He made a great point," records Sir James Knowles, "of his favourite motto, *Gwyt yor erbyn y byd,* being prominently emblazoned in tile mosaic at the threshold of the front door and in the pavement of the hall."

In English, it appears, the motto signifies: "The truth against the world."

The story of the last two decades of Tennyson's life is the story of Farringford written on an ampler, more confident scale. The success, the popularity, are more universal and more ecstatic; the voice of criticism, when it dares to utter, becomes but a defiant squeak of paradox; the etiquette is the same, but more serene, more confident and more convincing; the foreign journeys are the same, only more spectacular; the guests are the same except that the more distinguished among them appear at less irregular intervals; the readings from the *Ode to the Duke of Wellington* and *Maud* are exactly the same; and year by year the Tennyson legend expanded in ever-widening circles and carried his renown to the distant fringes of the English-speaking world.

The tourists in their hundreds debouched on Haslemere; anonymous correspondents and people glorying in their names would stoop to the basest of stratagems to secure an autograph or to elicit an opinion; his birthdays took upon themselves the solemnity of a national festival; his compatriots would send him presents of honey and garden chairs and rolls of tweed; they christened lakes after him in New Zealand; they christened agricultural colonies in South Africa; explorers would select the most remote of hyperborean ice-cliffs for the honour of the Laureate's name; rosarians would employ it to give a final lustre to their choicest blooms; his every movement, his every action, his clothes, his dogs, his walking-sticks and his tobacco were canvassed and proclaimed in the illustrated journals; quite serious people would make the round of Somersby, Mablethorpe, Cambridge, Clevedon, Epping, Cheltenham and Freshwater, and spend hours cross-examining Lincolnshire agriculturists and Grimsby fishermen; publishers grasped eagerly at the result of their researches, and the bookshops would display elaborate volumes on the "Homes and Haunts of the Tennysons" or the records of reverential adventures "In Tennyson Land."

And perched above it all up there at Aldworth the Laureate would fret and fume and contradict and be perplexed and indignant and rather gratified. And by every post would come the letters. Mrs. Tennyson was kept very busy. It is said by malicious and quite untrustworthy people that she spent wistful hours copying with one of her husband's pens that thick and authoritative autograph. In

1874 her health collapsed under the strain. The journal ends upon a pathetic note:—

> "On our return," the last entry runs, "I had to answer many letters from unknown correspondents, asking advice from A. as to religious questions and desiring criticism of poems, etc., and I became very ill, and could do but little. So my journal ends here."

But fortunately Hallam Tennyson had only just gone to Cambridge. He was at once recalled to fill his mother's place.

It is difficult for us to realise the extent to which the Laureate in his later life filled, and to some extent unwillingly, the thoughts and the imagination of his contemporaries. His views and opinions on all subjects were by the great majority of his countrymen regarded as decisive. Scattered throughout the newspapers of the period one finds evidences of the official communiqués which were from time to time issued from Farringford or Aldworth. Here is an early example from *The Times*:—

## "THE POET LAUREATE AND
## COLONEL RICHARDS

"The Poet Laureate, after consideration of the 'proofs' of Colonel Richards' claim to be considered the chief originator of the Volunteer Movement of 1859, has signified to Captain Bertrand Payne, Conservative Club, commanding the 4th Mid. V.A., and Hon. Sec. of the 'Richards' Volunteer Testimonial Fund,' his intention to become a subscriber, and has written to Colonel Richards himself, as follows:—

" '*Farringford, Freshwater, Isle of Wight,*
" '*April 19th,* 1867.

" 'I most heartily congratulate you on your having been able to do so much for your country, and I hope that you will not cease from your labours until it is the

law of the land that every man-child in it shall be trained to the use of arms. I have the honour to be,
" 'Yours faithfully,
" 'A. TENNYSON.' "

Nor were this veneration and confidence confined to the laity or the middle classes. The following is from the *Echo* of January 22, 1879:—

### "MR. HAWEIS'S EVENINGS FOR THE PEOPLE

#### "TENNYSON'S 'IN MEMORIAM'

"The fifth 'Evening for the People' at St. James's, Welbeck Street, Marylebone, was densely crowded by an audience who, as soon as the doors were opened, filled every part of the church and thronged the vestry.

"It was observed that many persons had brought their copies of *In Memoriam*, and studied the preacher's allusions, whilst copious notes seemed to be taken all over the church, from the full shorthand report to the mem. in the margin.

"The preacher said that here at length, etc. . . ."

And Mr. Haweis embarks for the enlightenment of the proletariate on an analysis of *In Memoriam*.

The intense, the passionate, interest which the Laureate aroused in his contemporaries did not always take so anodyne a form as the above. Every fresh poem, as it was published, evoked a stream of correspondence from unknown admirers. Nor was abuse less frequent than adulation. On the publication of *Maud* he had received the following:—

"SIR,

"I used to worship you, but now I hate you. I loathe and detest you. You beast! So you've taken to imitating Longfellow! Yours in Aversion. . . ."

When in 1882 he had recast and republished as a patriotic song the *Hands all Round* of 1852, with its opening lines:—

> "First drink a health this solemn night,
>     A health to England every guest;"

the Executive Committee of the Grand Lodge of Good Templars of England at once met in Birmingham and passed the following resolution:—

> "That this Executive observes with regret that the Poet Laureate's new national song invites to repeated drinking, as expressive alike of loyalty, patriotism and freedom, thus pandering to a fast-decaying convivial custom which inflicts manifest injury upon so many of her Majesty's servants, hinders national advancement, and impairs both body and mind."

The resolution was forwarded to the Laureate, who replied through his son asking them to remember "that the common cup has in all ages been the sacred symbol of unity," and that the word "drink" had only been used in reference to this symbol. "Further," comments Hallam Tennyson, in the Memoir, "I might have mentioned that my father had supported a movement for the closing of public-houses on Sunday throughout the Isle of Wight."

It is not surprising that Tennyson should have suffered acutely under the fierce light which beat upon his retirement. For under a very obvious and transparent layer of vanity he possessed a shrewd Lincolnshire sense of proportion. Of his vanity much has been said and written. In 1872 we find FitzGerald grumbling to Houghton:

> "I used to tell Tennyson thirty years ago that he should be a dragoon, or in some active employment that would keep his soul stirring, instead of revolving in his own idleness and tobacco smoke; and now he is sunk in coterie worship, and (I tremble to say it) in the sympathy of his most lady-like, gentle wife. . . .

I mourn over him as over a great man lost—that is, not
risen to the greatness that was in him, for he has done
enough to outlast all others of his time, I think, up to
1842."

Nor can it be denied that the "sweet incense" of his home
which "rose and never failed" had a rather narcotic effect
upon his sterner faculties. The sheltered isolation of this life
contributed further to his curious ignorance of the world,
to his astonishing misconception of the intellectual progress
of his age. For Tennyson did not possess the eager, mun-
dane curiosity of Browning, nor yet the practical intelligence and culture of Matthew Arnold, nor even the gentle
receptivity of Aubrey de Vere. As a result, we find that
unique simplicity of his character, which at its best gives
an abiding impression of stateliness, and at its worst merely
an effect of limpid naïveté which is quite engaging. "He
was accustomed," wrote Lecky, "to express his opinions
(about his own poetry) with a curiously childlike simplicity
and frankness. But at bottom his nature seemed to be singularly modest." Or again, as Sir A. Lyall has it: "He listened to applause with straightforward complacency." This
habit of his misled the superficial, nor can one blame them
if, on hearing Tennyson declare his poem *The Oak* to be
"clean-cut like a Greek epigram," or describe *Maud* as "a
little Hamlet," they thought the man quite indiscriminately
conceited.

The pathos of these last years is to be sought for rather
in the curious circumstance that Tennyson was not always
self-confident enough. The Duke of Argyll, on being introduced to him, said: "I am so glad to know you," and
Tennyson replied: "You won't find much in me—*after all.*"
Nor had he many illusions as to the inevitable reaction
which would follow his apotheosis: his garland, he knew,
was but "of a day"; and he would regret this, at times, as
in the lines to Mary Boyle when he sighs:—

"As I shall be forgotten by old Time
Laid on the shelf——"

Speaking once to Barnes, the Dorsetshire poet, he was even
more explicit: "Modern fame is nothing: I would rather
have an acre of land. I shall go down, down. I am up now.
Action and reaction." And finally, in one of Mrs. Warre
Cornish's articles there is a passage which strikes me as
very pathetic and illuminating. It was the year before he
died. He had been reading to her that disastrous poem *The
Death of Oenone*. He asked her how she liked it, and she
replied, "with warmth," that she liked it even better than
the first *Oenone*. "He said 'Why?' and scrutinised me with
his magnificent eyes as if he doubted my sincerity."

And thus, while his inherent modesty and simplicity, his
inherent good sense, were disturbed and angered by the
hysteria of his contemporaries, the other side—the sensitive,
diffident, timid side which had remained to him from childhood—was tortured by the publicity to which he was
exposed. At its worst this sensitiveness was the timid, self-
conscious quality which had angered Carlyle. "Yes," the
latter had said to Patmore in the late 'thirties, "he is a really
great man, but not quite: he stands on a dunghill with
yelping dogs about him, and if he were quite a great
man he would call down fire from heaven and burn them
up." Even in the old Cambridge days he would not suffer
his friends to criticise his poems, and Moxon told Browning
in 1842 that he had been instructed by Tennyson to hide
from him all but the most favourable reviews.

FitzGerald had once ventured to say that the later poems
lacked something of the old "champagne flavour," and for
many years Tennyson and FitzGerald ceased to meet. Patmore, who in the early stages of their friendship had "followed Tennyson about like a dog," was dropped for ever
the moment he showed signs of independent judgment. A
similar fate almost, but not quite, overwhelmed Jowett. For
on one occasion, when Tennyson was staying with his wife

at Balliol, someone had asked him after dinner to read them
a manuscript poem. He consented. The circle of chairs was
arranged, the manuscript was brought down from upstairs,
and the assembled company listened in an ecstasy of veneration to the trochaics which boomed from the lips of their
author. When the reading was over a respectful silence fell
upon the company. It was obviously for Jowett to voice the
emotion which was in all their hearts. The silence was long
and painful. In the end, even as by a little silver bell, it was
broken by Jowett's: "I wouldn't publish that, Tennyson, if
I were you." Poor Mrs. Tennyson, sitting there with her
pulses fluttering in anticipation of the impending storm; and,
Oh dear, that nice Mr. Jowett, who was so fond of Lionel
and Hallam. But the thunder, when at length it crashed,
glanced off miraculously into comparatively impersonal directions: "If it comes to that, Master," bellowed the
Laureate, "the sherry you gave us at luncheon to-day was
positively filthy." And ever after that evening, which still
lingers as an awful memory at Balliol, Jowett was careful,
if he did not like a poem, to become silent or "broken down."

And how Tennyson loathed "the pen-punctures of those
parasitic animalculæ of the press"! "I *am* thin-skinned," he
said to Tyndall, "I take no pains to hide it." Or again: "I
*hate* spite; I am black-blooded like all the Tennysons. I
remember all the malignant things said against me, but little of the praise."

Take this also, for a poem of 1874:—

> "Popular, popular, unpopular!
>     'You're no poet'—the critics cried!
>     'Why?' said the poet. 'You're unpopular.'
> Then they cried at the turn of the tide—
> 'You're no poet!' 'Why?' 'You're popular!'
> Pop-gun, popular and unpopular."

An important manifestation of this sensitiveness was an
abiding terror of being investigated or examined, a horror
of having his nakedness exposed—a very real gymnophobia,

if such a word exists. He relished fame, but he shrank in morbid fear from the consequences of fame; and hence the endless precautions and strategems and disguises which were adopted to prevent and deviate any but the most authorised and pre-arranged inquiry.

He loathed all gossip:—

> "The tiny trumpeting gnat can break our dream
>   When sweetest: and the vermin voices here
> May buzz so loud—we scorn them but they sting."

He called it "that foul bird of rapine whose whole prey is man's good name." He told Palgrave once that if Horace had left his autobiography and the only extant manuscript fell into his hand he would throw it into the fire. "I thank God," he would say, "day and night that we know so little of Shakespeare." And he was very rude indeed to an old lady who endeavoured to entertain him with an intimate story about Dr. Johnson.

He hated all biography. The following spirited verses were addressed, it appears, to Monckton Milnes on the publication of his Life of Keats, although they have been referred, less convincingly, to Medwin's book on Byron:—

> "For now the Poet cannot die,
>   Nor leave his music as of old,
>   But round him ere he scarce be cold
> Begins the scandal and the cry:
>
> 'Proclaim the faults he would not show:
>   Break lock and seal: betray the trust:
>   Keep nothing sacred: 'tis but just
> The many-headed beast should know.'
>
> Ah, shameless! for he did but sing
>   A song that pleased us from its worth
>   No public life was his on earth,
> No blazon'd statesman he, nor King.

He gave the people of his best:
    His worst he kept, his best he gave.
    My Shakespeare's curse on clown and knave
Who will not let his ashes rest!

Who make it seem more sweet to be
    The little life of bank and briar,
    The bird that pipes his lone desire
And dies unheard within his tree,

Than he that warbles long and loud
    And drops at glory's temple-gates,
    For whom the carrion vulture waits
To tear his heart before the crowd!"

Less justifiable, perhaps, is his secretiveness about his own bibliography and his loathing of all variorum editions. I prefer the attitude of Browning with his: "Leave out anything? Certainly not. What I have written I have written." With Tennyson it was different. He did his best to suppress his early poems or the earlier versions of those subsequently emended; he envied the days before variorum editions and other commentaries:—

"Hours, when the Poet's word and looks
    Had yet their native glow:
Nor yet the fear of little books
    Had made them talk for show;
But, all his vast heart sherris-warm'd,
    He flash'd his random speeches,
Ere days, that dealed in *ana,* swarm'd
    His literary leeches."

And in his later years he wrote a poem against bibliographers which is so good an example of his Horatian manner that it merits full quotation:—

"Old poets foster'd under friendlier skies,
    Old Virgil who would write ten lines, they say,
    At dawn, and lavish all the golden day
To make them wealthier in his readers' eyes;

And you, old popular Horace, you the wise
    Adviser of the nine-years-ponder'd lay,
    And you, that wear a wreath of sweeter bay,
Catullus, whose dead songster never dies;
If, glancing downward on the kindly sphere
    That once had roll'd you round and round the Sun,
    You see your Art still shrined in human shelves,
You should be jubilant that you flourish'd here
    Before the Love of Letters, overdone,
Had swampt the sacred poets with themselves."

"He wished," says Hallam Tennyson in the preface to the Memoir, "that the incidents of his life should be given as shortly as might be without comment, but that my notes should be final and full enough to preclude the chance of further and unauthentic biographies."

And it cannot be denied that the notes collected in the Memoir and the Eversley edition are very full indeed.

## II

The last twenty-two years of Tennyson's life were marked by an astonishing increase in his productive capacity. *The Holy Grail* volume, which included *The Higher Pantheism*, the *Flower in the Crannied Wall* and *Lucretius*, was published in 1870. The two final idylls, *Gareth and Lynette* and *The Last Tournament*, appeared in 1872. The plays begin three years later with *Queen Mary* in 1875, *Harold* in 1877, *The Falcon* in 1879, *The Cup* in 1880, *The Promise of May* in 1882, *Becket* in 1884, *The Foresters* in 1890–91. In 1880 Kegan Paul published *Ballads and other Poems* which included *The Ballad of the Revenge, The Defence of Lucknow, The Voyage of Maeldune*, and that remarkable poem *Rizpah*, which at once convinced Swinburne that Alfred de Musset was not, after all, as great a poet as our own Laureate. By 1885 Tennyson had left Messrs. Kegan Paul for Macmillan; and while under Macmillan the old poet of seventy-six was stimulated to a perfect frenzy of publication. In 1885 we have *Tiresias* and some twenty-six other poems, comprising *The Ancient Sage* and the magnificent Catullus and Virgil pieces. The next year comes *Locksley Hall Sixty Years After*, to which was attached the printed version of *The Promise of May*. In 1887 comes *The Jubilee Ode*, and in 1889 the large volume entitled *Demeter and other Poems*. Finally in 1892 there appeared *The Death of Oenone, Akbar's Dream and other Poems*, which was posthumous only in the sense that it was issued to the booksellers three weeks after Tennyson's death. The actual physical bulk of the volumes completed by Tennyson between the ages of sixty-one and eighty-three is stupendous, and even apart from their quality, which is surprising enough, they compel our admiration by their zest and vigour. In face of such productivity we can well believe that at the age of sixty he began to learn Hebrew in contemplation of a metrical version of the book of Job; that at sixty-three he scaled the Dent du Chat, and that he waltzed with Miss Brookfield in the ballroom when well over eighty.

Thus the years passed, and the nineteenth century entered with ponderous solemnity upon its last three decades; and year by year the conifers grew higher against the dim distances of the weald, and the ivy and the ampelopsis obscured the clear-cut corbels, the flamboyant finials, the heraldic reliefs, with which Sir James had so cunningly enlivened the facade of Aldworth; and Lionel married in 1878 and Hallam married in 1884; and grandchildren appeared; and one summer evening in the early 'eighties Mr. Allingham, walking up from Haslemere, came upon Tennyson and "golden-haired Ally" in the dog-cart, the child hidden under his grandfather's sombrero and the little sailor hat perched high upon the poet's Sophoclean forehead.

And through all those years the full-sailed galleon of the Tennyson manner maintained its course with stately continuity. There were moments, it is true, when it seemed as if the breeze of popular favour were shifting to a different quarter, moments when some new sail would be hoisted, when the direction would be altered by a point or so; but in the end the helm would be reversed again, the extra sail would be lowered, and the ship would lumber on upon her original course, with the old familiar canvas bellying to the south wind. It had happened first in the early 'fifties, when the spasmodics had ruffled the waters of literature with the first puff of symbolism. At once the wary mariner had marked the flapping of the sail; the course was altered; and *Maud* was hoisted to catch the changing breeze. But the breeze died down as soon almost as it had begun, and it was the old favonian wind which filled again the mainsail of the *Idylls*. It happened again in the later 'sixties, when the sensuous ecstasies of the Pre-Raphaelites blew dangerously from the west, and when *Lucretius* was run up hastily to meet this sudden squall. It happened finally in the 'seventies, when the wind of popularity blew strong against the plays. This was a serious and perplexing moment; but the ship was steadied by *Rizpah*, and the voyage ended with wind and tide bearing the vessel gently to the shore.

"Tennyson," said Mr. Gosse, "was a power of a static species; he was able, by the vigour and uniformity of his gifts, to hold English poetry stationary for sixty years, a feat absolutely unparalleled elsewhere; and the result of various revolutionary movements in prosody and style made during the Victorian age was merely in every case temporary. There was an explosion, the smoke rolled away, and Tennyson's statue stood exactly where it did before."

As in the previous period, we find a succession of foreign expeditions: to Grenoble in 1872, to the Italian lakes in 1873, to Pau and the Pyrenees in 1875, to Ireland in 1878, to the Dolomites and Lake Garda—"o venusta Sirmio"—in 1880. In 1883 a more elaborate excursion was arranged. As the guest of Sir Donald Currie, and in the company of Mr. Gladstone and other distinguished and amenable persons, the poet embarked upon the *Pembroke Castle* for a journey to the Orkneys, Norway and Copenhagen. The voyage was well advertised and a great success; the Laureate and the Prime Minister enjoyed it thoroughly—"were as jovial together as boys out for a holiday." At Copenhagen there was a dinner-party, at which the guests included the Emperor and Empress of Russia, the King and Queen of Greece, the King and Queen of Denmark, the Princess of Wales and other very eminent people. And after dinner Tennyson read to them all the poem entitled *The Grandmother*, which was much appreciated. In the last few years he would be lent a yacht for a week or two—the *Stella* in 1887, the *Sunbeam* in 1889 and the *Assegai* in 1891 and 1892, and on two occasions, the last in 1892, he took the opportunity to visit Frederick Tennyson at Jersey. They spoke together of the garden at Somersby and of the Lincolnshire dialect as they had known it; and passed on to a discussion—an animated discussion—on spiritualism. "Nevertheless," records the Memoir, "the brothers parted on the best of terms."

An advantage of Aldworth was its comparative accessibility from London, and visitors were frequent: Jowett was a biennial occurrence; Gladstone and the Dufferins came; we hear of Tourgueneff being there in 1891 and "having great games with A. at German backgammon"; in June of the same year he met his neighbour George Eliot, and thought her "very like the picture of Savonarola"; and there were countless others. The rehearsal of his plays, moreover, obliged him from time to time to take a house in London. We hear of Wimpole Street, of Upper Belgrave Street, of Eaton Place, of 86 Eaton Square. We hear of luncheon parties; of his meeting Russell Lowell, Joachim and Renan; of his refusing to be lionised; of his insisting on having dinner at 7:00; of his being mobbed at the Zoological Gardens.

The references are endless, and occur, indeed, in all the memoirs of the period. I select one almost at random:—

"He was the central ornament," writes Mr. Escott, "of the garden-parties at Clapham, and it was upon one of these

occasions that he sat together with Mr. Browning and
Lord Houghton for an entire hour under a spreading mul-
berry tree, while the whole company, drawn around, gazed
in mute admiration upon this trinity of veteran wielders of
the plectrum, deeply occupied the while in their oral
symposium."

Mention must also be made of the Metaphysical Society,
which had been founded by Knowles in 1869, and the
meetings of which, during its eleven years of existence, were
sometimes attended by the Laureate. He had occasion at
these meetings to hear the views of men like Huxley,
Froude, Tyndall, Gladstone, Manning, Alford, Frederic
Harrison, Mark Pattison, W. K. Clifford, Frederick Pollock,
John Morley, and Arthur Balfour. It does not appear that
he benefited very much from the discussions: even as in the
old days of the Apostles he would hesitate to exhibit his
own intellectual insufficiences to his fellow-members. "I do
not remember," records Grant-Duff, "that the Laureate took
any part in the discussion, but his mere presence added
dignity to a dignified assemblage."

Still less does he appear to have been interested in current literary movements or coteries. In fact, his views on
literature were uninfluenced by other people's opinions.
"The first poetry that moved me," he recorded later, "was
my own at five years old." This early influence was gradually succeeded by others: Byron at first, but Byron was
repudiated before he left Somersby; then had come Cambridge and the Shelley period, which lasted till about
1835. By then he was beginning to say that "Shelley lacked
common sense," that there was "a certain tenuity in his
poetry." And finally, his admiration centred upon such different idols as Keats, and Wordsworth, and the "sledge-
hammer thud" of Crabbe, and even on Alexander Smith.
He preferred, as his son adds, "in his weaker moments" the
sonnets of Shakespeare to the plays, and the *Odyssey* to the
*Iliad*. He pronounced Poe to be "the most original American
genius"; he admired Walt Whitman, who, in return, called

Tennyson "the boss," and he talked of Ruskin "as of one who has said many foolish things." There is scant record of how he regarded Arnold or the Pre-Raphaelites or Swinburne. "What," he would ask abruptly of some visitor, "do you think of Browning?" There was generally some murmured response about Browning's obscurity. "I don't understand him either," the Laureate would conclude; "he seldom attempts the marriage of sense with sound." But as a rule the Laureate's views on the compositions of others were not very illuminating.

## III

In the year 1873 Tennyson had been invited to Windsor. The visit was a great success, and on his return he was offered a baronetcy. He replied that he and his wife would prefer to remain Mr. and Mrs. Tennyson, but that they would be glad if Hallam, then aged twenty-one, could be created a baronet. This suggestion was not adopted. The next year Mr. Disraeli, who had then succeeded Mr. Gladstone, renewed the offer and was met with the same suggestion. The new Prime Minister replied that Tennyson's proposal would be contrary to all precedent, and the matter dropped.

In 1883, however, when on board the *Pembroke Castle,* Mr. Gladstone, being again in power, sounded Hallam Tennyson as to whether his father would now accept a peerage. Hallam replied that the offer was so startling that he did not know how it would be taken; it was just possible, however, that his father would accept "for the sake of literature." When the proposal was broached to Tennyson he showed some hesitation, and Hallam was obliged to scour the deck for Mrs. Gladstone, Sir A. Gordon and Sir Algernon West to reinforce his own representations. For a time the poet remained obdurate. In the end he gave way: "Why," he said, "should I be selfish and not suffer an honour to be done to literature in my name?"

He wrote to Gladstone in December 1883:—

"MY DEAR GLADSTONE,

". . . . Her Majesty must decide as to when I am to be Peered. The younger branch of my father's family who succeeded to the fortune took the name of Tennyson d'Eyncourt. Would that do? They say they are descended from the old branch of the d'Eyncourts who came in with William, and from the later creation of the same name in tempore Charles II. If they, then I. It is a small matter. I will let you know later on. Many thanks for your congratulations on Hallam's engagement. I trust that Mrs. Gladstone, to whom my best and kindest remembrances, is better.

                                        "Yours ever,
                                        "A. TENNYSON.

"P.S.—I heard of an old lady the other day to whom all the great men of her time had written. When Froude's 'Carlyle' came out, she rushed up to her room, and to an old chest there wherein she kept their letters, and flung them into the fire. 'They were written to me,' she said, 'not to the public!' And she set her chimney on fire, and her children and grandchildren ran in. 'The chimney's on fire.' 'Never mind,' she said and went on burning. I should like to raise an altar to that old lady and burn incense upon it."

Mr. Gladstone did not, however, accept the hint conveyed in this postscript. He appears to have kept Tennyson's letter.

The peerage was gazetted in January 1884, and aroused some ungenerous criticism in the Press. The prospect of taking his seat filled Tennyson with acute dismay. "I did not want it," he said to Rawnsley. "What can I do? How can I take off a cocked hat and bow three times in the House of Lords? I don't like this cocked-hat business at all."

It is difficult, indeed, to see how he could well have refused. The Queen had set her heart on the idea, and he could not have faced offending her or interrupting an intercourse which had become so candid and so emotional. There are records of many audiences at Osborne or at Windsor, and in the interval there was considerable correspondence of a warm and affectionate nature. Tennyson's letters begin:—

> "Dear and honoured Lady
> My Queen,"

and end "I am always your affectionate servant."

"I will not say," writes Tennyson on one occasion, "that 'I am loyal' or that 'Your Majesty is gracious,' for these are old, hackneyed terms, used or abused by every courtier, but I will say that during our conversation I felt the touch of that true friendship which binds human beings together, whether they be kings or cobblers."

Nor were this esteem and affection entirely one-sided. We find the Queen's letters signed "Always yours affectionately"; we find her sending him the "Journal of Our Life in the Highlands":—

> "Though a very humble and unpretending author, I send you my new book, which perhaps you may like to glance at. Its only merit is its simplicity and truth.
> "What a warm winter we have had!"

And Tennyson at once acknowledges the present:—

> "I am certain beforehand of finding the lofty and tender sentiments and the hearty enjoyment of nature, expressed in pure English, which cannot fail to make a book interesting."

She writes in her own hand asking him to the wedding of Princess Beatrice, and when he refuses, gives him a long account of it in a very personal manner. She writes regularly on his birthdays, and in her journal the audiences are recorded:—

"*Aug. 7, 1883.*—After luncheon saw the great poet Tennyson in dearest Albert's room for nearly an hour; and most interesting it was. He is grown very old, his eyesight much impaired. But he was very kind.

"Asked him to sit down."

And indeed with such a community of character and interests how could they have failed to achieve a common understanding?

## IV

And thus, one way and another, when the querulous posturing of the early Farringford days had passed into the wide certainty of his later manner, when the swirls and eddies of his early self-consciousness had been fused into the placid flow of his established legend, Tennyson emerges as a figure of extraordinary outrightness, of very admirable simplicity; and on his last years descends, even for us, a glow of esteem and of affection. Esteem for a character so courageous, so consistent and so unsullied. Affection for the figure of this fierce and humorous old man, for the width and magnificence of his simplicity, for his outright complacency; for the complacency, not of the smug or the softly self-satisfied, but the firm and engaging complacency of some large Newfoundland or St. Bernard dog. Affection, finally, for one who could be so persistently himself, who could deride with such confidence our later-day subtleties and intellectualism. And I cherish, as the final impression, the picture of a rugged octogenarian at the dawn of the flaming 'nineties striding through the woods of Aldworth with some reverent companion, talking the while about baptismal regeneration, falling prone on occasions over the roots of some pine tree, picking himself up undaunted, and proceeding undaunted with his discussion on baptismal regeneration.

It was thus that he appeared to Henry James, "so utterly

other" than had been supposed by the "fond prefigurements
of youthful piety," and it was thus that Henry James, after
facing "the full, the monstrous, demonstration that Tennyson was not Tennysonian," came to draw comparisons between the homogeneous breadth and weight of the Laureate, and the "heterogeneous and profane" manner of
Browning, "composed of pieces and patches that betrayed
some break of joints." Nor can I resist a passage, the
luncheon-party passage, from the *Middle Years:*—

> "I was to breathe from beginning to end of our visit,
> which began with our sitting again at luncheon, an
> air . . . in which it seemed to me frankly that nothing
> but the blest obvious, or at least the blest outright,
> could so much as attempt to live. These elements hung
> sociably and all auspiciously about us—it was a large
> and simple and almost empty occasion; yet empty
> without embarrassment, rather as from a certain high
> guardedness or defensiveness of situation, literally in-
> deed from the material, the local sublimity, the fact
> of our all upliftedly hanging together over one of the
> grandest sweeps of view in England. Remembered pas-
> sages again people, however, in their proportion, the
> excess of opportunity; each with that conclusive note
> of the outright all unadorned. What could have par-
> taken more of this quality for instance than the ques-
> tion I was startled to hear launched before we had left
> the table by the chance of Mrs. Greville's having hap-
> pened to mention in some connection one of her French
> relatives, Mademoiselle Laure de Sade? It had fallen
> on my own ear—the mention at least had—with a cer-
> tain effect of unconscious provocation; but this was as
> nothing to its effect on the ear of our host. 'De Sade?'
> he at once exclaimed with interest—and with the con-
> sequence, I may frankly add, of my wondering almost
> to ecstasy, that is, to the ecstasy of curiosity, to what
> length he would proceed. He proceeded admirably—

admirably for the triumph of simplification—to the very
greatest lengths imaginable, as was signally promoted
by the fact that clearly no one present, with a single
exception, recognised the name of the nature of the
scandalous, the long ignored, the at last all but un-
nameable author; least of all the gentle relative of Ma-
demoiselle Laure, who listened with the blankest grace
to her friend's enumeration of his titles to infamy,
among which that of his most notorious work was pronounced. It was the homeliest, frankest, most domestic
passage, as who should say, and most remarkable for
leaving none of us save myself, by my impression, in
the least embarrassed or bewildered; largely, I think,
because of the failure—a failure the most charmingly
flat—of all measure on the part of auditors and speaker
alike of what might be intended or understood, of
what, in fine, the latter was talking about.

"He struck me, in truth, as neither knowing nor
communicating knowledge, and I recall how I felt this
note in his own case to belong to that general intimation with which the whole air was charged of the want
of proportion between the great spaces and reaches
and echoes commanded, the great eminence attained,
and the quantity and variety of experience supposable.
So to discriminate was in a manner to put one's hand
on the key, and thereby to find one's self in presence
of a rare and anomalous, but still scarcely the less
beautiful fact. The assured and achieved conditions,
the serenity, the security, the success, to put it vul-
garly, shone in the light of their easiest law—that by
which they emerge early from the complication of life,
the great adventure of sensibility, and find themselves
determined once for all, fortunately fixed, all consecrated and consecrating. If I should speak of this impression as that of glory without history, that of the
poetic character more worn than paid for, or at least
more saved than spent, I should doubtless much over-

emphasise; but such, or something like it, was none the less the explanation that met one's own fond fancy of the scene after one had cast about for it. For I allow myself thus to repeat that I was so moved to cast about, and perhaps at no moment more than during the friendly analysis of the reputation of M. de Sade. Was I not present at some undreamed-of demonstration of the absence of the remoter real, the real other than immediate and exquisite, other than guaranteed and enclosed, in landscape, friendship, fame, above all in consciousness of awaited and admired and self-consistent inspiration?"

## V

The last years of his life were clouded by ill-health and domestic bereavements. In 1879 his brother Charles had died, and in the same year Mrs. Cameron was buried in Ceylon. In 1881 Spedding was fatally injured in a carriage accident in Hill Street, and in 1883 FitzGerald died at Woodbridge.

In 1886 a more serious blow, and one that affected him very deeply, was occasioned by the death of his second son Lionel on board the s.s. *Chusan* in the Red Sea. Lionel Tennyson had entered the India Office, where he had already made a name for himself by his charm and efficiency. In 1885 the then Viceroy, Lord Dufferin, had invited him to India, and while in Assam he caught jungle fever and was brought to Calcutta. He was nursed there by Lady Dufferin and was eventually considered well enough to bear the ordeal of the return journey. After passing Aden he had a relapse, and the fever mastered him before he could reach cooler latitudes. He was buried at sea.

The blow for Tennyson was terrible, and his sorrow lives in the beautiful lines in which he dedicated *Demeter and other Poems* to Lord Dufferin:—

"For he—your India was his Fate,
 And drew him over sea to you—
 He fain had ranged her thro' and thro',
To serve her myriads and the State,—

A soul that, watch'd from earliest youth,
 And on thro' many a brightening year,
 Had never swerved for craft or fear,
By one side-path, from simple truth;

Who might have chased and claspt Renown
 And caught her chaplet here—and there
 In haunts of jungle-poison'd air
The flame of life went wavering down;

But ere he left your fatal shore,
 And lay on that funereal boat,
 Dying, 'Unspeakable,' he wrote,
'Their kindness,' and he wrote no more;

And sacred is the latest word;
 And now the Was, the Might-have-been,
 And those lone rites I have not seen,
And one drear sound I have not heard,

Are dreams that scarce will let me be,
 Not there to bid my boy farewell,
 When That within the coffin fell,
Fell and flash'd into the Red Sea

Beneath a hard Arabian moon
 And alien stars. To question, why
 The sons before the fathers die,
Not mine! and I may meet him soon;

But while my life's late eve endures,
 Nor settles into hueless gray,
 My memories of his briefer day
Will mix with love for you and yours."

His health was seriously affected by this disaster: by
1888 he was confined to his room with rheumatic gout,
occupying himself by feeding the thrushes out of the window. By the next spring he had recovered, and we hear of
him sitting in the summer-house at Maiden's Croft at Farringford. But the sense of depression remained with him,
and he looked back upon his life with a sigh of disappointment and forward to the future with the darkest foreboding.
"It seems to me," he wrote in 1887, "as if there were much
less of the old reverence and chivalrous feeling in the world
than there used to be . . . I tried in my *Idylls* to teach
men these things and the need of the Ideal. But I feel
sometimes as if my life had been a very useless life." Palgrave in his diary for November 1886 records finding him,
"though saddened by the loss of Lionel, unbroken in
strength and mind. He stoops a little, but strode along
steadily down hill and up rough road, through rain and
mud, talking much, depressed by the state of England, and
his own loss. He read aloud to me a second part of *Locksley
Hall*, a long poem of great force; also the 3rd Act of *The
Promise of May*. This is certainly very tragic and fine."

This depression about the "state of England" lives in the
long, ranting and pathetic diatribes which he composed in
his last few years:—

"Fires that shook me once, but now to silent ashes
      fall'n away.
  Cold upon the dead volcano sleeps the gleam of dying
      day. . . .

  Gone the cry of 'Forward, Forward,' lost within a
      growing gloom:
  Lost, or only heard in silence from the silence of a
      tomb

  Half the marvels of my morning, triumphs over time
      and space,
  Staled by frequence, shrunk by usage into common-
      est commonplace!

'Forward,' rang the voices then, and of the many
    mine was one.
Let us hush this cry of 'Forward' till ten thousand
    years have gone."

He was himself puzzled by this depression: he could not
wholly make it out. His faith, when he tested it, was ampler
and more convinced than formerly. He did not know where
these black moods could come from:—

"... or am I conscious, more
Than other Masters, of the chasm between
Work and Ideal? Or does the gloom of Age
And suffering cloud the height I stand upon
Even from myself? Stand? Stood . . . no more."

One turns gladly from these despondencies to the more
serene aspects of his old age—to his eightieth birthday in
August 1889, when he received congratulatory odes from
Swinburne and Alfred Austin, and planted a blue Colorado
pine in the garden at Aldworth; to that autumn evening in
the same year when he composed his *Crossing the Bar;* to
the last flashes of that amazing vitality, the walks with
Princess Louise, the yachting expeditions, the lessons in
water-colours from Mrs. Allingham, the gymnastic exercises
on the floor of his bedroom; to the black velvet skull-cap
which so increased his resemblance to Titian.

The spring of 1892, except for an excursion to Jersey in
the *Assegai,* was spent at Farringford; the blossom, the lilac,
and the aubretia came together that year and gave him
great pleasure. He did not agree with Emerson's opinion
that only "to youth the Spring is Spring." "For age," he
said, "does feel the joy of Spring, though age can only
crawl over the bridge while youth skips the brook." In July
they moved up to Aldworth. At first he took his regular
walks of a mile out and a mile in over Blackdown, but the
walks dwindled down, and he sat more and more in one
of his two summer-houses. For a few days we hear of him

again in London, visiting the Royal Academy, "oppressed by the heat and the crowd," visiting the Ichthyosaurus at South Kensington, and then he returned to Aldworth. The summer of 1892 was wet and windy, and he felt the cold. In the middle of September Lord Selborne and Jowett came to visit him. He was suffering from gout. He begged Jowett not to "consult with him or argue with him, as was his wont, on points of philosophy and religious doubt." This request was felt by the family to be heavy with foreboding.

By the end of the month he was visibly failing, and Sir Andrew Clark was telegraphed for. The latter, assisted by Dr. Dabbs of Haslemere, saw no immediate cause for anxiety and returned to London. In a few days he was again sent for, and at once realised that the end was near. By Tuesday, October 4th, the poet had fallen into a coma broken by lucid intervals: he spoke of a journey to Farringford; he asked for his Shakespeare; he made them pull up the blinds—"I want the blinds up, I want to see the sky and the light"—he thought that he had been walking with Gladstone in the garden, showing him the trees. The next morning he asked for the proofs of *The Death of Oenone*, and they were put into his hand; the family gathered round him and waited. The end came in the early hours of Thursday, October 6th. The final scenes are recorded in the Memoir with very excellent simplicity:—

"For the next hours the full moon flooded the room and the great landscape outside with light, and we watched in solemn stillness. His patience and quiet strength had power upon those who were nearest and dearest to him: we felt thankful for the love and the utter peace of it all, and his own lines of comfort from *In Memoriam* were strongly borne in upon us. He was quite restful, holding my wife's hand, and, as he was passing away, I spoke over him his own prayer, 'God accept him! Christ receive him!' because I knew that he would have wished it. . . .

"Some friends and the servants came to see him. He looked very grand and peaceful with the deep furrows of thought almost smoothed away. . . . We placed *Cymbeline* with him and a laurel wreath from Virgil's tomb, and wreaths of roses, the flower which he loved above all flowers, and some of his Alexandria laurel, the poet's laurel. On the evening of the 11th the coffin was set upon our waggonette, made beautiful with stag's horn moss and the scarlet Lobelia Cardinalis, and draped with the pall, woven by working men and women of the north, and embroidered by the cottagers of Keswick; and then we covered him with the wreaths and crosses of flowers sent from all parts of Great Britain. The coachman, who had been for more than thirty years my father's faithful servant, led the horse.

"Ourselves, the villagers, and the school-children followed over the moor through our lane towards a glorious sunset, and later through Haslemere under brilliant starlight.

"The coffin was taken to Westminster Abbey. . . ."

# CHAPTER EIGHT

# TENNYSON AND HIS AGE

## I

The prophet was dead; the leaders of his age were there to do him honour—Argyll and Dufferin, Salisbury and Selborne, Jowett and Froude. The nave was lined by veterans of Balaclava. To the thunder of his own verses the coffin was lowered and the pall removed.

And then they all streamed out again into the autumn sunlight, into the noise of the 'buses and the hansoms jingling up from Victoria to Whitehall, and the cries of street boys selling broad-sheets of *Crossing the Bar*. For days a reverent line of people filed past the wooden barrier that framed the grave; and then the chrysanthemums and the laurels were removed, and the stone was let into the pavement, and on the pillar opposite was placed the Woolner bust. And to-day the feet of tourists pass and repass idly above the slab that marks his tomb.

The family returned to Farringford. In 1896 Lady Tennyson died at Aldworth and was buried at Freshwater. In October of the next year Hallam Tennyson produced the Memoir of his father, and thereafter proceeded to Southern Australia—and became Governor-General, and returned in 1904 to England. And gradually the old reverent circle of the devout was dispersed, and the voices of the young or the irreverent grew louder and more insistent. And in their turn these voices also were stilled, and people began to trouble less about Tennyson one way or the other. And the Boer War came, and the Great War, and the subsequent anxieties of peace and reconstruction; and slowly, majestically, the nineteenth century began to assume more accurate proportions.

We are thus encouraged, as we look back upon the many fluctuations which Tennyson's renown has undergone, to hope that once again he will survive the reaction against him, and that the present estimate of his poetry is but the last of the successive phases through which his reputation has already passed. For indeed, as one turns to the reviews of the 1832 volume, to the reviews of the 1842 volume, to the reviews of 1855, and even to the reviews of 1887, one is struck by the extreme diversity of the opinions expressed. The attacks against his early work centred upon his apparent affectation, upon the "feminine feebleness of his polluted muse," upon the "occasional absence of refinement, and failure of dignity and decorum." Fault is found with "his want of truth in imagery and diction," with his diffuseness; or, as a writer in the *Quarterly* expresses it, "Mr. Tennyson is not free from the fault of nimiety." By 1849 we find the following in *Blackwood's Magazine:* "Poetry of the highest order, coupled with much affectation, much defective writing, many wilful blunders, renders Alfred Tennyson a very worthy, and a very difficult subject for the critic." "He has," the same writer says later, "a morbid horror of the commonplace," and we are startled a few paragraphs further to learn that the admirers of *The Lady of Shalott* "must be far gone in dilettantism to make a special favourite of such a caprice as this, with its intolerable vagueness and irritating repetitions." *In Memoriam,* when it appeared, was attacked among other things for its atheism, and for conveying "no impression of reality or truthfulness to the mind"; and *Maud* created a storm of indignation for its "positively hideous cacophony," for being "altogether an ill-conceived and worse-expressed screed of bombast," for being "outrageously silly," and, above all, for being "morbid" and "degenerate." When the *Idylls* appeared, critics were not wanting to pronounce them "immoral"; *Merlin and Vivien* was particularly unpopular, and the readers of that idyll were, as *Blackwood's* reviewer put it, "truly sorry it should pollute the pages which tell, further on, of the manly—ay, the *Christian*—purity of Arthur." We find the *Quarterly* in 1859 countering this line of attack with the explanation that "the brutal element in man, which now only invades the conjugal relation in cases where it is highly concentrated, was then far more widely diffused, and not yet dissociated from alternations and even habits of attachment." "We tremble," says *Blackwood's Magazine* again, in reference to the *Idylls*—"we tremble now and then for the fate of the nineteenth century in the hands of some future Macaulay. He will have no difficulty in giving us a very bad character, if he ground his judgment on such facts as the admitted popularity of 'Traviata' and the passing of the Divorce Bill. And we fear that he will find some additional evidence against us in the very book we are now considering." *Blackwood's Magazine* has little need, perhaps, to be alarmed; but it is useful for us to realise that as late as the middle 'sixties there were many sincere and not unintelligent people who considered the Laureate to be degenerate, subversive, atheistic and immoral. With the publication of *The Holy Grail* the note changes, and the attack centres upon Tennyson's obscurity. *The Holy Grail* itself was accused of being "intricate and involved beyond any allowance of symbolic reference or justification," and as late as the year 1889 we find the *Echo* contending "that there are long passages in the *Idylls of the King* which are as difficult to understand as the pictures of Mr. G. F. Watts."

The reaction of the intellectuals against Tennyson had begun earlier: the first notes of this reaction were raised in diffident protest against the immense popularity of the

*Enoch Arden* volume of 1864. It is curious to observe the apologetic, tentative way in which the critics, or some of them, ventured to beat against the tide. "It is true," writes a critic in the *British Review* for October 1864, "that at each new gift of Mr. Tennyson to the public the wave of enthusiasm rises higher and higher, until his admirers . . . cease to criticise his talent, and can only heap together epithets of praise and liken the god of their idolatry to all the chief poets of the world in turn. On this occasion, however, we confess, though with fitting diffidence, that we do not share the rapture of Mr. Tennyson's reviewers." With this apology the *British Review* proceeds to the heart of the matter: "We think," it says, "that Mr. Tennyson's remarkable subjection to present and external influences explains, in some degree, both his empire over some, and the indifference to his poetry of other by no means less able judges. . . . His taste follows the fashion of the time, whether for great exhibitions or Gothic manor houses. . . . His preaching—and he is fond of preaching—is tinged by the cheerful paganism of muscular divinity, while his exaltation of doubt above dogma betrays the temper of modern criticism. In short, the age governs Mr. Tennyson's utterances, which are the accepted expression of its complex fashions. . . . Meanwhile, how we enjoy his gifts we need hardly describe to a public whose rapture is so general."

The *Quarterly* for January 1866, no less cautious in the form of its criticism, proceeded in substance to go even further. "Mr. Tennyson," we read, "does not often rejoice us with any sudden irradiation of the darker chambers of the mind; . . . we are obliged to admit that a want of freedom of inspiration is some drawback upon his charm. . . . In many ways the Laureate's work reminds us of that of our very best modern Gothic architects. The edifice is faultless. Every detail shows a delicate taste, and a love and understanding of the best works of the past, while the structure as a whole shows, if not grandeur, at least beauty in its proportions and simplicity in its effects: yet there lacks, after all, the indescribable freshness and vigour which are more often indeed attributes of times and peoples than of individuals." By 1869 the same Review could write as follows: "Mr. Tennyson . . . has not merely been over-praised, but qualities have been ascribed to him the very reverse of his real merits. He has been thought to have a profound original intellect, whereas he has merely a receptive intellect; he has been thought to have dramatic imagination, whereas few poets are more self-contained and self-respective. . . . He has the sobriety of language which is so impressive; but he has not the largeness of grasp . . . there is no long sweep, no single grave conception working itself out in details." And again in 1871 we find the *Quarterly* enunciating the opinion that "what his domestic life has gained in sobriety, his poetry has lost in intensity; and his voice is mild as the sucking dove's when he communes with Nature or rails against mankind."

Already, therefore, by 1871, a certain alteration is to be noticed in the audience to whom the Laureate appealed. Things had changed since the 'fifties; things had changed singularly since 1842; things had changed most of all from the old Cambridge days when the youth of England gloried in their admiration of Tennyson as in some delicious heresy. His later admirers were, of course, infinitely more numerous, but they were old, or at least middle-aged, and most of them, perhaps, were not very well educated. And as the 'eighties approached, the younger generation appeared almost indifferent to the spiritual elevation, the moral repressions, the tender compromises which the Laureate had so often preached and quite as often practised. But the old man up at Aldworth was not so easily dismissed: in his seventy-second year he astonished them all by writing *Rizpah*. He astonished Swinburne more than anyone; and the famous review which the younger poet published in the *Fortnightly* on February 1, 1881, should have gone far to stem the tide of reaction, and to appease the growing fury of the Laureate. Even in this panegyric, however, hidden among the ecstatic tributes which Swinburne tossed hysterically at the feet of the Laureate, there were some bitter wounding thorns. It was not pleasant to find the dying words of King Arthur described as "the last deliberate snuffle of the 'blameless King,'" or as "the acme, the apogee, the culmination of all imaginable cant." It was not fair to have a tender little piece such as *The Ringlet* dragged out and compared unfavourably with the "splendid and showy puberty of a Musset." It was not fair that one's sturdy, sensible remarks upon the condition of England and foreign countries should be described as having "the shrill unmistakable accent, not of a provincial deputy, but of a provincial schoolboy." It was true, perhaps, that one's early poems, largely owing to the omission of hyphens, were sometimes a little difficult to scan; but it was really going too far to say that "there are whole poems of Mr. Tennyson's first period which are no more properly to be called metrical than the more shapeless and monstrous parts of Walt Whitman." Nor, after a lifetime devoted to the study and perfectioning of prosody, to the production of the completed perfection of each line, was it tolerable to be told that: "idler men, or men less qualified and disposed to expend such length of time and energy of patience on the composition and modification, the re-arrangement and revision and reissue, of a single verse or copy of verses, can only look on at such a course of labour with amused or admiring astonishment, and a certain doubt whether the linnets, to whose method of singing Mr. Tennyson compares his own, do really go through the training of such a musical gymnasium before they come forth qualified to sing."

How deeply Tennyson was stirred and angered by the intellectual habits of the rising generation can be gauged from the high-pitched fury of his final invectives. "I tried," we read again, "in my *Idylls* to teach men these things and the need of the Ideal. But I feel sometimes as if my life had been a very useless life." It was all very tragic, and for the moment, at least, it was all very true. He had passed

through toil and storm before he had reached the purer air
in which the figure of his "blameless king" stood out as the
perfect personification of English character. And the young
men of 1880 were saying that King Arthur was not blameless in the least—that he was not even "real," whatever that
might mean; that he was "very German." The young men
of 1880 were wrong—of course they were wrong—and, what
was worse, they were un-English. Yes, that was it; the
whole unhappy business was the fault of those fellows
Baudelaire and Zola. The "poisonous honey" in which these
young men dipped their impudent arrows had been "stolen
from France." He had never liked the French. This proved
that he had been right all along. For did not all this new
shamelessness, this new intellectualism, this unhealthy æs-
theticism, this new nonsense about "art for art's sake"—did
it not all come over to our sweeter, simpler island from the
fœtid, feminine banks of the Seine? Of course it did; and
he would tell them so. After all, he was still the Poet Laureate of England.

And so he told them:—

"Authors—essayist, atheist, novelist, realist, rhymester,
    play your part,
Paint the mortal shame of nature with the living hues
    of Art.

Rip your brothers' vices open, strip your own foul
    passions bare;
Down with Reticence, down with Reverence—for-
    ward—naked—let them stare.

Feed the budding rose of boyhood with the drainage
    of your sewer;
Send the drain into the fountain, lest the stream
    should issue pure.

Set the maiden fancies wallowing in the troughs of
    Zolaism,—
Forward, forward, ay and backward, downward too
    into the abysm."

## II

I have dwelt at some length on the fluctuations which Tennysons's reputation underwent in his own lifetime, not only because it is useful to show how far the Victorian critics anticipated the strictures which are now made against him, but because the shifting taste of his contemporaries furnishes an interesting rubric to his own literary development. We have seen how, until the success of the 1842 volume, he was generally assailed for being diffuse, precious and effeminate; how later the line of attack centred on his alleged obscurity and lack of truth; and how by the 'sixties he was being blamed for the shallowness of his thought and intellect. It is thus interesting to observe how the poet endeavoured to trim his sails to the vacillating breezes of public taste.

We can discover, I think, four distinct phases in Tennyson's literary development. The first, which extends from the "Poems by Two Brothers" in 1827 to the publication of the 1842 volume, represents his luxuriant period—the period in which, whatever people may say, he was under the influence of Keats, and, in a lesser degree, of Coleridge. The poems composed or published between these years are, from a certain point of view, designed to catch the taste of various audiences: there are the Keepsake verses and the domestic idylls for the young ladies, the "classical" poems for the cultured, the "romantic" poems for the literary, the ethical poems for the serious. He sings throughout to "one clear harp in diverse tones," but beautiful as the poems are, there is little impression of any central or directing purpose or inspiration. The second phase, which the first slightly overlaps, begins with the death of Hallam in 1833 and concludes with *Maud* in 1855. To this period, which is clearly the most important of the four, belong *The Two Voices*, and *Break, break, break*, which were actually published in the 1842 volume, *The Princess* in 1847, and *In Memoriam* in 1850. The magnificent *Ode to the Duke of Wellington,* which appeared in 1852, falls also within this period. With 1857 we come to the third, the unfortunate mid-Victorian, phase of Tennyson's development, and we enter upon the series of the *Idylls,* the *Enoch Arden* poems of 1864, *The Holy Grail* of 1870, and the final *Idylls* of 1872. Already, however, by the end of this period there are indications that the advent of Swinburne was leading the Laureate to consider whether a little—a very little—wine might not with advantage be added to the limpid waters of Camelot. The experiment, which was afterwards abandoned, was not very edifying. He wrote *Lucretius:* he wrote:—

> "How the sun delights
> To glance and shift about her slippery sides,
> And rosy knees and supple roundedness,
> And budded bosom-peaks";

he inserted into *The Last Tournament* the following startling indelicacy:—

> "He rose, he turn'd, then, flinging round her neck,
> Claspt it, but while he bow'd himself to lay
> Warm kisses in the hollow of her throat. . . ."

Messrs. Macmillan were appalled. They asked, they begged, the Laureate to suppress these passages. The passages were suppressed. But the former passage, at least, reappeared in the collected edition.

From 1873 onwards there is an interval in which the Laureate was occupied, with amazing obstinacy, in writing plays, but in 1880 the fourth and last period, the splendid Aldworth period, opens with *Ballads and other Poems,* with *Rizpah,* and *Lucknow,* and *De Profundis.* In 1885 we find *Tiresias* and the *Ancient Sage* and the lines to FitzGerald, and the period closes only with the posthumous publication of *The Death of Oenone* in 1892.

It is important, I think, clearly to mark the difference between these four periods. For whereas the early period

has given us things like *Mariana* and *The Lady of Shalott;*
whereas the second period has revealed to us the essential
lyrical inspiration of Tennyson, and convinced us of his
greatness and permanence as a poet; whereas the last period
is a magnificent monument to his vitality and his mastery
of language; the third period, the mid-Victorian period, can
make no appeal whatever to the modern mind. And, unfortunately, it is by this third period, the Farringford period, by the *Idylls* and *Enoch Arden,* that he is now condemned. And that this should be so is both unfair and
unintelligent.

I have decided, therefore, in the pages that follow, to
ignore this third period, as I ignore the plays. It might be
possible, doubtless, to make out a defence for the *Idylls*
and for *Enoch Arden.* The thing had been done (as regards
the *Idylls* at least) quite recently by Dr. Boas for the Royal
Society of Literature. *The Passing of Arthur* is a magnificent
poem, magnificently treated; the story of *Lancelot and
Elaine,* with all its blemishes, is handled with admirable
delicacy; *The Last Tournament,* which is only an idyll in
retrospect, is a remarkable achievement in the creation of
atmosphere. And, after all, the *Enoch Arden* volume, although it contains *Sea Dreams, The Grandmother, The
Ringlet,* and *Aylmer's Field,* contains also *Tithonus* and
*Boadicea.* But in spite of this, it will be wiser, and in the
end fairer to Tennyson, to leave this period for the judgment of future generations. Its effect upon our own can
only, in spite of the magnificent poetry which the *Idylls*
contain, be one of estrangement and hostility, since it is
impossible for us to conquer the impression (doubtless an
incorrect and transitory impression) that these poems of the
Farringford period are for the most part intellectually insincere.

### III

It is obvious that by passing over the Farringford, or
mid-Victorian, element in Tennyson's production, by refus-

ing, except incidentally, to discuss the group of poems which cluster round the *Idylls* and *Enoch Arden,* one has at the outset disposed of what is most liable to offend the susceptibilities of to-day. It may be argued that anyone who sets out to write a monograph on Tennyson has no right to ignore what to many of his contemporaries, and certainly to the poet himself, were the crowning achievements of his genius. My answer is that I have not ignored them: I have mentioned them with due prominence and have admitted their importance as a phase in Tennyson's literary development. I will go further: I will own that personally I enjoy the *Idylls* very much indeed, and that *Enoch Arden,* with the exclusion of the last line, appeals to me as a well-constructed and a moving poem. All I contend is that given the peculiar adjustment to which our nervous system has attained in this year 1923, the mid-Victorian compositions of Tennyson, whatever their intrinsic virtues, are apt to irritate and to estrange; and, as such, at this psychological moment they are best omitted. Even as it is, there is enough, and more than enough, which has got to be explained away.

For if we base our defence of Tennyson on the thesis that all that is worst in his poetry can be ascribed directly to the taste and influence of his age; if we contend that the essential lyrical element in his genius wells up apart from, and indeed in spite of, the clogging, cloying influence of his contemporaries, we are led directly to the task of endeavouring to separate the one from the other, of trying to detach what is permanent from what is merely topical. And this task is more difficult than might at first sight be supposed. For in many of Tennyson's more Victorian compositions there occur, as in *Sea Dreams,* or in *The May Queen*, certain sudden spurts of lyrical beauty; while the silken fabric of many of his sincerest pieces is marred here and there by a thick woollen thread of mid-Victorianism. The more one examines the poems, and even the lyrics, the more is one startled by coming upon these sudden relapses into the conventional, and it is a real shock, for instance, to discover that the maid is called down from yonder mountain heights for the express purpose of founding yet another domestic idyll, or that the haunting music of *Come into the Garden, Maud,* is based on the rhythm of a mid-Victorian polka. The admirer of Tennyson should be warned to avoid the temptation of any such discoveries; for of all poets, Tennyson should be read very carelessly or not at all.

It is my intention, therefore, in this chapter to point out the more Victorian elements in Tennyson's poetry, in the hope that, since their nature and origin have been realised and isolated, they will cease to obscure the essential fabric of his genius. For these elements, I contend, are of parasitic, not of organic growth; and however much they may obscure the vision and disconcert the taste, it should be possible, by indicating where they begin and where they end, to convey some impression of their purely incidental and subsidiary importance.

I propose to group these Victorian elements under the three main headings of love, politics and religion. But before I approach the devastation wrought on Tennyson's poetry by the requirements of his contemporaries from these so comprehensive sources of inspiration, there are certain offshoots from the main tree of Victorianism which it will now be necessary to examine.

IV

As I have said in the opening chapter of this book, the nineteenth century was one of furious and spasmodic movement. The Victorians did not want to be joggled, but they were joggled all the time: it was like looking at life through a kaleidoscope. Conscientiously, carefully, they would adjust their minds to some fresh and startling scheme of existence, when flick! would come another jolt, and a new, even more eccentric, pattern would be interposed between the sun and their perplexed and blinking eyes. Outwardly they pretended to enjoy it immensely: they talked continuously of "our incomparable civilisation," they talked like this very loudly and without ceasing: but in their souls they longed—how passionately they longed!— for all this progress, if only for an hour or so, to stop. It did not stop. It went on. And as they bumped along with it, the Victorians forced their minds to dwell on nice, calm, sedative subjects, such as little birds and clergymen and sunflowers and the purity of the English home.

We find, scattered through the Reviews of the period, plaintive evidences and expressions of such perplexities, of their desire to be soothed and diverted and reassured. They did not want their poets to provide them with tremendous thoughts in a familiar shape, they wanted to be provided with their own familiar thoughts in a form which would appear tremendous. They wanted their poets (I am quoting from the *National Review* of October 1855) to "transport them from the cankering cares of daily life, the perplexities and confusion of their philosophies, the weariness of their haunting thoughts, to some entirely new field of existence, to some place of rest, some 'clear walled city of the sea' where they can draw a serene air undimmed by the clouds and smoke which infest their ordinary existence." The poet, for them, should be there to soothe and reassure, "even as the calm, gentle, self-reliant physician inspires the fevered sufferer." "We ask," continues the *National Review*, "for rest—for passionless calm, and silence unreproved"; and it is for this reason that they applauded Tennyson "for throwing a divine grace over the happier emotions," and for "giving roundness and completeness to those thoughts which were before dimly discerned and half apprehended, but which he for the first time sets before us in their true significance and in their fairest aspect." The last words are illuminating. For whereas the reviewer did not really mean much by his "true significance," he meant a very great deal by his "fairer aspect." What they wanted was, in truth, the "happier emotions." After all, what with democracy and science and atheism, life was ugly and painful enough. It was the function of the poet to assure them that all was really for the best. And thus they insisted on the "happy ending," or the "moral"; and with both of these, in the literature of the period, the Victorians were effusively provided.

We are apt, to-day, to criticise our forbears for their lack of humour. I do not think such a criticism is very helpful or intelligent. For humour, like taste, is an evanescent quality, a mere nervous equilibrium which changes with the fashion of the day. Our present brand of humour has well been defined as "a delighted acceptance of reality." We must recollect that the Victorians did not appreciate reality; it inspired them with feelings the very reverse of delight. What they dealt in was unrealities, and in the end it all amounts to much the same. For if a certain disadjustment of the proportions of any given reality produces in us that friendly cachinnation which we ascribe to a sense of humour, the Victorians, by a no less cunning adjustment of the proportions of unreality, produced the best literature of nonsense which, with the possible exception of Wilhelm Busch, exists in any language. And as sister both to our own sense of humour and to the Victorian genius for nonsense, there is a common rift of sentimentality. We may laugh at the Victorians for admiring *The May Queen;* but we must remember that we ourselves applauded *Mary Rose.*

Although, therefore, I do not admit that the difference between what amuses us and what amused the Victorians is a very important one, it is interesting as an illustration of a far more fundamental divergence—the divergence, that is, between what the two ages regarded and regard as an emotional reality. For whereas we demand primarily from a work of art that it shall render the intrinsic reality of a given personal emotion, and are indifferent to the external reality with which such emotion is conveyed; the Victorians, while terribly concerned with the external accuracy of presentation, were indifferent, and even blind, to the intrinsic reality of the emotion presented. It is not so much a question of ethics (although their ethics were affected by a similar process), as a question of æsthetics, and the manner in which it influenced contemporary literature in general, and Tennyson in particular, is of considerable interest.

## V

I have mentioned "the moral" and "the happy ending." They are obvious expressions of the Victorian mentality, and if they jar unbearably upon your nerves, it is better without further ado to look to some other century for literary enjoyment. More fundamental, perhaps, was the effect of the Victorian compromise upon the quality of imagination. For unless we comprehend this effect, we may fall into the error of conceiving that Tennyson was a man of very deficient imaginative power. Which would not be true.

For the point is that the Victorians preferred the element of "recognition" to that of imagination. It is all very well for us, who are pleasurably stirred by the strong-winged flight of *The Song of Honour*, by the coloured sweep of Flecker, to deride the sedentary complacency of that unhappy generation. The fact is that they were so flustered by all the surprising in life, that they preferred, in literature, to be faced only with the expected. The popularity, some of the popularity, of Tennyson's Nature poetry is to be attributed to this Victorian delight in "recognition." It was with a real pulsating thrill of emotion that they recognised that Tennyson was right—how right!—in stating that the ashbuds in the early weeks of March were almost black in colour; and what, oh what? in Wordsworth could equal the observation, the exact and yet tender observation, which could inspire such poetry as:—

> "But pure as lines of green that streak the white
>   Of the first snowdrop's inner leaves"?

Or:—

> "The spring, that down
> From underneath a plume of lady fern
> Sang, and the sand danced at the bottom of it"?

"No poet," exclaims Mr. Horton, with every justification, "has so many and such accurate references to the vegetable world, and yet at the same time references so poetic."

Not, be it understood, that I should wish to depreciate the sincerity of Tennyson's Nature poetry. He was, as we know, extremely short-sighted, and his observation, acute as it was, smacks often of the microscope. But however deficient his optics, his optical memory was extraordinary. He never forgot the herbaceous borders at Somersby; he never forgot the pines, the lupins, and the waterfalls at Cauteretz; he never forgot the effect, the exact photographic effect, of the waves breaking on the flat sands at Mablethorpe, or on the thrift-enlivened rocks of Tintagel. And even upon our own hectic sensibilities, observation so intense as to equal that of Dorothy Wordsworth, as to amount almost to "earth-worship," has its effect. Nor can we omit the purple irises of Sirmio, and *The Daisy*, and above all, the eternal spirituality of *Flower in the Crannied Wall*.

On Tennyson's Nature poetry there will be much appreciation to be lavished at a later stage; for the moment I am concerned not so much with his personal merits as with the quite impersonal defects which were forced upon him by his age. And more specifically I am dealing with the Victorian distrust of absolute imagination.

For we may observe in dealing with the Nature poetry of Tennyson that he placed accuracy of observation above the more imaginative qualities. The backgrounds of his poems are always scenes or landscapes which he had himself visited; their foregrounds and their similes are drawn from the flowers that he himself had culled. When he is obliged by circumstances to leave the Rectory garden, he proceeds very cautiously indeed: the flora of Bagdad appear vaguely in the *Recollections of the Arabian Nights* as "Eastern flowers large"; *The Voyage of Maeldune,* which takes him necessarily very far from Lincolnshire, Cornwall, or even Cauteretz, does not tempt him to wander from the safe ground of his own experience. The trees met with on that romantic Odyssey are confined to the poplar, the cypress and the pine; the fauna does not extend beyond the lark, the cock, the bull and the dog; the flowers are not more exotic than the clematis, convolvulus, passion-flower, lily, poppy, tulip, gorse and rose; whereas upon the Isle of Fruits are found only such products as might well have graced the dining-room table at Harrington Hall—grapes, melons, figs, plums, pears and apples. As we know, he suppressed *Anacaona* because he was not quite at his ease about the botany of Hayti, and even when he really let himself go in *Locksley Hall,* one feels (for the italics are mine) that the wings of his imagination could not rise for very long or very far above the hollies and the yews of home:—

"Or to burst all links of habit—there to wander far
    away,
On from island unto island at the gateways of the day.

Larger constellations burning, mellow moons and
    happy skies,
Breadths of tropic shade and palms in cluster, knots
    of Paradise.

Never comes the trader, never *floats an European
    flag,*
Slides the bird o'er lustrous *woodland,* swings the
    trailer from the *crag:*

Droops the heavy-blossom'd *bower,* hangs the *heavy-
    fruited tree*—
Summer isles of Eden lying in dark-purple spheres of
    sea."

It is a little distressing, perhaps, to realise the ease with
which one can identify the scenery of Tennyson's dramatic
poems. One quite expects *Enoch Arden* to be based on
Freshwater; one does not mind the scenery of *Oenone* being
drawn from the Valley of Cauteretz; the coincidence that
*Mariana in the South* draws its sense of drought from the
fact that it was written in a diligence near Perpignan is
fitting enough; and the prologue to *The Princess* accords
admirably with Maidstone. But to me, at least, it comes as
a slight shock to learn that the island of *The Lotos-Eaters*
is no more, after all, than an idealised Torquay.

Poetic imagination is a winged quality, and, as such, requires not only freedom, but exercise. In the Victorian era
the wings of fancy were, if not exactly clipped, at least confined within a cage which, though large enough, was very
carefully constructed. The result—the inevitable result—was
bathos and accuracy.

It is unnecessary, perhaps, to dwell at any length upon
the bathos of Tennyson. The concluding line of *Enoch
Arden*, the epilogue to *In Memoriam*, the "Sabbath-morn"
interlude in *The Two Voices* are sufficiently familiar. Such
lines as "he suddenly dropt dead of heart-disease"; such
incidents as the broken tumbler in *Sea Dreams*, "with little
Margaret's medicine in it"; such mistakes as the sudden
immersion of Princess Ida, or the introduction into the last
act of *Becket* of Fair Rosamond disguised as a monk; such
digressions as the "See, what a lovely shell," passage in
*Maud*—have already, and indeed often, been cited against
him. They can be explained away, perhaps, as being instances merely of the sudden lapses which come upon every
poet. More distressing are the occasions on which the sudden failure of Tennyson's visual imagination leads to some
startling incongruity and mars some exquisite poetic passage; for personally I can never forgive the introduction of
the Pilot into the last verse of *Crossing the Bar;* nor can I
believe that the conventions of any age can quite excuse

such an oversight as the following description of the martyr-
dom of St. Stephen:—

> "But looking upward full of grace,
>   He pray'd, and from a happy place
> God's glory smote him in the face."

For, in dealing with this particular incident, the impression
of any additional and quite gratuitous concussion was
surely, of all impressions, the one to be avoided.

Of the accuracy of Tennyson there is little that need be
said. It played an increasing and most deleterious part in
his literary development. As early as 1833 Jack Kemble had
warned Tennyson that "he had a touch of mathematics in
him." As the years progressed the thing became more than
a mere touch: it gripped him like a vice. One has only to
read the notes to the Eversley Edition, to see how constantly he was obsessed by the necessity, if not the desire,
to verify, to substantiate and to explain his references to
the beauties of Nature or the wonders of science. If he
made a mistake, which was not often, he altered the line
in a second edition; if he was unable to alter the line, he
took pains to instruct the reader as to how the mistake arose.
In the first *Locksley Hall*, for instance, he had indulged in
the following simile:—

> "Let the great world spin for ever down the ringing
>   grooves of change."

Most people would have left it at that. Not so Tennyson.
The inspiration of the verse had been drawn from a railway
engine and had been rendered inaccurately; for it appears
that railway engines do not, as he had at first supposed,
run in grooves. So he confesses his mistake in a note: "When
I went by the first train from Liverpool to Manchester
(1830) I thought that the wheels ran in a groove. It was a
black night, and there was such a vast crowd round the
train at the station that we could not see the wheels. Then
I made this line." And again, in *The Princess*, he had re-

ferred to an "April daffodilly." The *Quarterly* at once pointed out that daffodils came in March. "Daffodils," wrote the Laureate in a note to the collected edition, "in the North of England belong as much to April as to March. On the 15th of April in the streets of Dublin I remember a man presenting me with a handful of daffodils."

This obsession of accuracy, being a symptom of the Victorian dislike of imagination, was not so natural to Tennyson as might be supposed. It became a habit with him largely in self-defence. If he made an actual mistake he never heard the end of it: even if he allowed a certain vagueness to enter into one of his descriptions he was for ever pestered by people to explain what, exactly, he had meant. There is a passage in Rawnsley which illustrates this so vividly that it merits quotation:—

"We passed on to speak of the line in *In Memoriam*:—

"'Flits by the sea-blue bird of March.'

"'I don't know,' he answered, 'but I suppose it's the kingfisher.'

"'But,' I rejoined, 'you, with your accuracy of eye, would not speak of any kingfisher as flitting. A kingfisher shoots by, flashes by, but never flits.'

"He smiled and said, 'Yes, you are right, but then what bird could it have been?'

"'Well,' I replied, 'you alone can know that, but there is a bird that does seem in March to shine blue and blue-green with especial brilliancy, by reason, as I think, of the red contrast that has come into the thorn-bush buds. I have often been astonished at the March brightness of the blue tit, and that bird flits.'

"'Well,' said the poet, 'make it a tit: I daresay it was a tit, but I have quite forgotten, and I know I have told other folk it was a kingfisher.'

"The next day we were again sitting on a garden seat in the sun and fell to talking about . . ."

And so Rawnsley goes on and on and on; and our sympathy with the Laureate increases by leaps and bounds.

## VI

I have dealt summarily with these incidental effects of the Victorian spirit upon Tennyson's poetry. It is important to realise how deep and how universal was the current suspicion of the wilder flights of the imagination, how general was the yearning to find in poetry that simpler, sweeter dream-world which their jangled nerves desired. The excitements to which our own age has been exposed are more spectacular, perhaps; they are certainly less intense. For the present generation has grown up with but few illusions left to shatter: we have seen so much already that our eyelids, by now, are more than a little weary; we are resigned in advance to whatever misfortunes the future has in store for us; we have lost our faith in individual endeavour; we are losing our interest in posterity: we are content to cultivate our gardens and to know that there are few things, to-day, which could come to us as a surprise. It was different with the Victorians: they believed, with excruciating conviction, in the value of individual endeavour; they were obsessed with the tremendous responsibility of their own future; and as they watched uneasily the monster civilisation which they had fathered getting more and more beyond their control, they clung despairingly to the pretence that they were a serene generation of happy and enlightened people who knew exactly why and whither it was all progressing, who were delighted to observe that it was all progressing so fast. And it was on the basis of this pretence that Tennyson, the mirror of his age, treated the subjects of love, politics and religion.

# CHAPTER NINE

# LOVE, POLITICS AND RELIGION

## I

The optimism of the nineteenth century was not, in its essence, a very spontaneous quality; there was something
deliberate about it, something almost factitious. The Victorians lived, as Mr. Drinkwater has said, in an atmosphere
of "violent uncertainty." In their trouble they turned, as
timid people turn on such occasions, to subconscious suggestion; they assured themselves that they, and civilisation,
were getting better and better all the time; they assured
themselves of their "unrivalled happiness"; they assured
themselves that never had so pressing a demand for great
political and spiritual leaders been met by so abundant, so
miraculous, a supply; that the millennium was indeed real-
isable, and in fact imminent. As decade followed decade, it
became increasingly difficult for them to repeat this formula
with absolute conviction; it became obvious that something
indefinable was wrong with the condition of England. Their
commercial prosperity, glorious as it was, had brought with
it the increase of the industrial population, and this, in its
turn, was leading to radicalism, to trade unions; nay, even
worse: the discoveries of science, glorious as they were, had
already shaken religious opinion, and were driving men to
atheism or even to Rome; and what was, perhaps, most
disconcerting of all, human nature—that importunate and

stubborn heritage—kept on cropping up in unpleasant ways and in the most unexpected places.

The English race has always, and with justification, prided itself upon a scrupulous regard for truth. There are, however, many foreign observers who consider us to be of all nations the most perfidious and the most hypocritical. This curious misconception has arisen, I think, not from any conscious duplicity in the national character, but from our peculiar, and indeed unique, faculty for ignoring such facts as are unpleasant or inconvenient. The ancient Greeks invented the process of euphemia for occasions when they were obliged to speak of irksome or distressing things; we have carried this process a step further—we endeavour, whenever possible, to pretend that such things are non-existent; we endeavour not to speak of them at all. In this respect the Victorians were even more fortunate than ourselves; for whereas the worst that we can now say against the modern realist is that he displays deplorably bad taste, the Victorians were able triumphantly to escape from truth, if she showed signs of becoming unpleasant, by calling her "arrant cynicism." And, after that, there was no more to be said.

There were three truths, however—three quite unpleasant truths—from which even the Victorians failed to escape with their usual dexterity. There was democracy; there was the growth of unbelief; and there was sex. None of these three problems could be permanently dismissed as non-existent: they were problems which, however unpleasant they might be, it was essential in the end to face. And as the Victorians were singularly averse from facing anything, they approached these three problems obliquely and from the gentler angle of compromise.

## II

Of these three compromises, the one that covered what we call the sex problem was perhaps the most blatant, certainly the most persistent, and, for the moment, the most successful. Their object—and it was wholly laudable—was to discover some middle course between the unbridled licentiousness of previous ages and the complete negation of the functions and purposes of nature. For although they repudiated the voluptuarism of their fathers, although their first editions of Byron were kept, with the French engravings, in a locked drawer, yet the average Victorian (and it is curious how many of them rallied to the average) was not so narrow-minded as to preach the complete, the absolute mortification of the flesh. The doctrine of original sin savoured of the dissenters, or at least of the evangelicals; asceticism would not only be difficult, but even dangerous. It was essential, it was *right*, that the British race should be propagated. With a sigh of hope and of relief they decided that this biological necessity could be elevated into a moral—nay, even a civic—virtue. And in this way they evolved the ideal of the English home.

Tennyson, it will be agreed, was singularly well adapted to the reception and the exploitation of this ideal. He understood clearly, and from the very first, what was required. "In rude ages," says Mr. Horton in his biography of the poet—"in rude ages before marriage is sanctified by being treated as a symbol of the union between Christ and His Church, virginity is exalted as the true purity. But it is impurity that conceives such an ideal. The higher truth is that which the poet saw and constantly celebrated. The ascetic ideal is at the best but a sad thought in bad times. As it is the product of an impure age, so it adds to the impurity of the age which succeeds. It was to be not the least of the lessons to his time, that Tennyson from the first saw Paradise regained not in a monastery, but in a home. . . . Tennyson flung the light of romance over the familiar, and the home shone with unearthly radiance." And Mr. Stopford Brooke, in his discussion of *The Miller's Daughter*, has defined the position with even greater insight: "*The Miller's Daughter*," he writes, "is a simple story of true sweet-hearting and married love, but raised . . . into a steady and grave emotion worthy of a love built to last for life betwixt a man and woman. This was the sort of love for which Tennyson cared, for which Byron and Shelley did not care, which was not in the world where Keats lived at all. . . ."

The value to his contemporaries of Tennyson's treatment of the theme of love was not only that his attitude was uniformly, or almost uniformly, manly: it was also eminently wholesome. For Coventry Patmore, who imagined that he, too, had received a supernatural mandate "to sing the praises of nuptial love," was apt at moments to go a little too far. Yes, there were moments when Patmore was inspired by his subject to become almost sentimental; to become almost mawkish—to become, so to speak, mystical; to become, as one might say, un-English. Tennyson, on the other hand, retained his common-sense throughout. He was, perhaps, aided in this attitude by the fact that, as it appears, he was not himself very sorely exposed to the physical temptations to which he was endeavouring to minister. It is but rarely that we can detect in his poems any convincing note of physical passion. It may have been that he suppressed it; it may also have been that, for him, it did not, in any very persistent or formidable way, exist. For it is with real surprise that one comes, as in the 1832 volume, on such lines as:—

> "My whole soul, waiting silently,
>     All naked in a sultry sky,
>     Droops blinded with his shining eye:
> I *will* possess him or will die.
>         I will grow round him in his place,
>         Grow, live, die looking in his face,
>         Die, dying clasp'd in his embrace."

and it must be remembered that these lines (from the poem originally called *phainetai moi kēnos isos theoisin emmen anēr*, and subsequently re-christened *Fatima*) are, after all, conceived (as were also *Mariana* and the love passage from

*The Sisters* and *Oenone*) as being addressed by a woman to a man, and, as such, they can be only experimental in character. For in general, as in *The Vision of Sin, Lucretius* and that curious lazaretto poem entitled *Happy,* Tennyson concentrated very firmly upon the advantage of spiritual as opposed to physical love. The latter, he feels, should, wherever possible, be avoided: "Arise," he says:—

> "Arise and fly
> The reeling Faun, the sensual feast;
> Move upward, working out the beast,
> And let the ape and tiger die;"

and even in *Maud,* the hero, unbalanced as he was, exclaims:—

> "And most of all would I flee from the cruel madness
>     of love,
> The honey of poison-flowers and all the measureless
>     ill.
> Ah, Maud, you milk-white fawn, you are all unmeet
>     for a wife.
>
> Your mother is mute in her grave as her image in
>     marble above;
> Your father is ever in London, you wander about at
>     your will;
> You have but fed on the roses and lain in the lilies of
>     life."

It was not only his abhorrence of physical passion, his immunity from, or his control over, the coarser instincts of the male, which rendered Tennyson so naturally and so preeminently the poet of the domestic virtues. He possessed another quality; he possessed an almost feminine sympathy for the tender delicacies of the home. We have seen how, when a young man of twenty-three, he had proclaimed his preference for his own bedroom at Somersby over the more romantic allurements of a tour (even with Arthur Hallam)

LOVE, POLITICS AND RELIGION 249

on the Rhine. He was throughout his life to retain this instinctive preference; and indeed it was painful for him (at
least in his published works) to contemplate even the possibility of any relation between man and woman other than
the conjugal. The "shadows of the world," the reflection of
which so distressed the Lady of Shalott, included, it is true,
"two young lovers" walking together in the moonlight; but
we are at once reassured by the statement that these two
lovers were "lately wed." The maiden who, in *The Princess*,
is invited to find Love in the valley, is guaranteed at the
same time that she will be soothed on arrival by "the azure
pillars of the hearth"; and the love potion which caused
Lucretius to be visited by such remorseless visions, deleterious as it indubitably proved, was, after all, administered
to him by his wife. More curious even is the ultimate fate
of Oenone, who, although for sixty years she was allowed
to wander as a gentle little pagan among the respectable
English couples with which Tennyson peopled his intervening poems, was in the end caught and married, somewhat
posthumously, to Paris, who, whatever his subsequent ex-
travagances, had, after all, been "once her playmate on the
hills." One is sorry for Oenone. Even Mr. Stopford Brooke
is sorry for Oenone. "Nor do I understand," he writes, "the
husband and wife and widow business, unless it be that
Tennyson desired to express once again his devotion to the
eternity and sanctity of the marriage relation. This is wholly
out of place in the story. The union between Paris and the
nymph Oenone was not a marriage, nor anything that re-
sembled it."

    There are moments, such as this, when one is apt to
consider that domesticity was for Tennyson not so much an
ideal as an obsession. It is curious, for instance, to observe
how constantly, in his abhorrence of the illicit, he throws
a domestic atmosphere even over the preconjugal relations
of his characters. The young men and women of Tennyson's
stories are rarely allowed even the legitimate adventure of
selection: they are pledged to each other from their child-

hood. In almost every case they are either closely related or have played at man and wife together in the nursery. "When Harry an' I were children, he call'd me his own little wife"—such, more or less, is the prelude to nine out of ten of all the Laureate's romances. And for this purpose—for the purpose, that is, of giving a tender and wholly spiritual savour to his love-stories—the device works well enough.

It is absurd, of course, to suggest that Tennyson was prevented by his idealisation of the domestic from writing any love poetry of importance. The songs from *The Princess,* the whole of *Maud,* are of themselves sufficient to disprove such a contention. All that can be advanced—and I advance it rather indignantly—is that Tennyson would have written even better love poetry had he aimed at some adequate reality of emotion, had he been unhampered by the shackles of his own unhealthy compromise. It may be doubted, perhaps, whether the spirit of Poetry, a spirit in its essence winged for some divine excess, could, in any circumstances, find affinity with the spirit of compromise, whose only purpose is the negation of excess. But the gulf between the two becomes wide indeed when one realises—as one is forced in the present instance to realise—that the particular compromise, even as a compromise, was insincere, selfish and unintelligent. The eternal struggle between the spiritual and the material, between soul and sense, is not one which can be gaily brushed aside by fusing sense with sentimentality. We could have nothing but admiration for Tennyson had he succeeded in the difficult, but by no means impossible, task of conveying in his poetry some tenable or inspiriting theory of the institution of marriage. There are passages, indeed, in *The Princess* which furnish grounds for supposing that he himself was capable of visualising the relationship in proportions which are broad, interesting and unconventional. What we resent is that he should have consented to incorporate in his poetry the current Victorian fallacies as to the relation of the sexes, and to preach a compromise which has little justification either in honesty or even in eugenics.

For although, in *The Princess*, Tennyson showed clearly that he realised the illogical basis on which the relations of the sexes then rested, yet he deliberately set himself in all his other poems to perpetuate those fallacies, and was careful to provide the excuse that *The Princess* was merely "gamesome" and a "burlesque," and was not—of course it was not—to be taken seriously. And, indeed, the subsequent heroines of Tennyson bear as little resemblance to the Princess Ida as "moonlight unto sunlight, or as water unto wine." And what exasperates is that Tennyson had conceived Ida quite honestly, so that his subsequent repudiation of her can only be ascribed to cowardice.

The real and typical Tennysonian heroine is made of far daintier stuff. As early as the days of Lady Clara, he had expressed the view that:—

> "A simple maiden in her flower
>      Is worth a hundred coats-of-arms."

This opinion can scarcely be contested, but the ideal Victorian heroine was not only simple: she was also meek. Even as the astonished consort of the Lord of Burleigh, the representative Victorian wife:—

> "Shaped her heart with woman's meekness
>      To all duties of her rank;
> And a gentle consort made he,
>      And her gentle mind was such
> That she grew a noble lady,
>      And the people loved her much."

Such a result was admirable, and indeed any other course would have led to "confusion." The woman's place was the hearth; all extraneous interests and ambitions were ridiculous, and, what was more, pretentious: nature had ordained otherwise:—

> "Man for the field and woman for the hearth:
> Man for the sword and for the needle she:
> Man with the head and woman with the heart:
> Man to command and woman to obey;
> All else confusion."

The Victorian conception of marriage, of which to-day we suffer the inevitable result, appears to us as a dishonest and a selfish theory evolved by man for the greater comfort and satisfaction of his own sex. To the average Victorian husband, marriage came as the ultimate solution, the ultimate "hushing-up," of what might or might not have been a self-indulgent youth. Its dominant constituent was not romance, or even abnegation, but calm and comfort, and for him:—

> "The kiss,
> The woven arms, seem but to be
> Weak symbols of the *settled* bliss
> The *comfort* I have found in thee."

The italics are mine. The sentiment is wholly Tennyson's. The sentiment is similar to that which inspired him to write such devastating and jaunty lines as:—

> "Love for the maiden, crowned with marriage, no regrets for aught that has been,
> Household happiness, gracious children, debtless competence, golden mean."

And the woman? The woman was advised, if she questioned this arrangement, to repeat to herself: "I cannot understand; I love!"

And we, who have had to suffer for this fallacy, can only regard as an indefensible apostasy that the man who pandered to this illusion was the man who realised, who wrote, the following:—

> "At last
> She rose upon a wind of prophecy
> Dilating on the future; 'everywhere
> Two heads in council, two beside the hearth,

Two in the tangled business of the world,
Two in the liberal offices of life,
Two plummets dropt for one to sound the abyss
Of science, and the secrets of the mind:
Musician, painter, sculptor, critic, more;
And everywhere the broad and bounteous Earth
Should bear a double growth of those rare souls,
Poets, whose thoughts enrich the blood of the world!' "

### III

The attitude which Tennyson adopted towards the foreign and domestic politics of his time is so curious and so
characteristic that it also merits detailed treatment. It is
unnecessary, I suppose, to summarise the startling, and indeed fundamental, changes which took place in the life and
constitution of the British Isles and Empire between the
date of the composition of the first *Locksley Hall*, in the
early 'thirties, and the publication of the second *Locksley
Hall* in 1886. During those fifty-five years the English body
politic had passed from the phase of aristocratic Whiggism,
through a sound phase of middle-class Liberalism, to the
achievement of democracy as we enjoy it to-day; during
those fifty-five years Tennyson, for his part, passed from an
early suspicion of democracy, through a wholesome dislike
of democracy, to a loathing of democracy so fierce and so
violent that it upset not only his health and his temper, but
even his prosody.

In a sense the early Tennyson, the Tennyson of 1831, was
in advance of his time; for whereas his Cambridge contemporaries waited for middle age before repudiating
"that deep chord which Hampden smote," Tennyson became a reactionary at the age of twenty-two. The early
enthusiasm which had led him to ring the church bells at
Somersby on hearing of the passing of the Reform Bill had
already received a severe shock from the French Revolution
of July, and was not to survive our own rickfire days, or
that mysterious interview with Señor Ojeda in the Pyrenees.

Not that the Tennysonian reaction was ever carried to excess: he was careful never to give himself wholly away. The praise of freedom and progress was in the best tradition of English poetry; the muse of Liberty was one that could not wholly be ignored. He did not ignore her. He hedged. He was all for Liberty so long as she remained English and "sober-suited" and well behaved; and even when, at moments, he began to despair of her behaviour, he never disputed her undoubted qualities. He suggested merely that, however admirable, she was perhaps a little premature; he suggested that, if she would only wait "ten thousand years," she could then behave exactly as she liked. And thus, when people asked him for his opinion on the condition of England, he would reply: "I am of the same politics as Shakespeare, Bacon and every sane man." And there was obviously no more to be said.

For, indeed, Tennyson's views upon the principle of governance never advanced, in spite of the superficial influences of Coleridge, the Cambridge Apostles, and even Carlyle, beyond the opinions which he had imbibed at Somersby Rectory. They remained the views of any provincial squire; they are based upon the old territorial and not on the new industrial system. There is the instinctive distrust of the growing commercial aristocracy which is reflected in *Maud*; the instinctive worship of the older territorial aristocracy which we get in *The Lord of Burleigh* and other decorative poems. There is the same complacent confidence in the old order, the easy conviction that, provided the squire justified the privileges by fulfilling the duties of his position, all was really, and indeed gloriously, for the best. Although, therefore, he has little to say in defence of Sir Aylmer Aylmer, who was but one of:—

> "These old pheasant lords
> These partridge-breeders of a thousand years,"

yet Edith Aylmer, his daughter, who would visit bed-ridden women in their cottages and show them how to grow mignonette, appeared to him to represent not only an elegant, but also a practical solution of our social difficulties; and Sir Walter Vivian, with his collection of snowshoes, his models of Papuan lifeboats, his melons, his pineapples and his pamphlets on guano, had set his feet courageously on the ladder of enlightened progress by allowing the Maidstone Mechanics Institute to let off fire-balloons in his park:—

> "Why should not these great Sirs
> Give up their parks some dozen times a year
> To let the people breathe?"

And Tennyson concludes decisively that they should.

Although, however, the poet was pleased to delude himself by these facile compromises, although he endeavoured to ignore the menacing tide of the industrial population, and to solace his uneasiness by prescribing common-sense for the poor and district-visiting for the rich, we can trace, even in his earliest poems, an uneasy suspicion that things were beginning, and with distressing rapidity, to move. "Slowly," he had written in the first *Locksley Hall*:—

> "Slowly comes a hungry people, as a lion creeping nigher,
> Glares at one that nods and winks behind a slowly-dying fire."

But was it slow, after all? It was all very well for him to write in 1833 of:—

> "A land of settled government,
>     A land of just and old renown
>     Where Freedom slowly broadens down
> From precedent to precedent."

He was not sure—he was not wholly sure—that this represented any very convincing description of the England of 1833; he was not sure that the moment had not come when

it would be desirable and preferable to go, or at least to *be*,
somewhere else:—

> "Should banded unions persecute
>     Opinion, and induce a time
>     When single thought is civil crime,
> And individual freedom mute;
>
> Tho' Power should make from land to land
>     The name of Britain trebly great—
>     Tho' every channel of the State
> Should fill and choke with golden sand—
>
> Yet waft me from the harbour mouth,
>     Wild wind! I seek a warmer sky
>     And I will see before I die
> The palms and temples of the south."

This threat of emigration was never executed. Tennyson
remained in England. But as the years passed, his dislike
of what was coming, his dislike of what eventually came,
grew more and more vocal. Already before 1840 we find
him uttering a note of warning against "raw haste"; expressing the hope that the British electorate will not imitate "the
red fool-fury of the Seine"; preaching against the "falsehood
of extremes"; and begging his contemporaries to "regard
gradation." As the years passed, he decided that it was not
enough to progress slowly: one must also cultivate disci-
pline, loyalty and common-sense; one must cultivate:—

> "That sober freedom out of which there springs
>     Our loyal passion for our temperate kings";

and however "scared" one might be by the signs of storm,
by "wordy trucklings to the transient hour," by "Labour
with a groan and not a voice," one could, one should, find
solace in the thought of:—

>                                   "our slowly-grown
>     And crown'd Republic's crowning common-sense
>     That saved her many times."

With middle and later age he felt emboldened to express his views with greater self-confidence. It was not the people of England who were at fault: they were sound enough— the agricultural population especially. "Plowmen," he wrote in 1886,

> "Plowmen, Shepherds have I found, and more than
>     once, and still could find,
> Sons of God, and kings of men in utter nobleness of
>     mind."

Such encounters, such sentiments as these, proved, as he pointed out in a note to this passage, that he did not "by any means dislike democracy." No, the people were all right: it was all the fault of the politicians; it was the fault of "all the yells and counter-yells of feud and faction"; it was the fault of the "tonguesters": in the deluge of their demagogy they had succeeded "in drowning old political common-sense"; they had killed the love of man for man; they were directly responsible for the evil conditions of the poor; they had "pilloried Wisdom in their markets"; they had "pelted their offal in her face." "Are we devils?" inquires the poet in the second *Locksley Hall*. "Are we men?" And oh! Oh:—

> "Sweet St. Francis of Assisi, would that he were here
>     again."

He wasn't: there was only Mr. Gladstone. And Mr. Gladstone was stung to the quick by the invectives of the second *Locksley Hall*. He wrote a defence of his age in the *Nineteenth Century*. He explains that the politicians had since 1830 achieved many and considerable improvements; he outlines these improvements in a very stately and convincing manner; he leaves the facts, the records of legislation, to speak for themselves. He does not attack the Laureate for his views; he says only that "the voice of our Prophet in this poem, if taken as a whole, has undergone a change. . . . Perhaps the tone may even, at times, be thought to have grown a little hoarse with his years." And in any case he concludes that "justice does not require—nay, rather she forbids—that the jubilee of the Queen be marred by tragic tones."

But the tones, after all, were not wholly tragic. The Poet Laureate was too conscious of his age to fail to supplement the bitter pill of criticism with the jam of consolation. For, terrible as was the condition of England, we could all of us help, each in his own way, to make it better. It was the privilege of the Laureate to inspirit as well as to upbraid: "Clara," he had advised in the later 'thirties:—

> "Clara, Clara Vere de Vere,
>     If time be heavy on your hands,
> Are there no beggars at your gate,
>     Nor any poor about your lands?
> Oh! teach the orphan-boy to read,
>     Or teach the orphan-girl to sew——"

This was good advice. He repeated it all his life: he repeated it on the occasion of Queen Victoria's Jubilee:—

> "You, that wanton in affluence,
>     Spare not now to be bountiful,
> Call your poor to regale with you,
>     All the lowly, the destitute,
> Make their neighbourhood healthfuller,
>     Give your gold to the Hospital,
> Let the weary be comforted,
> Let the needy be banqueted,
> Let the maimed in his heart rejoice
>     At this glad Ceremonial,
>     And this year of the Jubilee."

And even the bitterness of the second *Locksley Hall* ends, as Mr. Stopford Brooke points out, "with an excellent morality." For we are there assured that "Love" (whatever the Laureate meant by that) "will conquer at the last."

It is sad, and very irritating, when we reflect upon all

this Victorian cant, upon all this selfish and timid adherence to the economic fallacy of *laisser-faire*, to remember that Robert Owen had perfected his experiment at the New Lanark Mills fully ten years before Tennyson had even gone to Cambridge. And that the Apostles, doubtless, had never heard of Robert Owen.

## IV

I have indicated how Tennyson, in his attitude towards the domestic politics of the day, reflected the prejudices, solaced the anxiety, and assuaged the conscience of the vast public by whom his poems were purchased and admired. I do not pretend that in regard to politics his "message" was forced upon him by the requirements of his age: we must admit, I fear, that his political poems welled up from the clear spring of personal conviction. The most that can be said in favour of his attitude, is that it was shared by a great number of people who, while no less high-minded than Tennyson, were better educated and informed than he was himself. For the extent to which the Victorians misinterpreted and mishandled the phenomena of their age is an historical disaster. And we must leave it at that.

In the region of foreign and imperial politics Tennyson was equally the product of the Victorian upper middle class. It needed the Great War, and one of the most poignant incidents of the Great War, to convince our own generation that "patriotism was not enough." The Victorians were serenely convinced that patriotism was all-sufficient, that it was the highest civic virtue; and this conviction flourishes in the poetry of their Laureate. At its best, the patriotic poetry of Tennyson, as indirectly in *The Revenge* and in *Lucknow*, as more directly in the *Wellington Ode* and in *The Fleet*, is of the highest order. His sense of England, of her achievements and her responsibilities, is in the main magnificent. Nor can we omit the splendid passage from *Tiresias:—*

"No sound is breathed so potent to coerce,
  And to conciliate, as their names who dare
  For that sweet mother land which gave them birth
  Nobly to do, nobly to die. Their names,
  Graven on memorial columns, are a song
  Heard in the future."

Had Tennyson confined himself to sentiments such as these, his contribution to the patriotic poetry of England would have been beyond all criticism. The complete assurance of his country's moral and physical supremacy, which goes well enough to such lines as:—

"her voice
  And meaning, whom the roar of Hougoumont
  Left mightiest of all peoples under heaven,"

degenerates with other passages into arrant jingoism. For on such matters he was ignorant, fire-eating and insular. Like the Tory member's elder son in the prologue to *The Princess,* he thanked God for the seas which kept "our Britain whole within herself." The mere mention of the Channel tunnel would send him into a frenzy. His attitude to foreigners was as simple as that of Sir Richard Grenville himself, and in the 'fifties he did his best to drive us into war with Napoleon III. Take the following as a specimen of English patriotic verse:—

"We quarrel here at home, and they plot against us
      yonder,
    They will not let an honest Briton sit at home at
      ease:
  Up, Jack Tars, my hearties! And the d—l take the
      parties!
    Up! and save the pride of the Mistress of the Seas!
      Up, Jack Tars! and save us!
      The whole world shall not brave us!
    Up! and save the pride of the Mistress of the Seas!"

Nor are *Britons Guard your Own, Hands all Round,* which
he wrote with tears of emotion, and *Rifleman Form,* although they inspired the Volunteer movement, on a much
higher level than the above verses.

Apart from what Swinburne called "his strident anti-
Gallican cackle," Tennyson's interest in foreign countries
and politics, unless there seemed some chance of a jolly
good war, was at most apathetic. The sonnet to *Poland* is an
early work, the sonnet to *Montenegro* was purely incidental.
The great struggle for Italian freedom and unity left him
almost unmoved. "He had," we learn from the diary of Mrs.
Rundle Charles, "read a poem of mine on Italy. He said he
felt 'great interest in the Italian movement, as in all movements for freedom; that perhaps all looked equally disor-
derly as they arose.' We went into the drawing-room. I
played Mendelssohn. . . ." And after that apparently the
Italian movement was left to look after itself.

In Imperial questions his attitude was more defensible—
one might almost call it advanced. He shared, of course,
the current convictions of the white man's burden: he was
convinced that subject races naturally preferred good
British government to bad self-government; he flaunted oc-
casionally in the gold and purple of Empire; and he was not
above such lines as the following:—

> "You saw the league-long rampart fire
>     Flare from Tel-el-Kebir
> Thro' darkness, and the foe was driven.
>     And Wolseley overthrew
> Arabi, and the stars in heaven
>     Paled, and the glory grew."

But he bitterly regretted the way the previous generation
had handled the American question. He urged his country,
"strong Mother of a Lion-line," to:—

> "Be proud of those strong sons of thine
>     Who wrenched their rights from thee";

he urged her to be very careful that it didn't happen again; and he possessed and inculcated a quite definite idea of the Commonwealth of English-speaking nations. For assuredly these lines, written for the opening of the Indian and Colonial Exhibition, are salutary and sensible enough:—

> "Britain fought her sons of yore—
>     Britain fail'd; and never more,
>     Careless of our growing kin,
>     Shall we sin our fathers' sin,
>     Men that in a narrower day—
>     Unprophetic rulers they—
>     Drove from out the mother's nest
>     That young eagle of the West
>     To forage for herself alone;
>         Britons, hold your own!
>
> Sharers of our glorious past,
>     Brothers, must we part at last?
>     Shall we not thro' good and ill
>     Cleave to one another still?
>     Britain's myriad voices call,
>     'Sons, be welded each and all,
>     Into one imperial whole,
>     One with Britain, heart and soul!
>     One life, one flag, one fleet, one Throne!
>         Britons, hold your own!' "

## V

"Mr. Tennyson's development," wrote the *Edinburgh Review* in 1881, "has coincided with two great events: the growth in England of the modern democratic principle and the general diffusion of modern religious scepticism." In the last section I have endeavoured to show how Tennyson, faithfully reflecting the anxieties of his public, viewed the rise of democracy with dislike and apprehension, and how he strove to sweeten such disturbing feelings with the sugar of human optimism and the milk of human compromise. His attitude towards the problem of faith and doubt, although more intense and painful, was not dissimilar.

It was fortunate for Tennyson that the theological controversies of his age were restricted, if not simplified, for him by the fact that he had gone to Cambridge. He escaped the Oxford Movement. He was not unduly troubled in those early years by such problems as the Council of Trent, or the doctrine of Apostolic Succession, or the Thirty-nine Articles; he was not exposed to the hectic atmosphere of Oriel Common Room, to the gentle eloquence of Newman, or the boisterous conviction of Hurrell Froude. Unlike his friend Ward, he did not feel forced to decide whether Arnold was right when he said that Tractarianism would end in popery, or whether Pusey was right when he foresaw that the logical outcome of the latitudinarian tendency was free thought; he was not exposed to the conclusion—the terrible conclusion—that both Arnold and Pusey were undeniably correct in their respective forecasts; he did not, like Clough, accidentally mislay his faith in the tangle of all these subsidiary controversies and spend the rest of a puzzled and unhappy existence in trying to recover it. He was able from the outset to face the problem in its essentials; he was not distracted from the central issue between doubt and faith by feeling obliged to read the Early Fathers or the Caroline Bishops, or even, we may hazard, "Tracts for the Times."

The theology of the Cambridge Movement was of a broader, and, we may add, of a vaguer character. Trinity, no less than Oriel, had felt the need of some spiritual reaction against the materialism of Bentham and the elder Mill; the Cambridge Apostles were equally convinced that some principle more vivifying than Evangelicalism was necessary if the Church was to recover from the lethargy into which it had fallen; but whereas the Oxford Movement was based on an emotional appeal to the authority of the past, the Cambridge Movement aimed at an intellectual appeal to the opportunities of the future. Thus, while the Puseyites

rummaged in agonised perplexity among the writings of
S. T. Coleridge. And in the end it was the Puseyites who
were found perhaps to have chosen the happier path. For
whereas the Early Fathers, the doctrine of authority, and
the appeal to the emotions led the more honest of the Trac-
tarians to the secure haven of the Church of Rome, the
theologians of Cambridge, the adherents of Arnold and
Whately at Oxford, having once admitted the applicability
of intellect and reason to theological discussion, having once
allowed the evidence of science and historical criticism,
were driven to the open sea; and as the century progressed
and the blasts of science and historical criticism became
more and more violent, these broader theologians had a
very trying time indeed. Some of them lost their faith completely; a few relapsed into a mystic form of theism; many
became merely agnostic; others, like F. D. Maurice, fell
back on the comforting if rather insecure theory that in the
end would come "the sure triumph of order, beauty and
love over confusions, divisions and hatred." But the great
majority—the vast perplexed majority—were frightened and
appalled by the logical position in which they found themselves. They desired to be assured that all was really for
the best; they desired to discover some compromise which,
while not outraging their intellect and their reason, would
none the less soothe their conscience and restore their faith
—if not completely, at least sufficiently to allow them to
believe in some ultimate purpose and, more important still,
in the life after death.

In voicing these doubts, in phrasing the inevitable compromise, Tennyson found, and endeavoured passionately to
fulfil, his appointed mission.

"Compromise," writes Mr. Stephen Gwynn in his brilliant
study of the Laureate, "is never very picturesque, and
Tennyson, British in this as well as in everything else, held
in religion to what was essentially a compromise." It was;
but it was not a facile or a feeble compromise, such as those
which he evolved for politics and love: it was a compromise

which caused him bitter searchings of heart, and devastating reactions, and agonising uncertainties. Nor can the mental suffering through which he attained to it, and the recurrent pangs of doubt which assailed him even after it had been attained, fail to throw over the whole process an atmosphere of sincerity which raises his theological poems far above the ordinary level of his other didactic work. We may, perhaps, question the logical and intellectual strength of the position he adopted, we may even feel out of sympathy with the problems which he raised: we may feel that at the end he erects a very convincing structure on the side of doubt and a very flimsy structure on the side of faith; but we cannot deny that he approached the subject in bitter earnestness, and that the solution which he evolved, though to us but a compromise, was for many of his generation a final and courageous answer to the moral uncertainties by which they were tormented.

## VI

The problem which Tennyson set himself to solve was in its essence that of reconciling science with religion. It was not an easy problem. For whereas religious revelation remained where it was, the scientists evolved some new and startling revelation every few months. It was difficult to know what to do. To draw back would imply a recognition of defeat; to go forward might—— Tennyson refused to contemplate what might happen if one went forward. He decided to remain where he was. At Cambridge he had faced undismayed the discovery that the first chapter of Genesis was scientifically inaccurate. He endeavoured throughout his life to face other and more disconcerting discoveries with similar equanimity. He was not very successful. In his later theological poems one can detect a note here and there of something akin to panic, and often, very often, a note of indignation—a note, even, of injured fury, at the cursed

spite which had landed him, without his asking, in so perplexing a position.

The vast majority of his contemporaries were confronted
with the same dilemma. They desired, in the spirit of the
time, to be liberal and broad-minded; so did Tennyson.
They were prepared—nay, anxious—to look beyond the dis-
putes of creed and dogma to something higher and more essential; Tennyson, from the first, had recommended just
such an attitude. They were anxious not to be dismayed by
the progress of science; Tennyson also felt that science was
both fruitful and important. They were determined not to
lose their ultimate faith in a Supreme Power, and in the life
after death; Tennyson shared and voiced this determination with passionate intensity. He went further: he showed
them, in *St. Simeon Stylites,* that the truly religious man
was the man of action; he showed them in *The Holy Grail*
that religion would lose rather than gain if they neglected
their business interests; he told them that their doubts, if
"honest," were more admirable than the superficial convictions of the less enlightened; he preached to them the importance of the individual, the actuality, within limits, of
Free Will, the survival of human personality, the immortality of the soul. He advised them, in their moments—their
inevitable and quite praiseworthy moments—of hesitation,
to keep to the "sunnier side of doubt," to "cling to Faith
beyond the forms of Faith," to trust in the "hidden hope,"
to look to:—

> "One far-off divine event
> To which the whole creation moves."

All this would have been very comforting and conclusive
if he had been able to convince himself. But he was not
able; and the interest—the very real interest—of Tennyson's
religious poetry resides not in the compromise with which
he sought to appease the anxieties of his generation, but
in the doubts which he himself raised as to the validity
of that compromise. For by temperament (as is proved by

his unending experiments in personality and by the "weird seizures" which they provoked) Tennyson was a mystic; it was only through circumstances that he became a casuist.

The realities of space and time, which astronomy and geology, those "terrible muses," were inculcating, filled him with dismay. Even as Pascal before him, he gazed in terror on the infinite silence of the stars:—

> "Innumerable, pitiless, passionless eyes,
>     Cold fires, yet with power to burn and brand
>     His nothingness into man. . . ."

Even as his own Lucretius, he saw:—

> "The flaring atom-streams
>     And torrents of her myriad universe
>     Running along the illimitable inane."

And it was with a feeling akin to despair that he "knew that their light was a lie":—

> "Bright as with deathless hope—but however they
>         sparkled and shone,
>     The dark little worlds running round them were
>         worlds of woe like our own."

The sense of time, the sense of human life "whirl'd for a million æons through the vast," would descend upon him at moments in a cloud of oppression, and crush all faith in human personality, crush utterly all faith in any Victorian compromise.

> "What is it all, if we all of us end in being our own
>         corpse-coffin at last,
>     Swallow'd in Vastness, lost in Silence, drown'd in the
>         deeps of a meaningless Past?"

We find him throughout his life endeavouring in anguish to rid himself of this obsession of Space and Time, of this crushing immensity, of this dread of eventual annihilation. We find him at times endeavouring to deny the evidence of

his own senses, endeavouring to convince himself that what
he knew and saw was no more than a "subjective condition
of our sensibility." For after all, he argues, how can we
know to prove the unknowable? What are we but children
crying in the night? And what is knowledge but:—

> "Half grown as yet, a child and vain
>     She cannot fight the fear of death.
>     What is she, cut from love and faith,
> But some wild Pallas from the brain
> Of Demons?"

Or again:—

> "For Knowledge is the swallow on the lake
>     That sees and stirs the surface shadow there
>     But never yet hath dipt into the abysm,
>     The Abysm of all Abysms. . . ."

But, supposing there wasn't any Abysm to dip into? Supposing that it was faith, and not infinity, which constituted
the "subjective condition of our sensibility"? What was there
then on which the weary human heart could fall for comfort? At moments he is able to find some solace, some temporary conviction, in the formula, "God is love." He is able
to know:—

> "altho' no tongue can prove,
> That every cloud that spreads above
> And veileth love, itself is love,"

and to feel that:—

> "Love himself will bring
> The drooping flower of knowledge changed to fruit
> Of wisdom. Wait: my faith is large in Time
> And that which shapes it to some perfect end."

But even in *In Memoriam*, of which this theory of Love
constitutes the central theme, he is confronted with the
problem of how to reconcile the supremacy of the Spirit

of Love with the existence of evil. Nature herself, God's living manifestation on earth, is "red in tooth and claw," is "one with rapine." "An omnipotent Creator," he said, "who could make such a painful world is to me sometimes as hard to believe in as to believe in blind matter behind everything." And thus he makes his hero in *Despair* exclaim:—

"Ah, yet—I have had some glimmer, at times, in my
        gloomiest woe,
Of a God behind all—after all—the great God for
        aught that I know;
But the God of Love and of Hell together—they can-
        not be thought,
If there be such a God, may the Great God curse him
        and bring him to nought."

And yet, in spite of all these doubts and terrors, it was not possible—it was intolerable!—to conceive of a Godless world whirling through space towards a purposeless annihilation. The "black negation of the bier" was not a negation that could be accepted; the "sacred passion of a second life" was implanted too firmly in the human soul. One could not, one should not, ignore this "heat of inward evidence":—

"Not only cunning casts in clay:
        Let Science prove we are, and then
        What matters science unto men
At least to me? I would not stay.

Let him, the wiser man who springs
        Hereafter, up from childhood shape
        His action like the greater ape,
But I was *born* to other things."

For what, in fact, was knowledge of the external universe compared with the soul's instinct and intuition? What could science avail against man's intuitive conviction of a divine purpose, the conviction which wells up from the soul of man:—

"In moments when he feels he cannot die,
And knows himself no vision to himself,
Nor the high God a vision, nor that One
Who rose again. . . ."

It was not only good to believe in the immortality of the
soul, it was necessary, it was essential, it was inevitable.
No other conception was possible or tolerable; on no other
understanding could one continue to live in hope and virtue:—

"By night into the deeper night!
The deeper night? A clearer day
Than our poor twilight dawn on earth—
If night, what barren toil to be!
What life, so maim'd by night, were worth
Our living out? Not mine to me . . ."

## VII

We observe, therefore, in Tennyson's treatment of the
religious questions a very interesting psychological process.
There can be no doubt, I think, that what he intended to
do, what he longed to do, was to evolve the happy compromise that "God is love." Had he allowed himself to be a
subjective religious poet, to the extent that Christina Rossetti or George Herbert were religious poets, he would have
floated off into a mystic ecstasy over this conception and
remained for ever entranced and beatific. Had he been a
hard-headed objective thinker, had he possessed any "insight into the devouring fact," had he possessed even
average *dianoia*, he would have thought *through* his perplexities and achieved some definite and absolute position—
either the grace of faith or the courage of agnosticism. But
he achieved neither the one thing nor the other. The practical circumstances by which he was surrounded obliged him
to repudiate mysticism; his nervous temperament quailed
before logic. He wandered despondently round and round

his own conceptions—with belief at moments, with a gloomy half-belief generally, and at moments in the bitter despair of active doubts. For if God so loved the world, why was the world both evil and unhappy? Why were there other worlds, myriads and myriads of other worlds, which must also claim the affection of this God of Love? It was all very well for Browning, that robust and bustling casuist, to exclaim:—

> "There's heaven above: and night by night
> I look right through its glorious roof."

Browning was made of sterner stuff. Tennyson would also, from the little platform on the roof of Farringford, gaze upon the "illimitable inane"; but it did not convince him that all was right with the world: it convinced him only that he must find some more effective compromise than "God is love." He therefore evolved the formula, the pathetically inadequate formula, that God must exist because the human heart felt an instinctive need of His existence; that the soul must be immortal because any other solution was unthinkable. "It is hard," he said, "to believe in God, but it is harder not to believe. I believe in God, not from what I see in nature, but from what I find in man." "I would rather," he said, "know that I was to be lost eternally, than not to know that the human race was to live eternally."

As a philosophical formula, as a logical statement even, these conclusions which Tennyson ultimately adopted are obviously defective; but according as his "message" loses its consistency, his poetry at once gains in interest. For whereas in such matters as love and politics Tennyson had no doubts as to the truth and value of his compromise, and delivered his message in a jaunty and complacent manner which strikes us as both foolish and irritating, yet on religious matters the compromise which he had hoped to evolve broke down before the depth and honesty of his own bitter perplexities, and the result is that we have, not the

objective enunciation of a doctrine, but the subjective confessions of a tortured human soul. And thus there are passages in some of his religious poems in which the essential
Tennyson, in which his sombre emotional genius, emerges
again, austere and tragic, above the little futile expedients
of optimism which had veiled him from our sight.

"That which we dare invoke to bless;
    Our dearest faith; our ghastliest doubt;
    He, They, One, All; within, without;
The Power in darkness whom we guess;

I found Him not in world or sun,
    Or eagle's wing, or insect's eye;
    Nor thro' the questions men may try,
The petty cobwebs we have spun:

If e'er when faith had fall'n asleep,
    I heard a voice 'believe no more,'
    And heard an ever-breaking shore
That tumbled in the Godless deep;

A warmth within the breast would melt
    The freezing reason's colder part,
    And like a man in wrath the heart
Stood up and answered, 'I have felt.'

No, like a child in doubt and fear:
    But that blind clamour made me wise;
    Then was I as a child that cries,
But, crying, knows his father near;

And what I am beheld again
    What is, and no man understands;
    And out of darkness came the hands
That reach thro' nature, moulding men."

# CHAPTER TEN

# LYRICAL INSPIRATION

## I

Were an anthology of Tennyson's poetry to be compiled
for the purpose of including only such poems as can appeal
directly to the literary taste of to-day, the result might well
be both curious and illuminating. Such a volume would, in
the first place, be far more bulky than might be imagined.
And, in the second place, it would be found, I think, that
in any honest and intelligent process of rejection and selection a great many of the more famous and popular poems
would be discarded—it would be found, that is, that in the
end of Victorian Tennyson, the didactic and the narrative
Tennyson, had disappeared, and that someone quite different had emerged in his place. Were I myself to make
such a selection, I should from the first be tempted to reject the *Idylls of the King*, the *Idylls of the Hearth*, or at any
rate *Enoch Arden*, *Dora* and *Sea Dreams*, the Keepsake
verses, most of the ballads and dramatic pieces, and some
of the later theological compositions. I should also, I think,
reject both the *Locksley Halls*. On the other hand, I should
include all the "Classical" poems, with the exceptions of
*Lucretius* and *The Death of Oenone*; I should include
nearly all the early Romantic poems, together with the
*Kraken* and the *Ode to Memory*; I should give *The Vision*

*of Sin* and *The Palace of Art* in their entirety; I should include *The Northern Farmer,* while rejecting the other dialect poems; I should give the lyrics from *The Princess* while omitting the main narrative; I should include the whole of *The Two Voices* and *Maud* and nearly the whole of *In Memoriam;* I should give *Boadicea* and the other experiments in quantity; and finally, I should retain practically all the occasional poems, the dedications, epitaphs and such pieces as *The Daisy* and *Will Waterproof's Lyrical Monologue.*

Such a selection would doubtless be arbitrary and personal. I do not think, however, that, as regards the two general categories of the selected and the rejected, there would to-day be much dispute. For these categories do actually represent a basic divergence of taste between the nineteenth and the twentieth century; they represent, that is, the divergence between absolute or, if you prefer it, "pure," poetry and applied poetry. For whereas the Victorians cared mainly for applied poetry, for poetry as a vehicle, either of instruction or diversion, for poetry either as a sermon or a novel; we, caring less for the object or even the form of a poem, insist that it shall possess an "absolute" quality, that it shall be an end unto itself. And it is because of this conviction of "poetry for poetry's sake," that we are particularly apt to resent the intrusion of any extraneous purpose. Now, the great mass of Tennyson's poetry is, as I have endeavoured to show, "applied" poetry; nor, even as such, is it of a very high quality. His didactic poetry suffers from a lack of intellect and education, his dramatic poetry is marred by the fact that, unlike Browning, he was not a creative analyst of character. But if we can isolate this great mass of his "applied," of his didactic and narrative, poetry, there remains a very important residue of "absolute" poetry, and it is because of the value, of the very remarkable value, of this "absolute" poetry that he will survive.

For should anyone doubt the real importance of this distinction between the "absolute" and the "applied" poetry of Tennyson, let him cast a glance at the many incidental or occasional poems which figure in the collected works. Although these poems constitute applied poetry to the extent that they are written for the avowed purpose of conveying some compliment or message, yet the object of the poem is in effect subsidiary to the subject. The occasional verses of Tennyson stand, that is, midway between his subjective and his objective poetry. For whereas in the latter we are continually disconcerted by the suspicion that the thing could be done far better either in the form of a novel with a purpose or in a volume of philosophical or religious essays, in the former, in his lyrical poetry, we are convinced that verse alone offers the accordant form of expression. In the intermediary category of his occasional verses we may feel, of course, that he could as well have put it all into a letter, yet we must admit that his choice of the forms of verse has raised the communication to a far higher and more memorable level. And the fact that we are so pleasurably surprised by the quality of Tennyson's occasional verse shows, I think, that the moment he can rid himself of the obsession of his "message" and his mission, from that moment he begins to write very good poetry indeed. And if so slight a thing as incidental and often perfunctory versification can cause us pleasure, how far more penetrating should be the effect of those subjective emotions which forced him, almost against his will, to give them lyrical expression!

And thus the subsidiary virtues which he possesses—and they are important enough—furnish a useful transition between the previous analysis of his Victorian aspects and the concluding exposition of his lyrical genius. I propose, therefore, after indicating what I mean by his occasional verses, to discuss his treatment of Nature and his mastery of language. For between Tennyson the bard of the Victorian age and Tennyson the lyrical poet, comes the intermediary Tennyson—Tennyson as a technician and an artist.

Tennyson's occasional verses are, as I have said, of considerable interest, not only because of their intrinsic quality, but also because they are generally exempt from the intention of striking some particular attitude or conveying some particular moral. They are taken, so to speak, in his stride, and they show, better than his didactic poems or his cautionary tales, how wide, and indeed lavish, was his range of interest. They show him, moreover, in a pleasant light as a quite human, quite urbane, almost genial man of culture. They are an invaluable antidote to the Victorian fog which obscures so many of his poems. Even the odes which he would write from time to time in his official capacity as Poet Laureate are better than those of his predecessors, infinitely better than those of his immediate successor and imitator in that office. They produce the same pleasurable feeling of satisfaction at the achievement of something intricate and deliberate, as is conveyed by a polished copy of Latin verses; and, of course, the Wellington ode is in a class by itself. But apart from the official poems, there is a great mass of incidental verse, dedications, epitaphs and the like, which, whether they be incised with the stately condensation of some Roman inscription, or composed with the flowing lucidity of some of the lighter odes of Horace, carry with them a very welcome and a very mellow savour of the humanities.

Take this, for instance, from the lines to F. D. Maurice:—

"You'll have no scandal while you dine,
    But honest talk and wholesome wine,
        And only hear the magpie gossip
    Garrulous under a roof of pine:

For groves of pine on either hand,
    To break the blast of winter, stand;
        And further on, the hoary Channel
    Tumbles a billow on chalk and sand;

Where, if below the milky steep
Some ship of battle slowly creep,
   And on thro' zones of light and shadow
Glimmer away to the lonely deep,

We might discuss the Northern sin
Which made a selfish war begin;
   Dispute the claims, arrange the chances;
Emperor, Ottoman, which shall win."

Even better, perhaps, are the lines to FitzGerald, in which, after recalling his visit to Woodbridge in 1876, and the pigeons and the vegetarianism of it all, Tennyson sends his friend *Tiresias:*—

"which you will take
My Fitz, and welcome, as I know,
   Less for its own than for the sake
Of one recalling gracious times,
   When, in our younger London days,
You found some merit in my rhymes,
   And I more pleasure in your praise."

One is pleased by the urbanity of this, by the supple Horatian felicity with which the last line closes the movement; and, indeed, there is a real place in poetry for the urbane. For it would be well if the detractors of Tennyson would read more often such incidental pieces as *The Daisy* or *June Bracken and Heather,* as the epitaphs on Simeon and Ward, or the lines to Jebb and Jowett, or even the intrinsically fine poem in which the *Idylls* are dedicated to the Prince Consort. The Virgil ode is familiar, as are the Alcaics to Milton and the lines to Dante, but how excellent also is the epitaph on Lord Stratford de Redcliffe; how suitable to its purpose is the poem on Helen's Tower! Nor do I know of any complimentary verses since the time of Horace which so well combine the intimate and the stately, the personal and the imperial, as the dedication of *Demeter* to Lord Dufferin:—

"At times our Britain cannot rest,
    At times her steps are swift and rash;
    She moving, at her girdle clash
The golden keys of East and West.

Not swift or rash, when late she lent
    The sceptres of her West, her East,
    To one, that ruling has increased
Her greatness and her self-content. . . .

But more, that you and yours may know
    From me and mine, how dear a debt
    We owed you, and are owing yet
To you and yours, and still would owe.

But since your name will grow with Time,
    Not all as honouring your fair fame
    Of Statesman, have I made the name
A golden portal to my rhyme:—

For he—your India was his fate . . ."

and with this perfectly graduated transition Tennyson proceeds to the sombre lines on his dead son which I have, in their place, already quoted.

## II

Equally intermediate in character is Tennyson's treatment of Nature. For although much of his Nature poetry is, it must be owned, written with the old desire to instruct, with the wish, even, to display his powers of observation, or his peculiar felicity in condensing such observation into accurate and concentrated expression, yet one has but to read through any of the longer poems to be pleasantly stimulated at recurrent intervals by some chance simile or illustration of Nature such as opens a sudden rift of blue in the heavy clouds which hang so often upon his poetry. It is not that Tennyson's Nature poetry is as a rule more

subjective or more "absolute" than his other themes—it is
that, in approaching the eternal and illimitable inspiration
of Nature, the emotional ecstasy depends perhaps more
upon the temperament of the reader than upon the imaginative impulse of the poet himself. For if the reader is at
all sensitive to the inspiration of Nature, it will require but
the slightest stimulus of "recognition," some incidental al-
lusion, vivid or merely accurate, in order to inflame his own
imaginative recollection, and to afford him that startled realisation of the identity of the personal with the eternal
which is, in effect, the essence of the highest poetic appreciation. As a theme, Nature herself contains all the necessary elements for such appreciation: she combines, in a
perpetual surprise, the minute and the infinite, the precise
and the unknowable, the momentary and the eternal. One
has but to feel assured that the poet is himself sensitive
to these sublime contrasts for his Nature poetry to be affected almost automatically, and by processes which, if applied to other themes, might well fail to produce any nervous vibration. And with Tennyson at least you have such
an assurance. One of the few subjective poems which he
wrote on this theme figures fittingly upon the base of his
most appropriate statue, that rugged masterpiece of Watts
which stands in shambling untidiness under the Lincolnshire sky and in the shadow of the three cathedral towers
which grace and dominate the wide, sad county of his
birth:—

> "Flower in the crannied wall,
>   I pluck you out of the crannies,
>   I hold you here, root and all, in my hand,
>   Little flower—but *if* I could understand
>   What you are, root and all, and all in all,
>   I should know what God and man is."

It is not, however, merely this sense of the spirituality of
Nature which gives to Tennyson's treatment of the subject
so peculiar an interest. It is also that his observation of

Nature is curiously concentrated and detailed. This concentration arises, not only from his unwillingness to record facts which he had not actually experienced, or to describe phenomena which he had not actually examined, but also from the more practical cause of his extreme short sight. The result is that the Nature poetry of Tennyson so often deals, on the one hand, with the tiny and incidental phenomena of the foreground, and, on the other, with the vast and illimitable movements in the background: there is no middle distance. And, as a result, the essential contrast of Nature—the contrast between the microscopic and the illimitable, between the speedwell and the stars—is continually, even if only indirectly, emphasised. And the emotional reality of this contrast gives to Tennyson's Nature poetry, whether he be speaking of the minute or of the infinite, a very peculiar significance.

It is important, in discussing Tennyson's powers of observation, to keep in mind this emotional reality, since there are moments when his habits of accuracy, his method of storing and "working up later" some observed phenomena —the rippled shadow on a cow's neck when drinking, the foam flakes scudding along the beach at Mablethorpe, the flat leaves of water-lilies tugging at their stems in a gust of wind, the little tufts of thrift upon some Cornish headland—might savour otherwise of the perfunctory, or even of the prosaic. And it must be admitted that at times Tennyson's habits of accuracy, his predilection for the scientific, his sudden relapses into botany, his interest in pond life, are apt to throw the shadow of "Madam How and Lady Why" over some of his most stimulating references to Nature. It is unfortunate, for instance, on reading in Section X of *In Memoriam* lines as good as:—

> "Than if with thee the roaring wells
>     Should gulf him fathom-deep in brine;
>     And hands so often clasp'd in mine
> Should toss with tangle and with shells,"

to turn to the note and find the following:—

"Section X, verse v, *tangle,* or 'oar-weed' (*Laminaria digitata*)."

But then the notes to the Eversley Edition should in any case be read only by the healthy-minded.

If we are resolved, therefore, to steel ourselves against these relapses into the accurate, and to bear in mind Tennyson's essentially emotional attitude towards Nature, his powers of observation and portrayal will then become for us of great value and interest. For how often, and with what economy of language, does he set before us such penetrating touches as the soft smell of the earth after rain, as the colours of the autumn woods reeling behind the smoke of burning weeds, as the crumpled leaf of a poppy when first liberated from its sheath, as the rustle of the poplar leaves like the patter of rain, as the breeze of early dawn stirring the flowers of a garden, or as the sound in every mood of falling waters? It may be said, of course, that his pictures of Nature savour too much of the Rectory garden, of the soft, steaming monochrome of the Isle of Wight, of the trim complacency of Surrey; that they recall a little too vividly the water-colours of Mrs. Allingham. There are moments when this is true enough, such as the description of the cottage-gardens in *Aylmer's Field:*—

"Her art, her hand, her counsel all had wrought
    About them: here was one that, summer-blanch'd,
    Was parcel-bearded with the traveller's-joy
    In autumn, parcel ivy-clad; and here
    The warm-blue breathings of a hidden hearth
    Broke from a bower of vine and honeysuckle:
    One look'd all rosetree, and another wore
    A close-set robe of jasmine sown with stars:
    This had a rosy sea of gillyflowers
    About it; this . . . .
    A lily-avenue climbing to the doors;
    One, almost to the martin-haunted eaves
    A summer burial deep in hollyhocks."

All this perhaps is too sweet to be wholly true. But in the

main the Nature poetry of Tennyson, restricted as it is to his actual range of observation, is a faithful and stimulating picture of English country scents and sounds and habits. Take this, perhaps, from the *Grandmother:*—

> "And I cried myself well-nigh blind, and all of an eve-
> ning late
> I climb'd to the top of the garth, and stood by the
> road at the gate
> The moon like a rick on fire was rising over the dale,
> And whit, whit, whit, in the bush beside me chirrupt
> the nightingale."

Or this as a description of East Kent:—

> "The happy valleys, half in light, and half
> Far-shadowing from the West, a land of peace;
> Gray halls alone among their massive groves;
> Trim hamlets; here and there a rustic tower
> Half-lost in belts of hop and breadths of wheat;
> The shimmering glimpses of a stream: the seas;
> A red sail or a white: and far beyond,
> Imagined more than seen, the skirts of France."

How full also of such impressions is the central portion of *In Memoriam,* whether it be the sunbeam scudding along the fens, the pastures on Warder Hill winking through the noonday heat, the sound of the scythe in the dew of morning, the murmur of the bees in the limes, or the bubbling of the warm milk within the pail; whether it be "the long backs of the bushless downs," or even:—

> "the goodly hills of Somerset
> And white sails flying on the yellow sea."

Water-colours, perhaps, but water-colours of the utmost delicacy and precision.

Nor can we omit the endless loving references to the English birds—references made curiously vivid by Tennyson's delicate sense of sound and his power of onomatopœia. The "sightless" song of the lark is familiar, and indeed his descriptions of birds are generally based on their song rather than on their plumage, since Tennyson's ear was far more acute than his eyesight. Thus we have such vivid touches as "the starling's tiny castanets," the "clamour of the daws," the "sudden skritches" of the jay, the "laughter" of the woodpecker, the cry of the partridge—"like a rusty key turned in a lock"—the "hum of dropping snipe," the "human whistle" of the great plover, the "myriad shriek of wheeling ocean fowl." Such evidences of observation may, perhaps, be incidental, but they show at least an interest which, when all is said, is more affectionate than scientific, and in their aggregate they do provide a theme which should even now come to many readers with the pleasure of surprised recognition.

If Tennyson's appreciation of the more tender processes of Nature has, perhaps, too domestic a flavour, his sense of the infinities of sea and sky is on a larger, and indeed a sterner, scale. Ever since his schoolboy days, the sense of water, the sound of water, had meant a great deal to him, and his earlier poems abound with impressions of the great North Sea rollers booming along the flat beach at Mablethorpe. The Isle of Wight, when it came, furnished him with other scenes and echoes, and with the scream of the shingle sucked back by the retreating wave. His visits to Cornwall gave him one simile, at least, of arresting truth and beauty:—

> "So dark a forethought roll'd about his brain
>     As on a dull day in an Ocean cave
>     The blind wave feeling round his long sea-hall
> In silence."

His voyage to Norway in 1858 remains in one of his few deep-sea similes:—

"as a wild wave in the wide North Sea
Green-glimmering toward the summit, bears, with all
Its stormy crests that smoke against the skies
Down on a bark, and overbears the bark . . ."

And finally it was the slow movement of Lymington har-
bour-mouth which inspired what is perhaps the finest of all
his references to the sea:—

"But such a tide as moving seems asleep,
    Too full for sound and foam,
  When that which drew from out the boundless deep
    Turns again home."

Of his sense of the infinity of space I have already spoken,
but some further mention must here be made of the many
striking passages in which he speaks of the stars. His knowledge of astronomy was slightly above that of the ordinary
amateur, and we hear of him in the 'sixties going down
frequently to Fairfax road to look through Lockyer's six-
inch equatorial. And after dinner, sometimes, at Farringford, he would take them all on to the roof and point out
Venus. "Can you imagine," he would say, as he said later
in the second *Locksley Hall*, "roaring London and raving
Paris *there* in that point of peaceful light?" "While I said
*there*," he would add, "the earth has whirled twenty miles."
Scattered throughout his poems there are many passages
which show how deep was the feeling which possessed him
for the majesty and the distance of the stars. As early as
the first *Locksley Hall* we hear of "great Orion sloping
slowly to the West," or we find him watching the Pleiades:—

"rising thro' the mellow shade,
  Glitter like a swarm of fire-flies tangled in a silver
    braid."

And later, when his renown had grown to wider proportions, he would gaze at the Nebula in the sword of Orion

and be filled with dismay at the insignificance of human
fame:—

> "A single misty star
> Which is the second in a line of stars
> That seem a sword beneath a belt of three,
> I never gazed upon it but I dreamt
> Of some vast charm concluded in that star
> To make fame nothing."

## III

If, therefore, we can find in the felicitous humanism of
Tennyson's incidental verses a relief from the heavy shallowness of his didactic and narrative poetry; if we can discover in his loving and precise observation of Nature an
interest which is quite detached from the usual conception
of him as devoted only to the applied purposes of poetry;
we can also, I think, look to his technical proficiency as a
master of the English language to provide a genuine stirring of purely literary enjoyment.

I have not the aptitude, nor indeed the space, to discuss
in detail the technical aspects of Tennyson's prosody and
language. Much has been written on the subject, notably
by Schipper and by Saintsbury. It may be said, perhaps,
that he never fully justified the prosodic promise of his early
poems, which, tentative as they were, yet showed a metrical originality such as causes us to wonder at the contemporary strictures of Coleridge and the later criticisms of
Swinburne. The extraordinary dexterity with which, by the
shifting of the stress, by the interchange of vowel sounds,
and by the use, and sometimes the abuse, of alliteration, he
was able to vary the inherent monotony of *In Memoriam;*
the mastery which he abundantly displayed in the trochaic
measure—a measure so naturally adapted to the English
language; the success of his experiments in quantity, of
such pieces as the Phalaecian hendecasyllables, or *The Bat-*

*tle of Brunanburh,* make one regret that he was not more often, as in *The Daisy,* tempted to adopt original verse forms, and that he confined himself predominantly to blank verse, in which, proficient as he indubitably was, he did not possess the skill of Browning or the mellow movement even of Matthew Arnold. One has only to read the panting, spasmodic interjections of *Maud,* or the frenzied sweep of *Boadicea,* the rattling galliambics of which, so unlike the effeminacy of the "Attis," have all the fire of Borodine's *Igor,* to realise what a remarkable talent Tennyson possessed for accommodating the movement of his verse to its subject, for marking the gradations of his theme by the subtlest changes of key or intonation.

His skill in this important and intricate branch of his art is conveniently illustrated by his famous lines to Catullus. He had, in the summer of 1880, been travelling in the Dolomites with his son, Hallam Tennyson. They had gone down to Garda and had rowed out one evening to the peninsula of Sirmio. As they rowed across the lake the poignant movement of the old Catullan choriambics, fused with the elegiacs to his brother, mingled in the poet's consciousness with the rhythmic beating of the oar:—

"Paene insularum, Sirmio, insularumque."

and he produced the following famous stanza:—

"Row us out from Desenzano, to your Sirmione row!
  So they row'd, and there we landed—'O venusta
    Sirmio'—
  There to me thro' all the groves of olive in the summer
    glow,
  There beneath the Roman ruin where the purple
    flowers grow,
  Came the 'Ave atque Vale' of the Poet's hopeless woe,
  Tenderest of Roman poets, nineteen hundred years
    ago,
  'Frater Ave atque Vale'—as we wandered to and fro

Gazing at the Lydian laughter of the Garda Lake
 below
Sweet Catullus' all-but-island, olive-silvery Sirmio!"

The subtlety with which these lines are constructed, instinctive and subconscious as they probably were, merits some
analysis. For, of the two currents of emotion which gave
birth to the poem, the first is the actual beauty of the moment—the flat lake, the encircling mountains and the Italian
boatmen, singing, doubtless, to their oars—and the second
is the plangent recollection of Catullus—of how, so many
years ago, he had looked upon this little jutting strip of
olives as his own, how he had come so gaily back to it
from Bithynia, and how he had lost the brother whom he
loved. There are therefore two musical *motifs* in the poem
—the *motif* of the rowers, represented by the vowel "o,"
and the *motif* of Catullus, represented by the broad Roman
"a." The music is set to eight rhythmic beats, as is general
in all such water songs from the Volga to the Elbe, and in
the first line, as well as in the first two beats of the second,
the rowing motif predominates. With the broader vowel
of "landed," however, it ceases to obtrude—becomes indeed
an undertone to what follows and passes in recurrent echoes
among the hills. The transition between the "o" motif and
the "a" motif is marked by the intermediately broad vowel
of "there," which word is repeated and echoed predominantly in the two lines that follow. In the fifth line, the
"a" *motif* is definitely introduced by the "Ave atque Vale,"
which is repeated in the opening of the seventh line, and
echoed in the lesser tones of "wandered," "at," "Lydian,"
"laughter," "Garda" in the verse that follows. And the poem
ends with the sighing rustle of the concluding line, in which
the two dominant *motifs* are fused in a crowd of gentler
vowels.

Should anyone consider the above analysis as artificial,
let him then read the poem of Flecker written on the same
subject, with the same Catullan original in his ears, written

in identical metre and with the same terminal and predominant rhyme; and let him explain why the later poem conveys none of the effect which is implicit in the lines of Tennyson. It is but fair, of course, to Flecker to add that he was only writing a translation of the Catullus poem, and had clearly no desire to combine the two elements in the way that Tennyson attempted and so miraculously achieved.

This very dexterous manipulation of vowel sounds can be illustrated from other poems of Tennyson, and might be said, indeed, to constitute his most original contribution to the harmonics of the English language. We have the authority of Sir C. Stanford that "it was his perfection of vowel balance which made his poetry so difficult to set to music," and he was himself fully aware of his talent in this direction, and would at times exploit it somewhat unduly. He would take infinite trouble to exclude the harsher gutturals and sibilants from his verse, and he had a prejudice against the vowels "i" and "ē." He even went so far on one occasion as to inform Rawnsley that "the finest line he had ever written" was:—

"The mellow ouzel fluted in the elm."

It must be admitted, indeed, that Tennyson was apt to exaggerate the importance of harmonics, and to rely a little too often and too lavishly upon the mere devices of verse —upon onomatopœia, epanaphora and alliteration.

In Mr. Bram Stoker's reminiscences of Henry Irving there is a story which illustrates entertainingly enough how serious an importance Tennyson attached to onomatopœia:—

"In the course of our conversation, something cropped up which suggested a line of one of his poems, *The Golden Year*, and I quoted it.

" 'Go on,' said Tennyson, who seemed to like to know that anyone quoting him knew more than the bare quotation.

"I happened to know that poem, and went on to the end of the lyrical portion. There I stopped.

"'Go on,' he said again, so I spoke the narrative bit at the end, supposed to be spoken by the writer:—

"'He spoke; and, high above, I heard them blast
  The steep slate-quarry, and the great echo flap,
  And buffet round the hills, from bluff to bluff.'

"Tennyson listened attentively. When I had spoken the last line he shook his head and said:—

"'No!'

"'Surely that is correct?' I said.

"'No!'

"There was in this something which I did not understand, for I was certain that I had given the words correctly. So I ventured to say:—

"'Of course one must not contradict an author about his own work; but I am certain those are the words in my edition of the poem.'

"He answered quickly:—

"'Oh, the words are all right—quite correct!'

"'Then what is wrong?'

"For answer he said:—

"'Have you ever been on a Welsh mountain?'

"'Yes! On Snowdon!'

"'Did you hear them blast a slate quarry?'

"'Yes. In Wales, and also on Coniston in Cumberland.'

"'And did you notice the sound?'

"I was altogether at fault and said:—

"'Won't you tell me—explain to me? I really want to understand.'

"He spoke the last line, and further explanation was unnecessary. The whole gist was in his pronunciation of the word 'bluff,' twice repeated. He spoke this word with a sort of quick propulsive effort, as though throwing the word from his mouth. 'I thought anyone would understand that,' he added.

"It was the correct muffled sound which the exploding charge makes in the curves of the steep valleys.

"This is a good instance of Tennyson's wonderful power of onomatopœia."

The passage on which, at this interview, Mr. Bram Stoker was so unfortunate as to embark, is, it is true, one of the better instances of Tennyson's use of the onomatopœic device. It was a talent which was inherent in him, and as early as *Mariana* we find:—

> "The sparrow's chirrup on the roof,
>     The slow clock ticking, and the sound
> Which to the wooing wind aloof
>     The poplar made. . . ."

In later years the thing became a habit, and of almost irritating frequency. For while one can well admire the "moan of doves in immemorial elms," the "murmuring of innumerable bees," and the "long wash of Australasian seas," one cannot wholly welcome such expressions as "oilily bubbled up the mere," or such a simile as:—

> "like an iron-clanging anvil banged
> With hammers."

Nor can the device be wholly legitimate when applied to visual and not to aural impressions, as in the following:—

> "And I rode on and found a mighty hill
> And on the top a city wall'd: the spires
> Prick'd with incredible pinnacles into heaven."

But at its best the use which Tennyson makes of onomatopœia is effective enough, and one cannot but respect the skill with which the introduction of the four leading labials in the last two lines of the following passage marks the transition from the preceding gutturals:—

"Dry clashed his harness in the icy caves
  And barren chasms, and all to left and right
  The bare black cliff clang'd round him as he based
  His feet on juts of slipping crag that rang
  Sharp-smitten with the dint of armed heels—
  And on a sudden, lo! the level lake
  And the long glories of the winter moon."

Coupled with Tennyson's use of onomatopœia must be
mentioned his employment of the devices of epanaphora,
or repetition, and alliteration. The former he could use, at
times, with great effect, as when:—

"The rain of heaven and their own bitter tears,
  Tears, and the careless rain of heaven mixt
  Upon their faces";

or even when:—

"The lizard, with his shadow on the stone
  Rests like a shadow";

but in his narrative poems, and with the purpose of giving
an impression of speed and continuity to his blank verse, he
is apt to employ the device with too much frequency, and
we find, for instance, in a passage of *The Princess*, fourteen
out of seventeen consecutive lines beginning with the same
word "and."

His abuse of the trick of alliteration has been severely
commented on. He derived it, doubtless, as he derived his
onomatopœia, from too appreciative a study of the *Æneid*.
But at times, and in combination with onomatopœia, he
can use it with almost miraculous effect, as in the interchange of the letters "d," "s," and "h" in the famous Wye
passage of *In Memoriam:*—

"The Danube to the Severn gave
  The darken'd heart that beat no more;
  They laid him by the pleasant shore,
  And in the hearing of the wave.

> There twice a day the Severn fills;
>  The salt sea-water passes by,
>   And hushes half the babbling Wye,
> And makes a silence in the hills.
>
> The Wye is hush'd nor moved along,
>  And hush'd my deepest grief of all,
>   When fill'd with tears that cannot fall,
> I brim with sorrow drowning song."

I have dealt hitherto with the more technical aspects of Tennyson's style, its general beauties being sufficiently obvious and familiar. The development of his style was, in truth, as has been said, a progression "from the luxuriant to the heroic." The early affectations, the lispings of *Claribel,* the abundance of epithets, the abuse of double or archaic words disappeared with his increasing power of selection and condensation. This power of condensation, which was indeed remarkable, led him at times into irritating tricks of periphrasis and elaboration. The sea becomes "the ocean mirrors rounded large," a poacher appears as "the nightly wirer of the innocent hare," and "the foaming grape of Eastern France" is, I suppose, to be interpreted as champagne. Such tricks are harmless enough, and have their precedent in even greater poetry, but there are occasions when Tennyson's use of periphrasis is illegitimate, in that it deliberately produces a false sense of beauty. The lines, for instance:—

> "Or where the kneeling hamlet drains
>  The chalice of the grapes of God,"

do not, as one vaguely hopes, refer to some village in the Alban hills, but to early service at Clevedon parish church; and the simplicity essential to his meaning is marred by the elaboration of the language in which that meaning is conveyed. Nor am I one of those who relish the verbal contortions in which the game-pie of *Audley Court* is so in-

tricately involved; for food, apart from drink, is a subject
for epic poetry alone.

Such elaboration is not, however, the dominant characteristic of Tennyson's maturer style, and indeed, one can
observe in his later poems a determined endeavour to prefer the direct to the elaborate, and even the Anglo-Saxon
to the Latin word. Nor does he indulge over-much in the
device, so popular with English poets from Milton to
Flecker, of enlivening the grey colours of our native speech
by the introduction of resonant and flamboyant foreign
names. He is at his best, and he knows that he is at his
best, in the flow of direct and simple narrative, as in the
nine initial lines with which the scenery of the sea-village
is sketched as the introduction to *Enoch Arden*. And indeed the impression which emerges from any unbiassed
reading of Tennyson is not that of his many tricks and affectations, but of a very outright simplicity, continuity and
stateliness; more definitely, perhaps, of a remarkable gift of
condensation, of a condensation which could produce such
lines as the following:—

> "And one, the reapers at their sultry toil.
>     In front they bound the sheaves. Behind
> Were realms of upland, prodigal in oil,
>     And hoary to the wind,"

and of a directness which could evolve:—

> "Not wholly in the busy world, nor quite
>     Beyond it, blooms the garden that I love.
> News from the humming city comes to it
>     In sound of funeral or of marriage bells;
> And, sitting muffled in dark leaves, you hear
>     The windy clanging of the Minster clock;
> Although between it and the garden lies
>     A league of grass, wash'd by a slow broad stream,
> That, stirred with languid pulses of the oar,
>     Waves all its lazy lilies, and creeps on,

Barge-laden, to three arches of a bridge,
Crown'd with the Minster towers.
                              The fields between
Are dewy-fresh, browsed by deep-udder'd kine,
And all about the large lime-feathers blow,
The lime a summer home of murmurous wings . . ."


## IV

Mr. John Drinkwater has defined the lyric as "the product of the pure poetic energy unassociated with other energies." This definition is useful in itself, and particularly
valuable in its application to Tennyson's lyric poetry. For,
as I have already stated, and perhaps with wearisome iteration, the poetic genius of Tennyson was essentially lyrical
in quality, and was marred only by the fact that he was
unable, except in isolated moments, to dissociate his lyrical
energy from other energies—dramatic, narrative, ethical,
theological and didactic. In the preceding sections of this
chapter I have endeavoured to show how, from the moment that his poetic energy was even incidentally dissociated from other energies, the quality of his poetry was at
once enhanced; and how in his occasional verses, in much
of his Nature poetry and in his mastery of the technique
of language, he reached a level which is quite out of proportion to the esteem which his more important poetry now
enjoys. Such evidences of his quality are but secondary:
the primary force of Tennyson's poetry is his central lyrical
energy, an energy which is, unfortunately, often obscured
by other and less vital elements, and which has, as a result,
been profoundly and very generally misconceived. I have
endeavoured in this book to detach, one by one, these several parasitic growths which from the first encumbered and
almost strangled the organic development of Tennyson's intrinsic genius. His lyrical quality has now been adequately
isolated. I shall attempt, in the concluding pages, to describe that quality and to indicate some at least of its more
remarkable and excellent manifestations.

In its technical and narrow sense lyrical poetry implies a
form of words written to be sung to the lyre or other accom-
paniment; in its applied and extended meaning it is interpreted as the poetry of personal experience or emotion.
The latter interpretation is the more comprehensive and important. The former, however, is not without its interest
and its instances. For the songs of Tennyson, written sepa-
rately as interludes to break the flow of narrative, are among
the best in the English language, and in them we find, as
rarely in his other poems, the absolute vatic ecstasy; the
"purest" poetry, perhaps, which he ever composed. For in
his songs, and predominantly in the songs incorporated in
*The Princess*, his poetic energy was concentrated wholly
on the magic of words. He sang, for once, "but as the linnets sing"; he sang, for once, "without a conscience and an
aim." The result comes to one with a shock of delight. For
they vibrate, these songs of Tennyson, with something
vague and poignant, with:—

> "I knew not what of wild and sweet,
> Like that strange song I heard Apollo sing
> While Ilion like a mist rose into towers."

And they vibrate with more than this—they vibrate, at last,
with that "divine excess," with that glimpse of the Dionys-
iac, that unmistakable sense of impulsive continuity falling
haphazard upon the right, the only word; they vibrate with
that conviction of the inevitable and the inimitable, with
that conviction of the inspired, which only the greatest lyric
poets can achieve in the moments when they feel the force
and beauty of their own genius:—

> "For Love is of the valley, come thou down
> And find him; by the happy threshold, he,
> Or hand in hand with Plenty in the maize,
> Or red with spirted purple of the vats,
> Or fox-like in the vine; not cares to walk
> With Death and Morning on the silver horns,"

or again:—

"Now sleeps the crimson petal, now the white;
Nor waves the cypress in the palace walk;
Nor winks the gold fin in the porphyry font:
The fire-fly wakens: waken thou with me.

Now droops the milk-white peacock like a ghost,
And like a ghost she glimmers on to me.

Now lies the earth all Danäe to the stars,
And all thy heart lies open unto me.

Now slides the silent meteor on, and leaves
A shining furrow, as thy thoughts in me.

Now folds the lily all her sweetness up,
And slips into the bosom of the lake:
So fold thyself, my dearest, thou, and slip
Into my bosom and be lost in me."

This poem is clearly beyond criticism and even elucidation. The sheer melody of the verse, unaided as it is by
the agency of rhyme, is by itself remarkable. The poem
can stand, I think, second only to the odes of Keats, to
which, in the quality of its inspiration, it bears a resemblance, faint but unmistakable. And unconscious, also. For
although the critic may find in the skill with which the
word "up" is placed at the end in the last stanza an echo
of the even greater skill which induced Keats to construct
the Ruth stanza of the *Nightingale* upon the corner-stone
of "hath," yet with Tennyson it is evident and welcome
that this song at least came all unconsciously, and with such
elaboration only as is given to something born already essentially completed from the soul.

Nor are his other songs, although they seldom reel to
the same drunken sense of beauty, much inferior in quality.
The first verse, at least, of *Ask Me no More*, with the sad
echo of the hollow-toned vowels in which he so delighted,
and with the skilful shifting of the stress in the fourth line,
is haunting enough:—

"Ask me no more: the moon may draw the sea;
　　The cloud may stoop from heaven and take the
　　　　shape,
　　With fold to fold, of mountain or of cape;
But O too fond, when have I answer'd thee?
　　　　Ask me no more."

Nor can I see how the two following verses, familiar as they are, can fail to be classed in the first rank of lyrical poetry:—

"Ah, sad and strange as in dark summer dawns
The earliest pipe of half-awaken'd birds
To dying ears, when unto dying eyes
The casement slowly grows a glimmering square;
So sad, so strange, the days that are no more.

Dear as remember'd kisses after death,
And sweet as those by hopeless fancy feigned
On lips that are for others; deep as love,
Deep as first love, and wild with all regret;
O Death in Life, the days that are no more."

And with what relief from the panting spasms of *Maud* do we slide into:—

"There has fallen a splendid tear
　　From the passion flower at the gate.
She is coming, my dove, my dear;
　　She is coming, my life, my fate;
The red rose cries, 'She is near, she is near,'
　　And the white rose weeps, 'She is late.'
The larkspur listens, 'I hear, I hear,'
　　And the lily whispers, 'I wait.'"

Few indeed are the occasions when Tennyson rises to his own poetic level, when the tremulous intensity of his emotion wells up suddenly within him and passes into that plangent wistfulness to which his lyre was so perfectly attuned. "A little flash" will come to him at moments, "a mystic hint," and, suddenly, he will write songs such as these, or let fall a verse such as:—

"Between the loud streams and the trembling stars,"

or conceive *Ulysses*, and the inspired line:—

"And see the great Achilles whom we knew,"

or strike upon the infinite beauty of the conclusion to *Tithonus:*—

"Thou seest all things, thou wilt see my grave:
Thou wilt renew thy beauty morn by morn;
I earth in earth forget these empty courts,
And thee returning on thy silver wheels."

It is with an almost melancholy satisfaction that one cites these scattered instances of poetic ecstasy, regretting, as one cannot but regret, how few they are, how seldom they occur, how rarely—how very rarely—the wide and continuous middle level of his poetry is relieved even by the swallow-flights of song. One feels that, like the youthful horseman of the *Vision of Sin:*—

"He rode a horse with wings, that would have flown,
But that his heavy rider kept him down."

This may be so. But even if we are of those who resent the fact that Tennyson was so emphatically not "of the howling dervishes of song," we must admit, I think, that his "middle level" is in itself a remarkable achievement of stately continuity and craftsmanship. Nor can one lightly dismiss a poet who in his eightieth year could give to the world a poem of such mellow Virgilian movement as *Demeter and Persephone:*—

"Once more the reaper in the gleam of dawn
Will see me by the landmark far away,
Blessing his field, or seated in the dusk
Of even, by the lonely threshing-floor

Rejoicing in the harvest and the grange . . .
        and thou that hast from men,
As Queen of Death, that worship which is Fear,
Henceforth, as having risen from out the dead,
Shalt ever send thy life along with mine
From buried grain thro' springing blade, and bless
Their garner'd Autumn also, reap with me,
Earth-mother, in the harvest hymns of Earth
The worship which is Love, and see no more
The Stone, the Wheel, the dimly-glimmering lawns
Of that Elysium, all the hateful fires
Of torment, and the shadowy warrior glide
Along the silent field of asphodel."


## V

And then there is *In Memoriam*. Not that artificially
constructed synthesis which appeared in 1850, with its prologue and its epilogue, with its three arbitrary divisions of
Despair, Regret and Hope, ticked off symmetrically by the
successive Christmas Odes; not the theological treatise on
the conflict between faith and doubt, religion and dogma,
belief and science; but the original *Mēnis*; those plangent
elegies which were scribbled in the old account-book, scribbled in odd unhappy moments during the seven years from
1833 to 1840; those lonely, wistful, frightened elegies.

For one would wish that the interdict which lies upon
the manuscript of *In Memoriam* could be removed; that
Spedding's pencil notes had not been all erased; that one
could be more certain of how the poem grew, of what was
omitted, of what was inserted after 1842. It is easy enough,
of course, to analyse the construction of the poem after
Tennyson had fiddled with it between 1842 and 1850. The
main divisions are emphasised with almost mechanical precision; the changes of mood are heralded deliberately, as
in the two visits to 67 Wimpole Street—the first (Section

VII), the one where the dawn breaks ghastly through the rain, being obviously an actual experience, the second (Section CXIX), with the "chirp of birds" and the smell of new-mown hay, coming to us with less convincing reality. One cannot but gain the impression that some at least of these sections which mark a date, or introduce a transition, are wholly mechanical, and instinctively one allows this impression to permeate some at least of the theological sections. The problem will not be solved until the original manuscript has been collated, and such additional cantos as may, for all we know, still linger in the archives at Farringford become available. For the moment it is possible only to draw attention to the essential lyrical and elegiac nucleus of *In Memoriam*, and to emphasise with what reality it reflects the essence of Tennyson's poetic temperament.

For the most durable impression of *In Memoriam* is that of a poem which renders, with an infinitely subtle melody, the "muffled motions" of a human soul overwhelmed by some immense personal disaster, of a soul crushed suddenly by irreparable grief. There is the first numbed insensibility to what has happened—his mind dwells only on the physical aspect, the dumb thought that "he is gone," the instinctive fusion of Arthur Hallam with the ship sailing slowly with his coffin from Trieste; the relief at feeling that he is at last in England; the incredible fact that one so vivid and so intimate should suddenly have become speechless and unreveal'd—the cry "Where wert thou, brother, those four days?" And, on the heels of this, the identification of his own blind sorrow with the dumb movements of Nature:—

> "But Summer on the steaming floods,
>     And Spring that swells the narrow brooks,
>     And Autumn, with a noise of rooks,
> That gather in the waning woods,

And every pulse of wind and wave
    Recalls, in change of light or gloom,
    My old affection of the tomb,
And my prime passion in the grave."

In section after section we have the sensitive response of
his bruised and languid nerves to the moods of Nature.
Whether it be that first sad October:—

"Calm is the morn without a sound,
    Calm as to suit a calmer grief,
    And only thro' the faded leaf
The chestnut pattering to the ground:

Calm and deep peace on this high wold,
    And on these dews that drench the furze,
    And all the silvery gossamers
That twinkle into green and gold:

Calm and still light on yon great plain
    That sweeps with all its autumn bowers,
    And crowded farms and lessening towers,
To mingle with the bounding main:

Calm and deep peace in this wide air,
    These leaves that redden to the fall;
    And in my heart, if calm at all,
If any calm, a calm despair,"

or the wilder month that followed:—

"To-night the winds begin to rise
    And roar from yonder dropping day,
    The last red leaf is whirl'd away,
The rooks are blown about the skies;

The forest crack'd, the waters curl'd,
    The cattle huddled on the lea;
    And wildly dash'd on tower and tree
The sunbeam strikes along the world:

> And but for fancies, which aver
>     That all thy motions gently pass
>     Athwart a plane of molten glass,
> I scarce could brook the strain and stir
>
> That makes the barren branches loud;
>     And but for fear it is not so,
>     The wild unrest that lives in woe
> Would dote and pore on yonder cloud
>
> That rises upward always higher,
>     And onward drags a labouring breast,
>     And topples round the dreary west,
> A looming bastion fringed with fire."

With this despair mingles the galling sense of waste, of resentment almost, that he who bore "the weight of all the hopes of half the world," that so radiant a promise, should have been quenched as if gratuitously. Such thoughts flit sombrely, with sad, incessant wings pulsating in the dim recesses of the poet's grief, and

> "circle moaning in the air
> Is this the end? Is this the end?"

They kill within him the interest of life itself, the joy even of the coming spring, the love of home; they "make a desert in the mind"; the "purple from the distance dies"; the "bases of his life" are drowned in tears. And through this veil of tears looms gradually the great problem of immortality, the agonised faith in ultimate reunion, the struggling hope, the torturing doubt, the dread of Nature's vicious cruelty:—

> "I falter where I firmly trod,
>     And falling with my weight of cares
>     Upon the great world's altar stairs
> That slope thro' darkness up to God
>
> I stretch lame hands of faith, and grope,
>     And gather dust and chaff, and call
>     To what I feel is Lord of all,
> And faintly trust the larger hope."

In the pauses of such bitter spasms he dwells with almost morbid insistence on the past: he forces himself to recall the features and the accents of his friend, he visualises little vivid incidents in that dawn-golden time, he traces lovingly the course of those four years of friendship, the "tracts that pleased us well," the "path by which we twain did go"; and in an agony he cries:—

> "How changed from when it ran
> Thro' lands where not a leaf was dumb;
> But all the lavish hills would hum
> The murmur of a happy Pan."

And thus gradually, through bitter reactions and long pauses of uncertainty, he works out his conviction of love and immortality. But the interest of *In Memoriam,* to me at least, centres not in the triumphant notes of its conclusions, but in the moods of terror and despair through which the ultimate conviction is attained.

Again and again this terror would seize and rack him, leaving him with quivering pulses sobbing as:—

> "An infant crying in the night,
> An infant crying for the light
> And with no language but a cry."

There are moments, such as the first anniversary of Hallam's death, when the wan hopelessness of it all descends upon him as a cloud:—

> "Risest thou thus, dim dawn, again,
>     And howlest, issuing out of night,
>     With blasts that blow the poplar white,
> And lash with storm the streaming pane?
>
> Day, when my crown'd estate begun
>     To pine in that reverse of doom,
>     Which sicken'd every living bloom,
> And blurr'd the splendour of the sun;

Who usherest in the dolorous hour
    With thy quick tears that make the rose
    Pull sideways, and the daisy close
Her crimson fringes to the shower; . . .

Lift as thou may'st thy burthen'd brows
    Thro' clouds that drench the morning star,
    And whirl the ungarner'd sheaf afar,
And sow the sky with flying boughs,

And up thy vault with roaring sound
    Climb thy thick noon, disastrous day;
    Touch thy dull goal of joyless gray,
And hide thy shame beneath the ground."

And there are moments, "in the dead unhappy night, and when the rain is on the roof," when he is in the dark and alone, when he lies there with the moon upon his bed, and the sense of night around him—moments when his nerves ache with fear and loneliness; moments when he sees:—

"A gulf that ever shuts and gapes,
    A hand that points, and palled shapes
In shadowy thoroughfares of thought;

And crowds that stream from yawning doors,
    And shoals of pucker'd faces drive;
    Dark bulks that tumble half alive,
And lazy lengths on boundless shores."

It was at moments such as this, when "the blood creeps and the nerves prick," that he would yearn with passionate intensity for Hallam, that he would lie there crushed by his own fear and loneliness, and that he would cry out in agony:—

"Speak to me from the stormy sky!
    The wind is loud in holt and hill,
    It is not kind to be so still,
Speak to me, dearest, lest I die."

## VI

This haunting wail of fear and loneliness piercing at moments through the undertones of *In Memoriam,* echoes a note which runs through all the poetry of Tennyson, and which, when once apprehended, beats with pitiful persistence on the heart. It proceeds from that grey region between the conscious and the unconscious; from that dim glimmering land where mingle the "Voices of the Dark" and the "Voices of the Day"; from the uncertain shadow-edges of consciousness in which stir the evanescent memories of childhood or the flitting shapelessness of half-forgotten dreams. It is a cry that mingles with the mystery of wide spaces, of sullen sunsets or of sodden dawns; the cry of a child lost at night time; the cry of some stricken creature in the dark; "the low moan of an unknown sea":—

> "The first gray streak of earliest summer-dawn
> The last long stripe of waning crimson gloom,
> As if the late and early were but one—
> A height, a broken grange, a grove, a flower
> Had murmurs 'Lost and gone and lost and gone':
> A breath, a whisper—Some divine farewell—
> Desolate sweetness—far and far away."

And thus, in that "ever-moaning battle in the mist" which was the spiritual life of Tennyson, there were sudden penetrating moments when he would obtain:—

> "A glimpse of that dark world where I was born";

when, once again, the "old mysterious glimmer" would steal into his soul, and when, in a sombre flash of vision, he would see his life:—

> "all dark and red—a tract of sand,
> And someone pacing there alone,
> Who paced for ever in a glimmering land,
> Lit with a low large moon."

To the vibration of so sad a cadence I should wish to leave him, trusting that the ultimate impression, thus attuned, will prove more poignant and more durable than any hollow reverence for what was once admired. The age of Tennyson is past; the ideals which he voices so earnestly have fallen from esteem. The day may come, perhaps, when the conventions of that century will once again inspire the thoughtful or animate the weak. But, for the moment, it is not through these that any interest can be evoked. And thus, if we consider it reasonable and right that Tennyson should also stand among the poets, let us, for the present, forget the delicate Laureate of a cautious age; the shallow thought, the vacant compromise; the honeyed idyll, the complacent ode; let us forget the dulled monochrome of his middle years, forget the magnolia and the roses, the indolent Augusts of his island-home; forget the laurels and the rhododendrons.

Let us recall only the low booming of the North Sea upon the dunes; the grey clouds lowering above the wold; the moan of the night wind on the fen; the far glimmer of marsh-pools through the reeds; the cold, the half-light, and the gloom.

1

# AFTERWORD

## 1960

### I

Since this book was first published in 1923, there has occurred a reaction in favour of Tennyson. The young intellectuals of the present generation do not regard it as either interesting or fashionable to despise the Victorians; the astonishing clarity and melody of Tennyson's verse stand in welcome contrast to the obscurity and tunelessness of modern poetry. The critics, while recognising his mastery of technique, still deny him the virtue of "universality"; still reproach him for shallowness of thought and emotion; and still blame him for surrendering too readily to the popular taste of his time. Yet when I compare the almost complete disregard into which, since my youth, the poetry of his rival Swinburne, has fallen, I rejoice to feel that the work of Tennyson possesses sufficient survival value to have conquered the inevitable reaction against it. The pendulum has found its equilibrium.

When I wrote this book nearly forty years ago, my intention was to induce people to read a great poet who was at that date neglected. While rejecting those poems which I thought would make no appeal to my own generation, I emphasised the value and beauty of those which I regarded as of lasting importance. While admitting that Tennyson was not a profound thinker, while agreeing with those who accused him of paying undue respect to the bourgeois taste of his time, I contended that his poetry should be approached as that of a melancholy mystic and that as such it possessed enduring significance. I was therefore surprised to hear a modern wireless critic assail my book for having been written with "cruel bias," and as being a typically insensitive onslaught on the Laureate of the Victorian age. It was not intended to be an attack on Tennyson: it was intended as an objective scrutiny of the transitory causes which rendered him unwelcome to the post-war generation, and as an attempt to indicate that it was not the complacency of Tennyson that could appeal to a cynical generation, but his intellectual and spiritual anxieties. So far from being intended as an attack, it was intended as a defence. That my book should to-day be defined by a responsible critic as destructive criticism, written with "cruel bias," shows me that the reaction against Tennyson has now spent its force and that we can approach his work anew, without any of the old Edwardian sneers or prejudices. I rejoice at this transformation.

The change of opinion has been fortified by the appreciation of Tennyson that has been expressed by such authoritative writers as Mr. T. S. Eliot and Mr. Wystan Auden. If these two most influential critics and poets can emphasise the serious aspects of the Laureate, then the younger generation will be less inclined to dismiss him as the author of much melodious verse which is far too dated to have any relevance to modern perplexities or conditions. Mr. Eliot, judging by the range of Tennyson's interests, and his astonishing power of giving popular expression to theological perplexities, regards him as worthy to be classed among the "great" poets. Matthew Arnold might contend that no creative writer who did not possess a philosophic mind and a depth of feeling could be classified as "great." I think that John Sparrow, the Warden of All Souls, would agree that a poet who deserves the title of "great," as distinct from the title of "good," must possess, not depth of feeling only, but also strength of mind. Scope and variety in themselves are not enough. Thus, although I should not claim that Tennyson is a "great" poet in the technical sense of that term, I should certainly argue that he is far greater than he seemed in 1923.

Fortified as they now are by two leading pioneers of modern poetry no critics of to-day need hesitate to express their admiration of Tennyson, nor need any young reader feel ashamed of deriving pleasure from what was once considered old fashioned and utterly out of date. Mr. John Betjeman moreover, who is our most popular writer of verse to-day, has frequently expressed his reverence for the Victorian poet and has pointed out that, so far from being no more than a highly gifted prosodist, Tennyson was able to give expression in memorable terms to the spiritual unrest of those who are disturbed by the conflict between science and religion and who feel abandoned by faith. So far from surrendering to the optimistic standards of the nineteenth century bourgeoisie, Tennyson sincerely detested the materialism of his age, and was profoundly moved by the gulf that had widened between the ideal and the real. There is much in his poetry that should make a direct appeal to the sad uncertainties of this angry world.

I warmly welcome the opportunity to add an Afterword in the Anchor Book edition of my original volume. In the last forty years certain facts have been disclosed which render it necessary either to extend or to correct my original version. Sir Charles Tennyson, the poet's grandson, has published new facts which confirm my theory that in childhood and early youth Tennyson suffered deeply from the wrong done to his father and a sense of shame due to his father's own conduct. The fact that the Rev. George Tennyson was disinherited by his father, the old man of Bayon's Manor, in favour of his younger brother, and forced to enter the Church for which he had no vocation whatsoever, brooded as a constant grievance over the Rectory at Somersby. But it was worse than I had supposed. The Rev. George, driven to desperation by the injustice done to him, took to drink and created much scandal in the county by mounting the pulpit in Somersby Church in a state of obvious intoxication. To the sense of wrong which I had realised as a cloud over his childhood must now be added a sense of family shame.

This is an important revelation, since it explains both Tennyson's early sensitivity and his later excessive regard for the respectable. It also explains how deeply Tennyson, coming from this injured and sullied background, welcomed the affection of Arthur Hallam, the phoenix of the century, the idol of contemporary Cambridge. Such mists of inferiority as he brought with him from Lincolnshire to the University were dissolved by the sunshine of Hallam's friendship. One cannot rightly interpret *In Memoriam* unless one can estimate the feelings of passionate gratitude, the sense of brilliant protection, which Hallam inspired. It was possible to recover from the shame of having as a father an alcoholic clergyman, if one possessed as a friend a man who was regarded as the social and intellectual leader of the university. Hallam for young Tennyson was a radiant justification. I am grateful to Sir Charles Tennyson for revealing to us this important aspect of his grandfather's adolescent state of mind.

There is a statement made in the original edition of this book which now calls for correction. On page 112 and the following pages I have attributed to Lockhart the criticism of the 1832 poems in the Quarterly Review which plunged Tennyson into such acute discouragement and led to the ten years' silence. Professor Grierson of Edinburgh University has since revealed that the review was not by Lockhart, as I had supposed, but by John Wilson Croker. From a letter now preserved in the William Clements Library at the University of Michigan, it is proved beyond doubt that the review, although approved of by Lockhart, was actually written by Croker. It is, as Professor Grierson remarks, "an unfortunate experience for a critic to have been in the ob-

servatory when two stars of the first magnitude, Keats and
Tennyson, rose successively in the firmament and to have
missed them both."

I apologise to Lockhart for having taken his name in
vain.

## II

I repeat that my object in writing this biographical and
critical study in 1923 was to induce my own generation
to discard their prejudice against the Laureate of the Victorian age and to approach him with renewed interest and
appreciation. With this in mind I deliberately ignored the
*Idylls of the King,* realising that of all Tennyson's poems
these, to my own generation, were the most ill-attuned.
Most of us had been taught them in childhood and on
reaching adult age had come to regard them with aversion.
To us they represented what we regarded as the repulsive
hypocrisy and sentimentality of the Victorian age; they
seemed to us as false and artificial as a theatrical costumer's
suits of armour; sham tapestries they appeared to us, on
which the knights and ladies of the age of chivalry were
portrayed in clumsy colours and with total unawareness of
the moral and social standards of the medieval world. They
seemed as irritating and as comic as a seventeenth century
pavane danced by gentlemen wearing the side whiskers of
the nineteenth century. Their form struck us as no less artificial than their content.

Irritating always is Tennyson's preoccupation with my-
opically observed nature, as when he refers to the sparkle
in the hard-stone "avanturine," or when he employs as a
metaphor the death of a cypress in the garden at Farringford, "root-bitten by white lichen." There is the all too frequent use of archaic words, such as "thrall," "caitiff," and
"Paynim." Above all, perhaps, is the artificial use of what
the Greek dramatist called "anagnôrisis," namely the
"recognition" of superiority in one deemed inferior. The

Cinderella story is an extreme example of this dramatic device. Gareth, derided by Lynette as a kitchen scullion, turns out to be a doughty knight and a Prince of royal descent. Guinevere takes refuge at Almesbury without revealing her identity. Geraint conquers in the disguise of a discarded shield and rusty armour. Balan in his wrath mistakes Balin for the demon of the wood. Arthur himself, when he fights Balin, is disguised as a second-rate Knight. These deceptions and disguises render the modern mind impatient of people who cause endless trouble by pretending to be someone else. With us anagnôrisis has become too faded a dramatic device to cause either pleasure or surprise. It is merely boring.

The variations between the slow and the quick movements of blank verse, the studied alternations of the melodious with the discordant, the all too frequent employment of such metrical devices as onomatopœia, and anaphora, confirmed our suspicions that the much lauded music of Tennyson was no "wood-note wild," but a studied effect worked out upon the pianos of Farringford or Aldworth. The metaphors and similes drawn from nature seemed to us even less spontaneous and to have owed their origin to jottings taken in a note-book when walking through the coppices of the Isle of Wight or striding across the downs.

In short, the *Idylls of the King* appeared to confirm all our prejudices against Tennyson and to display him as a gifted craftsman who manufactured his verses to suit the ears and sensibility of his age. Compared to the *Brut* of Layamon, the *"Conte del Graal"* of Chrétien de Troyes, the stories of Malory and William of Malmesbury, or even Wolfram von Eschenbach's *"Parzifal,"* the *Idylls* seem as unauthentic and irrelevant as glee-singers or maypole-dancers in Pittsburgh; or the stocks of Williamsburg.

Such prejudices may, in this later age, appear superficial. We have discarded the old Edwardian theory that the Victorians were hypocritical or complacent. They really did strive to lead pure and selfless lives, and they were profoundly distressed by the decline in religion and the spread of materialism. We are less inclined than we were in 1923 to deride as artificial all attempts to reconstruct the art, the architecture or the sensibility of the twelfth century; the lyrics of the troubadours can still reach us, fresh with the scent of thyme, across the hills of Provence. One does not need to be an antiquarian to be moved by the scents and colours of the age of chivalry. Yet even if we discount these prejudices and cease to attribute insincerity to our grand-parents, we must I think still feel that the *Idylls* are re-grettably artificial and that many of them utterly fail to interest or move the modern generation. Yet we should realize that the attraction exercised upon Tennyson by the Arthurian legend was a perfectly authentic attraction and that throughout his life he continued to revert to the theme. At first his feelings were stirred by the beauty and the ro-mance of chivalry; thereafter, when he became convinced that his duty as Laureate was to instruct his contemporaries, when he became infected by the moral earnestness of the age, he assumed a didactic attitude towards the myths and ruined the poetry in an attempt to teach. The sharp tones of the preceptor are out of tune with romance or even al-legory; Spenser with his butterfly touch would write pages of allegory without changing the key; in trying to combine twelfth century romance with nineteenth century earnest-ness Tennyson ruined the harmony and the beauty of his poems. And that is why, when seeking nearly forty years ago to convert my generation to the significance of Tenny-son I ignored the *Idylls* as bad art. Let me, now that I have reached a wiser age, re-examine them with a less jaundiced eye.

## III

The first thing to realise is that the Arthurian romance at-tracted Tennyson throughout his life. The "Lady of Shalott" appeared as early as the 1832 volume and was written when Tennyson was little more than a boy. The *Morte d'Arthur* was published in 1842. In 1859 appeared four of the Idylls, namely "Enid," "Vivien," "Elaine," and "Guinevere." In 1869 Tennyson added "The Coming of Arthur," "The Holy Grail," "Pelleas and Ettarre," and "The Passing of Arthur." "The Last Tournament" was not published until 1871, "Gareth and Lynette" in 1872, "Balin and Balan" in 1885. Thus for seventy-five long years the Arthurian myth shimmered on the edge of Tennyson's poetic inspiration. It would be tempting to suggest that the romantic poems date from the time when Tennyson was basking in the sun of Hallam's friendship and that the didactic poems only come to cloud the sequence when he had reached middle age. Yet we should realise that the gayest and most romantic of all the *Idylls*, namely "Gareth and Lynette," was written when Tennyson was over sixty and that the lovely lyric quality of the "Lady of Shalott" is already scarred by moral implications. The "Lady of Shalott" could not resist staring at the beauty of Lancelot and for this transgression her life was taken from her and she died on a barge. Yet I agree with Edward FitzGerald that the "Lady of Shalott" survives as one of the most beautiful poems that Tennyson ever wrote.

The Laureate always denied that the *Idylls* were composed as an allegory; all he would admit was that some allegorical implications accompanied the theme. Admittedly, the *Idylls* are not consistently based on allegory, in the sense that Spenser's *Faerie Queene*, or Bunyan's *Pilgrim's Progress*, are allegorical. Yet underneath the "fable or romance of Uther's son" there runs the allegory of the soul of man warring with the senses and of human beings passing from the mystery of birth to the mystery of death and in the end finding eternal life. It is evident also that King Arthur is depicted as the symbol of the rational mind "working out his will to cleanse the world." Guinevere is the beating human heart; the Knights of the Round Table rep-

resent the best faculties of human nature. "My knights,"
Arthur remarks:—

> "My knights are sworn to vows
> Of utter hardihood, utter gentleness,
> And, loving, utter faithfulness in love,
> And uttermost obedience to the King."

Arthur himself is portrayed as an unattractive hero. We are
told of the "mild face of the blameless King":—he is represented as "a selfless man and stainless gentleman" and "pure
as any maid." It was certainly ungentlemanly of him, when
Guinevere the queen of dignity grovelled at his feet, to take
such an occasion to deliver her a lecture on the social significance of conjugal fidelity. People of my generation had
little esteem for Albert the Good, and did not relish his being
presented to us in the guise of King Arthur. Nor did we
really derive much exaltation from the picture of the
Knights of the Round Table who were bound:—

> "To lead sweet lives in purest chastity
> To love one maiden only, cleave to her
> And worship her by years of noble deeds."

Such a prospect seemed to us discouraging. But to return
to the allegory.

The Three Fairies symbolise Faith, Hope and Charity.
It is the Lady of the Lake who presents King Arthur with
Excalibur, the magic Sword of the Spirit, wherewith he will
be enabled to make war against lust and weakness.

The Rev. Augustus Stopford Brooke, whose study of Tennyson remains among the most enlightened and sympathetic criticisms of the poet, contends that the attempt to
combine high romance with didactic ethics accounts for the
failure of the *Idylls* as great poetry. He calls them "gigantic
struggles for success," and admits that the didactic element which obtrudes throughout the series is "not good
art." He argues sensibly that when the allegory is imposed
upon the story, both become confused and dim; but when

they are distinct, as in "Gareth and Lynette" or in the "Holy Grail"—in the first of which the story dominates the allegory, and in the second of which the allegory is more consistent and insistent than the story—then the stream of pure poetry flows clear and strong. "No one," writes Stopford Brooke, "a hundred years from hence will care a straw about the allegory; but men will always care for the story and how the poet has made the persons in it set forth their human nature on the stage of life." Thus it is the humanity of the *Idylls,* not their metaphysics, that should compel our admiration.

I should wish to agree wholeheartedly with Mr. Stopford Brooke, but I fear that is impossible. I am unable to see Tennyson's heroes or heroines as real people, in the sense that we can immediately recognise and love Chaucer's characters as real people; to me they seem, at their best the figures in a faded tapestry, and at their worst the figures in a modern tapestry, woven at Kidderminster in 1852. I fully admit the romantic charm of the Arthurian legend, "about which" wrote William of Malmesbury, "the Britons rave to this day (*hodie delirant*)." I am quite prepared to believe that Arthur was a historical personage, of Celtic origin, but trained by Roman instructors in the military art. I am quite prepared to believe that he won twelve victories against the Romans and the heathen Saxons, culminating in the battle of Mount Badon in 516 A.D. I like to believe that there really did exist such faery sites as Lyonesse, Camelot, and Caerleon upon Usk. I am prepared to believe that in the end Arthur succumbed to treachery in his own family, that he was taken away by the Three Fairies to the vale of Avilion, and that, at the very crisis of atomic war, he will return to us armed with some mystic, magical deterrent. I am not as disconcerted as was Mr. Stopford Brooke by the fusion of the romantic with the allegorical. What I do mind is the incessant moralising, since I believe that only the greatest poets, such as Lucretius, can successfully fuse poetry with preaching, and in the *Idylls* Tennyson preaches almost all the time.

He has two main themes. The first is the destruction, or more accurately the gradual and progressive sapping, of the spiritual by the physical, the decline of idealism brought about by the advance of materialism and by surrender to the lusts of the flesh. The second theme represents Tennyson's obsession against all mystic or supernatural religion, his hatred of asceticism. He believed profoundly in the life of action, holding that the truly moral man should not hold himself aloof from the world around him but should devote such capacities as he may possess to the betterment of his fellows and the enhancement of moral values. Thus "Merlin and Vivien" is intended in its clumsy way to show the danger of even the most intelligent man being submerged by sensual desire. Thus "The Holy Grail" is intended to show that emotional or sensational religion is akin to superstition. As such it is destructive of the balance of the normal mind and of the integration and even security of the State. Again and again did Tennyson repeat his doctrine that birth and death are two dark mysteries and life a lit platform between these two wells of darkness. It is our duty while on the platform not to escape into ascetic holiness or mystic visions, but to exercise as usefully as we can the talents with which God has endowed us. At the age of eighty Tennyson, who was always furious when asked to explain himself, bellowed out "My meaning in the Idylls was spiritual . . . I intended Arthur to represent the ideal soul of man coming into contact with the warring elements of the flesh." His passion for conjugal fidelity, which arose from his boyhood yearning for the respectable, was a perfectly sincere passion; he really did loathe adultery; and throughout his poems he likes to imagine that his lovers are either "newly wed," or about to have their marriages solemnised in the village church. Thus, although both Lancelot and Guinevere are represented as noble characters, they set a bad example to weaker souls, such as Vivien and Tristram; it was their single sin that debauched the ideals of the Round Table. The weakness of Tennyson is that, whereas his noble characters tend to become pompous, his ignoble characters tend to become coarse. This to my mind is due to the fact that Tennyson lacked humour even as he lacked taste. His grandson, I am aware, has striven to depict the Laureate as an excruciatingly witty man; I fail to agree with him. Such humour as Tennyson possessed was a rustic humour, which is akin to a sense of farce. He was devoid of intellectual humour, and insensitive to the intellectually absurd. He is always allowing the incongruous to intrude even into his most solemn scenes. When, as in "Merlin and Vivien" he finds it necessary to describe lust in action, he treats the physical aspect with crudity. I have been much abused for advising young people "to read Tennyson carelessly or not at all." It is not merely that to my mind exaggerated accuracy, as didactic purpose, is generally destructive of pure poetry; it is rather that when we scrutinise too closely his descriptions of physical passion, we find him to be lacking in taste. It was, I am sure, very "noble" and "tender" of the bard to describe physical relationships in such unattractive terms, but, if you read "Merlin and Vivien" attentively, you will realise that old Tennyson had not the taste or sensibility to realise that they were unattractive. Thus, if on reading this you contemplate taking another look at the *Idylls*, which may well have remained on a dusty shelf among your school books since you went to college, I beg you not to begin with "Merlin and Vivien" or with "Guinevere," but to start reading "Gareth and Lynette" as a romantic story and "The Passing of Arthur" as a world tragedy beautifully told. And I beg you to read them inattentively, without searching for allegories or morals, and turning a deaf ear to all the alliteration, anaphora and other prosodic devices. And I should ask those who contend that they remain wholly unmoved by the *Idylls* whether they can guarantee that they could read the "Passing of Arthur" aloud without becoming what Tennyson would have called "broken down."

## IV

The twelve idylls collected together in the Macmillan edition of 1908 are not, as I have already noted, printed in order of composition. Thus "The Coming of Arthur," which is printed first in the collected edition, was written thirty-seven years after the "Lady of Shalott" and twenty-seven years after the first version of the "Passing of Arthur." Yet in deciding on this final sequence Tennyson was evidently anxious to give form and continuity to the whole series.

Thus "The Coming of Arthur" is intended to introduce the myths in an atmosphere of youth and hopefulness. Even as the concluding *Idylls* are shrouded in the mists of mystery, the fog eddying round the marshes and the sullen sea, so in the opening idyll all is clear and bright and spring-like. We are at the dawn of a new age, radiant in May sunshine:—

> "the world
> Was all so clear about him that he saw
> the smallest rock far on the faintest hill,
> And even in high day the morning star."

Once Arthur is crowned and married he gathers round him the knights of his Round Table and addresses them with "large, divine and comfortable words." The knights are so inspired by the occasion that for a moment they take on a resemblance to their Lord and Master and their features flash with confidence, high-mindedness and loyalty. Under such almost divine guidance they will free their island from foreign invasion, banish paganism from the land, and establish a new order of faith and chastity, and peace. With this in mind they are resolved to unite together to do battle for the right:—

"Flash brand and lance, fall battleaxe upon helm,
   Fall battleaxe and flash brand! Let the King reign."

The second of the series, "Gareth and Lynette," which
of all the *Idylls* was the one most favoured by that acute
critic, Edward FitzGerald, is composed in the same mood
of youthful confidence and gaiety. Gareth was the young-
est son of King Lot and Queen Bellicent and as a boy was
determined to join the Round Table and to become:—

"A knight of Arthur, working out his will
   To cleanse the world."

His mother the queen, not wishing to lose her remaining
son, makes him promise that he will enter the court disguised as a menial and serve for a year as scullion in the
kitchen. Her hope was that the boy would in such menial
servitude be cleansed of his dreams of glory and would
come back to his home cured of all further desire for adventure. He may tell the King that he is in fact the son of
a royal house but to all others, with the exception of Lancelot, he must never disclose his identity. On arrival at Camelot he is fascinated by:—

"Those tall knights that ranged about the throne
   Clear honour shining like the dewy star
   Of dawn, and faith in their great king, with pure
   Affection, and the light of victory
   And Glory gained and evermore to gain."

Gareth is assigned to the care of Sir Kay, the palace
seneschal, who is unaware of his princely lineage and who
treats him harshly. Thus it came that Gareth:—

"all for glory underwent
   The sooty yoke of kitchen-vassalage;
   Ate with young lads his portion by the door,
   And couched at night with grimy kitchen-knaves."

Old Sir Kay might treat him as a scullion, but the mighty

Lancelot recognised his virtue and admired his appearance:—

> "Broad brows and fair, a fluent hair and fine,
> High nose, a nostril large and fine, and hands
> Large, fair and fine—Some young lad's mystery."

Gareth resigns himself with gay humility to this servitude, knowing that in the end he can count on the protection of the gentle King. Then one day the maid Lynette arrives at the court and pleads for help to rescue her sister Lyonors who is confined by three caitiff knights in the Castle Perilous. She entreats the King to send Lancelot to free her sister from captivity. The King cannot spare his greatest warrior and entrusts young Gareth with the task of penetrating into the Castle Perilous and rescuing the damsel in distress. Lynette is furious at being thus fobbed off with a kitchen scullion. She was an uppish girl, her nose "tip-tilted like the petal of a flower." She behaves towards Gareth with offensive scorn. Being still under his promise to his mother Gareth is unable to reveal that he is in fact a Prince of the blood but does so well in his combat against the three wicked knights and in delivering the Princess Lyonors that Lynette apologises for her rudeness and admits that never before had she met a kitchen-lad of such strength, virtue and courage. In the end Gareth achieves full knighthood and, we may suppose, marries Lyonors, or even Lynette herself. The reader is left with the satisfactory impression that Lynette repented of her scornful attitude to the boy Gareth once she discovered that in fact he was not a scullion but the son of "good King Lot and good Queen Bellicent." She was a little snob.

To me the story of Gareth and Lynette is the most pleasing of all the *Idylls,* since the allegory is not insisted on whereas the romance is as gay and flowered as a copse in May. Gareth is a charming man, so young, so young, that his voice carols through the spring orchards and his laugh-

ter rings out on every page. It is in truth the dawn of a
new and happy order.

We then come to the "Marriage of Geraint" followed by
"Geraint and Enid." A cloud comes over the sunshine of
May and we first hear hints of the doom that is to destroy
the Round Table and bring King Arthur to his death.
Geraint acquires Enid as his bride after defeating the
wicked knight, known as the Sparrow Hawk, who held her
and her aged father in durance vile. Geraint is a suspicious
character and on marrying the saintly Enid decides he must
remove her from the corrupting influence of the court, away
from the fetid breath of scandal which is already linking
the name of Lancelot with that of Arthur's Queen. Then
one morning on waking Enid contemplates the magnificent
torso of the sleeping Geraint and, overcome by her love for
him, drops tears upon his chest, feeling that she was utterly unworthy of so heroic a husband. He wakes to hear
her murmuring that she is a bad wife and leaps to the conclusion that she is confessing to adultery. He tells her to
put on her meanest dress and to ride before him into the
wilderness. She is not in any circumstances to address a
word to him again.

Geraint is an abominable character and behaves to his
innocent wife with utter brutality. What renders this idyll
so unpleasing is that we detect in it some of Tennyson's
personal prejudices and his low estimate of women. Enid
was foolish to submit to Geraint's bullying and to be so
anxious to obey his instruction not to speak to him as to be
unable to explain that the whole incident was an utter misunderstanding. All she can do is to turn towards him her
"meek blue eyes," in silent and heart-broken appeal. There
is none of this brutality in Malory or in the Mabinogion
and the fierceness and injustice is due to Tennyson's own
obsession with the "meek unconscious dove" type of woman
and his fierce loathing of conjugal infidelity. This idyll has
nothing to do with the central Arthurian romance and bears

no relation at all to the coloured charm of chivalry. Geraint is a cad and Enid a noodle.

Another story based on Tennyson's preoccupation with "the purblind race of miserable men" who bring misery on themselves and others owing to their failure to give or to listen to rational explanations, is "Balin and Balan." The theme of this story is that anger if undisciplined can prove an enemy to the soul. Balin is a very angry knight whose rage "yelpt within him like a hound." Instead of learning gentleness and self-restraint from Lancelot and Arthur, he allows his passion to master him and in the end, owing to the inevitable misunderstanding, he kills the brother whom he loves. I do not care for this cautionary tale.

I care even less for "Merlin and Vivien," which was composed in 1856 and published when Tennyson reached the age of fifty in 1859. It describes the seduction of the aged Merlin by the harlot Vivien and is intended to presage the corruption which, with Guinevere's infidelity, gradually spread through Camelot and destroyed the ideals and the prowess of the Round Table. Merlin is supposed to symbolise pure intellect and Vivien is supposed to symbolise the senses. Yet instead of treating these two characters symbolically, Tennyson renders them living characters, with the result that we identify Vivien as a lascivious harlot and Merlin as a dirty old man. It is an abominable tale and confirms the impression that Tennyson could not describe physical passion with delicacy or taste. I agree with those who regret that the Laureate refused to follow the advice of those who urged him to eliminate "Merlin and Vivien" from the collection.

As a contrast to Vivien, who is the incarnation of lust and hatred, we are then given Elaine who is the embodiment of purity and love. She falls hopelessly in love with Lancelot and nurses him when he lies wounded and near to death. She confesses her passion and Lancelot tells her tenderly that he can never love any woman other than his Queen. In his fever and delirium even Lancelot, the prince of courtesy, had made remarks liable to wound his devoted nurse:—

> "but the meek maid
> Sweetly forbore him ever, being to him
> Meeker than any child to a rough nurse,
> Milder than any mother to a sick child,
> And never any woman yet, since man's first fall,
> Did kindlier unto man, but her deep love
> Upbore her . . ."

In the end this "little helpless bird" realised that she could never obtain her hero's love and she pined away and died:—

> "Sweet is true love, tho' given in vain, in vain
> And sweet is death who puts an end to pain."

Tennyson, in order to ease the tragedy, provides her "with gorgeous obsequies." I agree with Stopford Brooke that "Lancelot and Elaine" is one of the "tenderest" of the *Idylls*. My only regret is that Tennyson should have once again represented his heroine as an innocent moron and that he should have introduced the soothing notes regarding the costly funeral. He was lacking in emotional as well as physical delicacy and it was this defect which debars him from being placed upon the level of greatest poets.

V

Of all the *Idylls*, my favourite, after the "Passing of Arthur," is "The Holy Grail." In this the allegory is clear cut; it does not confuse the story and it contains some of the best blank verse that Tennyson ever composed. Even as the theme of most of the idylls is dictated by Tennyson's obsessive hatred of conjugal infidelity, so is this fine idyll devoted to his curious hatred of mysticism and his deep distrust of all forms of hysterical or emotional religion. Although he admitted that a few individuals of exceptional chastity and spirituality might find fulfilment in such ecstasies of abnegation, he felt that for the ordinary mortal it was a sin to renounce the world entirely and a duty to execute his function among his fellow mortals and to do so within the orbit of practical service. He thus writes the "Holy Grail" as a warning to those who think they can attain salvation by sundering themselves, not from the temptations only, but also from the useful activities of the world.

The Holy Grail was supposed to be the chalice in which Joseph of Arimathea caught the blood of the crucified Christ and brought it with him to Glastonbury. The vision of the Grail was only vouchsafed, as a roseate flame pulsating as a heart, to those of absolute chastity. Fired by the ambition to see the Grail the knights of the Round Table make a vow to be abstinent for a whole year and to go out in search of this divine vision. To be granted a direct vision of the Grail pulsating meant that one had been granted complete "union" with Christ. Arthur is absent in the north when his knights undertake this vow and when he returns he is furious at what had happened, foreseeing that if they all leave on this selfish quest the Round Table will disintegrate and his own rule collapse. He dreads the dispersal of his knights, of those great champions who were pledged:—

"With strength and will to right the wronged, of power
 To lay the sudden heads of violence flat,"

When he hears of the vow they have taken his face darkens and he exclaims:—

"Woe is me, my knights,
 Had I been there, ye had not sworn the vow . . .
 The chance of noble deeds will come and go
 Unchallenged, while ye follow wandering fires
 Lost in the quagmire . . ."

Queen Guinevere shares the sense of doom and cries aloud "This madness has come on us for our sins." Thus the knights ride off: to few of them is accorded the sight of the Holy Grail: Lancelot in despair realises that, because of his guilt, the quest is not for him; he loses his triumphant arrogance and becomes "beaten down by little men, mean knights." When Sir Bors returns after his quest to Camelot, he finds the hall deserted and the King sunk in gloom. Sir Percivale, who tells the story, recounts how the vow and the quest, sapped all their ambitions and all their energies. He himself was offered the fairest and most loving princess in the world with a great realm as dowry. But he cared "not for her, nor anything upon earth." The cohesion of the Round Table was destroyed by this mad pursuit of wandering fires that flickered across the marsh. Only Sir Percivale's sister and the "bright boy knight" Sir Galahad were allowed, owing to their utter purity, to see the grail floating in a beam of sunlight, throbbing with the passion of the sacred heart:—

"I saw the Holy Grail," cries Galahad, "and heard a cry
O Galahad, and O Galahad, follow me!"

So off goes the boy knight in his shining silver armour and enters the Spiritual City in a blaze of light.

The contrast between a life of selfless utility and the life of those who believe they can secure salvation for themselves by renouncing all the pleasures and all the responsibilities of this wicked world, is emphasised by confronting the retired knight of the Round Table, Sir Percivale, with the humble parish priest, Ambrosius, to whom the whole story is narrated. This old priest prefers his simple round of duty, his love and understanding of his village parishioners to all the excitements of these wild quests. "Rejoice," he mumbles:—

"Rejoice, small man, in this small world of mine,
Yea even in their hens and in their eggs."

To Ambrosius, as to Tennyson, the simple round the common task brings a man closer to life-fulfilment and to union with Christ, than any transcendental ecstasies. In "The Holy Grail" he drives home the lesson that the great Arthurian ideal was destroyed by mysticism as well as by adultery. And he does it with skill.

The slow decay of the Round Table is again described in the two following *Idylls*, "Pelleas and Ettarre" and "The Last Tournament." In the former Tennyson illustrates the reaction that is bound to succeed a puritan revival and religious "enthusiasm." Pelleas worships Ettarre with the old fervent chivalry, but in the end, after she has rejected and reviled him, finds her in the arms of Gawain. He reels away from this horrible spectacle, leaving his sword lying across their bare throats. He returns shattered to Camelot to learn that the Queen herself has violated her vows of chastity. "I have no sword" he groans brokenhearted and on hearing this cry of despair, the usurper Modred, sensing the collapse of Arthur, mutters the fell words "The time is hard at hand." With "The Last Tournament" we reach the stage when the knights have lost all faith in themselves. In Arthur's absence, Lancelot has to preside over the tournament but does so listlessly:—

> "sighing wearily as one
> Who sits and gazes on a faded fire
> When all the goodlier guests are past away."

The loss of all the old ideals, the intrusion of lust and cynicism, are illustrated by Tennyson's handling of the Tristram and Isolde myth. For whereas the passion of Lancelot for Guinevere is allowed to retain a certain nobility, the lust of Tristram for Isolde is degraded into a squalid intrigue. "Free love, free field" sings the voluptuary Tristram, "we love but while we may." And we say farewell to Lancelot, sitting heart broken in Arthur's chair and moaning "The glory of the Round Table is no more."

> "Then fell thick rain, plume droopt and mantle clung
> And pettish cries awoke and the wan day
> Went glooming down in wet and weariness."

Gone are the gay sunshine and the clear hopes of "Gareth and Lynette."

And then comes "Guinevere," when we find the Queen in the convent of Almesbury hoping by remorse and prayer to pay penance for her sin. The King comes to visit her and she grovels in abasement at his feet. He then tells her that her lack of chastity has "spoilt the purpose of his life," that he forgives her, but will never see her again in this world. "Yet I must leave thee, woman, to thy shame." The scene when Guinevere rolls in abasement on the convent stones and the King in full armour delivers to her a lecture on the merits of conjugal fidelity is almost intolerable.

It remains to me a mystery why the "Idylls of the King" should to this day be admired by many excellent judges of poetry. The central theme of allegory was intended to be the degradation of a high spiritual ideal owing to the weakness of human nature. King Arthur, "the blameless king," was, I suppose, intended to personify this ideal, but he fails to do so. He is too vague and allegorical to become a convincing human character, and too much the English gentleman of Victorian convention to become a spiritual example. Moreover Tennyson allows his obsession against conjugal infidelity and mystical religion to obscure and divert the central allegory, so that the reader is bewildered by such moral cruelty and intolerance. The style, moreover, is not on the level of Tennyson's higher standards of poetic diction, and those verbal and prosodic devices to which he was addicted are so intrusive as to become irritating. The fabric of fairy stories, romances and tales of chivalry is too delicate a fabric to bear the weight of moral teaching; the didactic element is far too insistent and is not, as in Spenser's lovely tale, merely implicit. Several of the *Idylls*, notably "Merlin and Vivien," "The Last Tournament," "Guinevere" and "Pelleas and Ettarre," are, even as stories, palpable failures. They bear no relation at all to the beauty and fantasy of the age of chivalry. The colours and the design are totally out of harmony, and out of scale.

The reason, I suppose, why the *Idylls* are still popular is that we were all taught at school to recite some passages from "The Passing of Arthur," which is indeed a fine poem, well constructed and written in the most majestic of Tennyson's many manners. If all the *Idylls* were on the same level as this early work, then the collected sequence would certainly deserve to live as a masterpiece of allegory and romance. In this, assuredly, is admirably depicted the collapse of a fine ideal and the defeat of a superb character. The dying king realises that his efforts have been in vain, that the Round Table is dissolved for ever and that:—

> "all my realm
> Reels back into the beast and is no more."

Thus Arthur, while the white mist swirls around him, is wafted to the Vale of Avilion, and as he leaves this earth that has proved unworthy of him there rises:—

> "A cry that shiver'd to the tingling stars
> And as it were one voice, an agony
> Of Lamentation, like a wind that shrills
> All night in a waste land, where no one comes,
> Or hath come since the making of the world."

In this we find an echo of what I have always believed to be the essential Tennyson, the mystic melancholy of the Lincolnshire wolds.

# INDEX TO TITLES

# INDEX TO PROPER NAMES

The Best of Tennyson
p. 13
p. 14-5
mainly p.29
p 273-274
p. 318

Tiresias
Tithonus
Ulysses
Lotus-Eaters
Mariana
The Kraken
Dying Swan
Frater Ave atque Vale
Ode to Memory
Ode of Death of Duke of Wellington